Athene Series
Feminist Scholarship on
Culture and Education

"Stalwart Women"
A Historical Analysis of Deans of Women in the South
Carolyn Terry Bashaw

Pedagogies of Resistance
Women Educator Activists, 1880–1960
Margaret Smith Crocco, Petra Munro, & Kathleen Weiler

The *Feminist Teacher* Anthology
Pedagogies and Classroom Strategies
Gail E. Cohee, Elisabeth Däumer, Theresa D. Kemp, Paula M. Krebs, Sue Lafky, & Sandra Runzo, Editors

Feminist Science Education
Angela Calabrese Barton

Disciplining Sexuality
Foucault, Life Histories, and Education
Sue Middleton

Privilege in the Medical Academy
A Feminist Examines Gender, Race, and Power
Delese Wear

Re-Engineering Female Friendly Science
Sue V. Rosser

All the Rage
Reasserting Radical Lesbian Feminism
Lynne Harne & Elaine Miller, Editors

Creating an Inclusive College Curriculum
A Teaching Sourcebook from the New Jersey Project
Ellen G. Friedman, Wendy K. Kolmar, Charley B. Flint, and Paula Rothenberg, Editors

Teaching the Majority
Breaking the Gender Barrier in Science, Mathematics, and Engineering
Sue V. Rosser, Editor

The Will to Violence
The Politics of Personal Behavior
Susanne Kappeler

Crucial Conversations
Interpreting Contemporary American Literary Autobiographies by Women
Jeanne Braham

Women's Studies Graduates
The First Generation
Barbara F. Luebke & Mary Ellen Reilly

Men Who Control Women's Health
The Miseducation of Obstetrician-Gynecologists
Diana Scully

The Transsexual Empire
The Making of the She-Male
Janice G. Raymond

Surviving the Dalkon Shield IUD
Women v. the Pharmaceutical Industry
Karen Hicks

Making Violence Sexy
Feminist Views on Pornography
Diana E. H. Russell, Editor

Father Knows Best
The Use and Abuse of Power in Freud's Case of Dora
Robin Tolmach Lakoff & James C. Coyne

Living by the Pen
Early British Women Writers
Dale Spender, Editor

The Knowledge Explosion
Generations of Feminist Scholarship
Cheris Kramarae & Dale Spender, Editors

All Sides of the Subject
Women and Biography
Teresa Iles, Editor

Calling the Equality Bluff
Women in Israel
Barbara Swirski & Marilyn P. Safir, Editors

Black Feminist Criticism
Perspectives on Black Women Writers
Barbara Christian

Narodniki Women
Russian Women Who Sacrificed Themselves for the Dream of Freedom
Margaret Maxwell

Speaking Freely
Unlearning the Lies of the Fathers' Tongues
Julia Penelope

The Reflowering of the Goddess
Gloria Feman Orenstein

Female-Friendly Science
Applying Women's Studies Methods and Theories to Attract Students
Sue V. Rosser

The Sexual Liberals and the Attack on Feminism
Dorchen Leidholdt & Janice G. Raymond, Editors

Between Worlds
Women Writers of Chinese Ancestry
Amy Ling

(continued)

ATHENE SERIES *(continued)*

Whence the Goddesses
A Source Book
Miriam Robbins Dexter

Made to Order
The Myth of Reproductive and Genetic Progress
Patricia Spallone & Deborah Lynn Steinberg, Editors

Exposing Nuclear Phallacies
Diana E. H. Russell, Editor

Teaching Science and Health from a Feminist Perspective
A Practical Guide
Sue V. Rosser

Taking Our Time
Feminist Perspectives on Temporality
Frieda Johles Forman & Caoran Sowton, Editors

Educating for Peace
A Feminist Perspective
Birgit Brock-Utne

Men's Studies Modified
The Impact of Feminism on the Academic Disciplines
Dale Spender, Editor

Stopping Rape
Successful Survival Strategies
Pauline B. Bart & Patricia H. O'Brien

Feminism Within the Science and Health Care Professions
Overcoming Resistance
Sue V. Rosser, Editor

Feminist Perspectives on Peace and Peace Education
Birgit Brock-Utne

Feminist Approaches to Science
Ruth Bleier, Editor

Science and Gender
A Critique of Biology and Its Theories on Women
Ruth Bleier

"Stalwart Women"

A Historical Analysis of Deans of Women in the South

Carolyn Terry Bashaw

Foreword by Linda Eisenmann

TEACHERS COLLEGE PRESS

Teachers College, Columbia University
New York and London

Published by Teachers College Press, 1234 Amsterdam Avenue, New York, NY 10027

Copyright © 1999 by Teachers College, Columbia University

Library of Congress Cataloging-in-Publication Data
Bashaw, Carolyn Terry.
   "Stalwart women" : a historical analysis of deans of women in the
South / Carolyn Terry Bashaw.
     p.   cm. — (Athene series)
   Includes bibliographical references (p.) and index.
   ISBN 0-8077-6300-4 (cloth : alk. paper). — ISBN 0-8077-6299-7
(pbk. : alk. paper)
    1. Deans of women—Southern States—History. I. Title.
II. Series.
LC1620.B37   1999
378.1'12—dc21   99-31310

ISBN 0-8077-6299-7 (paper)
ISBN 0-8077-6300-4 (cloth)

Printed on acid-free paper
Manufactured in the United States of America

06 05 04 03 02 01 00 99   8 7 6 5 4 3 2 1

To
Jean E. Friedman
Emily S. Gibson

and

the memory of Bernice Cottrell Terry

Contents

Foreword   *by Linda Eisenmann*   ix

Acknowledgments   xiii

Introduction   **"Stalwart Women"**
*Deans of Women and Their Significance in the History
of Collegiate Women in the United States*   1

1   **"The Alternative Story"**
Early Life and Challenging Careers   19

2   **"A Legitimate Place on Campus"**
Academic Women and Space on the Coeducational Campus   41

3   **"A Bright Mind and a Lean Purse"**
Academic Women and Financial Challenge   53

4   **"The Academic Dignity of the Campus"**
Collegiate Women, Academic Societies, and Campus Ritual   67

5   **"That Physique Which Is So Essential"**
College Women and Athletic Opportunity   79

6   **"We Who Live 'Off on the Edges'"**
Academic Women and Professional Organizations   95

7   **"Always a Dear Friend"**
Academic Women, Family, and Friendship   111

Epilogue   "Lost Down in Kentucky"
         Deans of Women and the Challenge of Historical Recovery   123

Notes   133
Primary Sources   145
References   149
Index   157
About the Author   165

Foreword

In this important study of four southern deans of women and their institutional settings, Carolyn Terry Bashaw describes Sarah Gibson Blanding, Katherine S. Bowersox, Agnes Ellen Harris, and Adele H. Stamp as consistently "conscious of the challenge of marginality." These deans indeed demonstrate some "marginal" characteristics when compared with more-recognized female leaders of 20th-century academe. The four attended nonelite colleges, worked their way through school, held initial jobs outside academe with clientele like industrial workers and farmers, and spent most of their careers in southern institutions.

Yet Bashaw wisely makes these differences the center of her analysis, thereby expanding a too-often "prestige-centric" focus in women's academic history (Eisenmann, 1997). Recognizing the near-infancy of solid scholarship on deans of women, Bashaw extends our knowledge in five important directions.

First, she *establishes the significance of deans of women* as academic advocates and actors. Refuting the stereotypic view of deans as petty, rule-minded matrons, Bashaw invigorates their image as risk-takers who challenged campus constituencies for women's share of space, prestige, and resources, while simultaneously building a profession among like-minded colleagues.

Second, she *studies southern academic women* in a field dominated by the Northeast and the Midwest. Bashaw notes that the South actually sustained a wider variety of higher education options for women, some of which developed because of regional discomfort with coeducation: private, denominational women's colleges; coeducational land grant and private institutions; coordinate colleges attached to older men's institutions; and public single-sex schools.

Third, Bashaw helps redress a notable historiographic imbalance by *focusing on coeducational institutions*. Although three-quarters of college women attended coeducational schools by 1900, studies of women's colleges (particularly the Seven Sisters) dominate early historiography. Further, she examines, in addition to the state universities of Alabama, Kentucky, and Maryland, a thoroughly nonelite institution through Bowersox's deanship at the labor-cooperative Berea College in Kentucky.

Fourth, Bashaw *examines academic women who remained single*. In studying women on coeducational campuses, she adds to Patricia Palmieri's (1995) important study of unmarried academics at the all-female Wellesley College, here analyzing ways in which single women forged personal and professional lives amid a more traditional setting.

Finally, by examining mid-20th-century administrators, Bashaw *focuses on a little studied era in women's higher education.* Recent scholarship generally investigates either the 19th-century push for educational access or the early-20th-century excitement of the Progressive Era. Bashaw finds her four deans grounded in Progressivism, yet building their careers during economic depression.

In her Epilogue, Bashaw recommends a template that assesses academic women's contributions by examining five areas: institutions, impediments, initiatives, infrastructure, and intimacy. This useful model characterizes her own analysis. In institutions, these deans challenged a setting where women's role was uncertain and shifting. In the South, especially during the Depression, women's curricular and career demands were questioned and often devalued; the four deans creatively enhanced women's presence. Impediments ranged from scarce financial resources to territorial athletic directors who valued women's sports solely for the notoriety of successful teams. Initiatives focused particularly on building academic viability, including financing women's buildings, establishing honor societies, and creating academic rituals. Infrastructure needs were particularly acute for women in a new profession operating in far-flung settings. These four deans assumed leadership in the National Association of Deans of Women (NADW), the premier organization for the young profession. Established and led by prominent northeastern and midwestern deans, the NADW found new and vigorous leadership from these southerners during the Depression. Conscious of the upstart nature of their activism, three of these deans sought national leadership that sustained NADW during a decade when the national headquarters nearly dissolved from lack of finances and support. In examining the intimacy of her subjects, Bashaw situates her work within a growing tradition of women's biography that prizes both the professional and the personal in determining benchmarks for women's narratives. She traces the deans' meaningful relationships, noting the special importance of older women mentors and long-term companions.

With this expansive study, Bashaw provokes reinterpretation of 20th-century academic women's history. Conscious of her contributions to both southern and mainstream history, she carefully delineates her findings with the historiography of those fields. More than a group biography, this analysis of women removed from the center impressively extends our understanding of women leaders throughout higher education.

Linda Eisenmann
July 1998

REFERENCES

Eisenmann, L. (1997). Reconsidering a classic: Assessing the history of women's higher education a dozen years after Barbara Solomon. *Harvard Educational Review, 67,* 689–717.

Palmieri, P. A. (1995). *In Adamless Eden: The community of faculty women at Wellesley.* New Haven: Yale University Press.

Acknowledgments

Archivists have played a central role in this study. Appropriately enough, I began research for this work at the Milbank Library of Teachers College, where David Ment introduced me to primary materials essential to understanding the role that Teachers College assumed in the founding of the National Association of Deans of Women (NADW) and in the development of the profession of dean of women. Anne Terkos, at the McKelden Library, University of Maryland–College Park, located sources that revealed the women's culture that Adele Stamp was instrumental in creating. Marilyn Levinson and Lee McLaird of the Center for Archival Collections at the Jerome Library, Bowling Green State University, shared with me the extensive National Association of Women Deans and Counsellors (NAWDAC) Collection so crucial to this study.

The W. Stanley Hoole Special Collections Library of the University of Alabama houses the Agnes Ellen Harris Collection, easily the largest personal collection used in this project. Archivist T. I. Jones answered numerous questions concerning the Harris collection and sent additional items long after my visits.

As a consequence of this work, I made two wonderful friends—Terry Birdwhistell, at the Margaret I. King Library, University of Kentucky, and Shannon H. Wilson, at the Hutchins Library, Berea College. A scholar of women and higher education in the South, Terry took a special interest in my research. He not only identified sources for me but also spent much time discussing the significance of Sarah Blanding.

Berea College is unique for many reasons. Shannon Wilson is surely one of them. Seldom have I met an archivist with so much knowledge of and fondness for his materials. Methodically, Shannon led me through the Berea archive and made me appreciate both the institution and Katherine Bowersox even more.

Crucial to understanding Bowersox's achievements at Berea was her employment at the Indian Industrial School in Carlisle, Pennsylvania. John J. Slonaker, of the Historical Research Branch at the United States Army Military History Institute, Carlisle Barracks, Pennsylvania, introduced me to the rich primary sources concerning this controversial chapter in U.S. history. The extensive newspaper and photographic archives provided invaluable insight into Bowersox's subsequent contributions to life at Berea.

At various stages of this work, I assiduously employed the Interlibrary Loan Service. Inga Barnello, Ann Waterbury, and Gretchen Pearson of the Noreen Falcone Library at Le Moyne College meticulously and successfully pursued my requests, however singular. I sincerely appreciate their patience and good humor.

Through Berea College, I fortunately met William B. Welsh, of Boothbay, Maine. A descendant of Mary E. Welsh, Katherine Bowersox's longtime professional colleague and friend, Mr. Welsh welcomed me to Boothbay, where the two women spent so many summers. Sitting on the same porch where they watched the sunset, sang hymns, and said their prayers, Mr. Welsh and I discussed Dean Bowersox and examined the family collection of primary sources. I treasure his gift of a book that belonged to Katherine Bowersox.

Financial support and release time were essential to the completion of this book. I thank the Department of History, University of Georgia, for a Heggoy Fund Travel Grant and the Research and Development Committee, Le Moyne College, for a series of Summer Research grants. Le Moyne also provided, through the good offices of Edward Judge, former Chair of the Department of History, a favorable course schedule so that I could complete revisions for this work.

I benefited from consultation with many scholars. At the University of Georgia, Sharon Price, Lester Stephens, Numan V. Bartley, and William F. Holmes commented on this project from its inception. At various points in the revision process, John W. Langdon and Douglas R. Egerton of Le Moyne College read the manuscript and offered encouragement and valuable advice. I am also grateful to Margaret Rossiter of Cornell University for her observations concerning this work.

Fortunately, I obtained exceptionally skilled and patient assistance in the technical production of this book. Dora M. Ervin, at the University of Georgia, assured that I made every deadline and remained sane in the process. I extend profound appreciation to Carol A. Miller for her extensive technical and editorial contributions to this work and for her friendship.

Although most scholars are fierce individuals, few of us could survive without a core of friends. I sincerely thank Linda Eisenmann, Jana Nidiffer, Glenn Eskew, Sherree Dendy, and Judith Shoen for their loyalty and concern for my welfare and for this project.

At various stages in the writing process, I presented portions of this work to scholarly organizations. Colleagues in the History of Education Society, Division F of American Educational Research Association (AERA), the Southern Historical Association, and the Southern Association of Women Historians encouraged my work and offered shrewd advice.

I won two writing awards for articles concerning Katherine S. Bowersox and Agnes Ellen Harris. The Filson Club Historical Society, Louisville, Kentucky, presented me with its Otto Rothert Award for the best article published in *The Filson Club History Quarterly* in 1991. I also received the Milo B. Howard Award, from the Alabama Historical Association, for the best article published in *The Alabama Review*, 1991–1993.

I have been extremely fortunate to work with the staff at Teachers College Press, two of whom merit particular notice. Faye Zucker saw the value of this project and served as its successful advocate. I am especially grateful to Susan Liddicoat, my editor, for graciously and patiently answering all too many questions and allaying concerns significant and otherwise.

W. Louis Bashaw—my husband, critic, and partisan—has been with me for every step in this circuitous journey. In face of my perennially shifting combination of ego and anxiety, grief and exhilaration, he relentlessly forced me to confront, with the bark off, some home truths about myself and this profession and what ultimately matters in life. I am a better scholar and human being because he shares his life with me.

I dedicate this book to three stalwart women, who have sustained me with their affection and have inspired me through their example. Jean Friedman introduced me to women's history and changed my professional life. Emily Gibson introduced me to the beauty of the Episcopal Church and the adventure of the committed spiritual life. My late mother, Bernice Terry, in 1938, at age 16, left the family farm and her 11 siblings in central Kentucky, with $10 and a borrowed suitcase, to earn her undergraduate and graduate degrees. Consistently, she held me to a high standard, the value of which I at last discern and cherish.

.

"STALWART WOMEN"

A Historical Analysis of Deans of Women in the South

"Stalwart Women"

Deans of Women and Their Significance
in the History of Collegiate Women in the United States

In the spring of 1939, at the age of 70, Katherine S. Bowersox retired from Berea College, Berea, Kentucky, after 32 years as dean of women. Students, administrators, and faculty colleagues celebrated her contributions to the women of Berea College. "We bring to you tonight . . . the thanks of a thousand freshman girls," noted a student, speaking at a dinner honoring Bowersox, "for the care you have used in watching over us and for the rights and privileges we should not have had, had you not won them for us."[1] No less adamant in his praise, President Francis Hutchins cited her equally significant initiatives on behalf of women faculty members: "It would be hard for the women of the faculty, who have come in recent years, to know how Miss Bowersox invested herself in the material welfare of [these] women" ("President Gives Recognition," 1939).

Faculty colleague May Smith (1939), writing in the *Berea Alumnus*, unambiguously cited Bowersox's contributions: "To a pioneer institution she brought pioneer gifts: physical strength . . . a mind, quick, operative, and a sense of humor." Bowersox brought an additional quality to Berea, Smith observed, something any coeducational institution sorely needed—"a woman's point of view and a woman's set of values" (p. 203). Putting these gifts to wise use, the dean instituted changes that tangibly improved the lives of women students and faculty members. For the former, she oversaw the establishment of extracurricular opportunities and the expansion of dormitory facilities. For the latter, college authorities, responding to "her foresight and championship," established "weekend houses" to provide a respite from daily dormitory responsibilities. In the end, Smith (1939) concluded, "her best gift to Berea has been to and through its women" (p. 205).

Ceremonies such as those honoring Katherine S. Bowersox occurred in colleges and universities throughout the South, and indeed the nation. During the 1940s and 1950s numerous pioneer deans of women retired after careers of distinguished service. Indeed, this generation of women made essential contributions to the fortunes of academic women—students, faculty, and professional colleagues.

Why does Bowersox's story matter? Was she part of a cohesive regional network? Why study members of a profession that no longer exists? What do her life and the lives of her colleagues reveal concerning the fortunes of academic women in coeducational institutions in the South in the first half of this century?

The best-kept secret in the history of higher education for women, particularly in the South, is the leadership that deans of women exercised in defining the quality of institutional life for women students, faculty members, and professional colleagues. By 1900, the majority of American college women attended coeducational institutions of higher learning. Within 20 years they comprised approximately half of the entire undergraduate population. In response, institutional authorities hired a new administrative official, the dean of women, charged with their supervision. Although most college and university presidents considered the position a necessary expedient to reassure skeptical parents, many of the women whom they hired did not. As the highest-ranking woman on the coeducational campus, deans of women increasingly expanded their role from one of supervision to one of advocacy. Such a challenging strategy invariably produced both nagging failure and notable achievement.

Between 1920 and 1970, virtually every coeducational institution—Black or White—in the United States employed a dean of women. Nevertheless, historians of women's higher education have consistently dismissed or ignored this administrative officer. Margaret W. Rossiter (1982), in her study of women scientists, defined the position as a variety of "academic 'women's work'" (pp. 71–72), which some women accepted in order to obtain employment in higher education.

Pioneer deans of women, many of whom were competent scholars—albeit in feminized fields, quickly perceived the position as an "entering wedge" (Rossiter, 1982, p. 2) by which they could demonstrate their organizational skills and enhance women's visibility both on the coeducational campus and in the larger society.

Aspiring women professionals such as these chose between two options: either to enter a traditional field with its various obstacles, or to build new, female-dominated professions. Whichever path they followed, Nancy Cott (1987) suggests that women professionals confronted similar problems: the battle for "professional credibility" and the need "to outperform men in their rigor and standards" (p. 238). Such formidable obstacles, however, did not deter dedicated women. Penina M. Glazer and Miriam Slater (1987) identify four strategies—superperformance, separatism, subordination, and innovation—by which women achieved productive professional careers. Of special interest are the innovators, women who created professional employment opportunities by appropriating "areas ignored by the established professions" (p. 217).

LEGITIMIZING THE PROFESSION

Deans of women were just such innovators. In 1900, despite the dramatic increase in the number of women attending coeducational institutions and in the number of deans of women, the position possessed none of the components of a profession—formalized graduate training programs, a coherent body of research literature, and a professional association. However, between 1900 and 1916, dedicated deans of women began transforming a nonstandardized job into a legitimate profession.

Beginning in 1834, with the appointment of Marianne Dascombe as principal of the Female Department at Oberlin College, institutions of higher education sporadically hired this new administrative official, who eventually became the dean of women, to be responsible for the welfare of college women. Although numerous other institutions hired "lady" principals, deans, and advisors of women, Gertrude S. Martin (1911), Dean of Women at Cornell University, in one of the earliest studies of the position, maintained that "it was the University of Chicago that really made it [the office] fashionable" (p. 66). Since this institution was committed to coeducation from its founding in 1892, President William Raney Harper hired one of the most prominent woman administrators in the country, Alice Freeman Palmer, as the first dean of women. The president of Wellesley College between 1881 and 1887, Palmer clearly defined the conditions of her employment at Chicago: that she be in residence only 12 weeks each year and that she bring as her assistant Marion Talbot, a Wellesley faculty member (Bordin, 1993, pp. 232–233). Palmer's choice of an assistant proved to be significant, both for women's education at the University of Chicago and for the future leadership of this nascent profession.

Born into a prosperous but progressive New England family, Marion Talbot graduated in 1881 from Boston University, coeducational since its founding 8 years earlier. Like so many of the first generation of women college graduates, Talbot had scant opportunity to obtain meaningful employment. Keenly aware of the problem, she joined with other college-educated women in the area to found the Association of Collegiate Alumnae (ACA) in 1881. Subsequently, Talbot accepted a faculty position at Wellesley College, and, in 1892, accompanied Alice Freeman Palmer to the University of Chicago (Fitzpatrick, 1990; Rosenberg, 1982).

Following Palmer's unexpected resignation in 1895, Marion Talbot became

Dean of Women at the University of Chicago. She assumed this post during a critical period in the development of higher education in the United States. Students, faculty members, and administrators all felt the effects of the middle-class preoccupation with professionalization. Deans of women eventually joined the ranks of the legitimate professions as a consequence of the determination of Talbot and of a group of professional colleagues.

Eighteen deans of women met in December 1903, at the invitation of Talbot and of Martha Foote Crow, Dean of Women at Northwestern University. Of that number only one, Dean Laura Drake Gill of Barnard College, worked at an institution outside the Midwest. Although no formal organization resulted from that meeting, Talbot was finally instrumental in establishing, in 1905, the Conference of Deans and Advisors in State Universities, the majority of whose members worked at public colleges and universities in the Midwest. Meeting biennially until 1922, the conference eventually became a division of the National Association of Deans of Women.

Furthermore, in 1911 a group of deans of women began meeting informally at the annual convention of the Association of Collegiate Alumnae (Potter, 1927). Significantly, however, the ACA included no southern chapters until 1921, when it merged with the Southern Association of College Women to form the American Association of University Women (Talbot & Rosenberry, 1931).

In their pursuit of professional status, pioneer deans of women sought to establish not only professional associations but also reputable graduate training programs. A significant number of deans of women enrolled in the well-known summer sessions at Teachers College, Columbia University. Despite the recognized quality of this program, it included no specific courses involving the profession of dean of women.

Determined that it do so, Kathryn Sisson McLean, Dean of Women at State Teachers College, Chadron, Nebraska, in 1915 founded an informal discussion group of graduate women at Teachers College. These women, along with sympathetic faculty, persuaded Teachers College to offer, in the summer session of 1916, its first graduate courses designed exclusively for deans of women (Phillips, Kerr, & Wells, 1927). These modest course offerings formed the basis of what became the major graduate training program in the United States for deans of women. Employing such eminent scholars as Sarah Sturtevant and Ruth Strang, the Teachers College program not only trained deans of women but also produced definitive research in the field.

However essential graduate training programs were, McLean knew that these alone could not define the profession. Like Talbot, she perceived the value of a national network, which only a professional organization could effectively establish and maintain. Taking advantage of the substantial number of deans of women in New York City in July of 1916, attending the annual convention of the National Education Association, McLean and her colleagues engaged the Horace Mann Auditorium at Teachers College for a meeting on Thursday, July 6, 1916.

To her surprise, approximately 200 people gathered for the session. Anxious that the audience discern the degree of support for the establishment of a professional society, McLean invited Gertrude S. Martin, Advisor of Women at Cornell University, and Virginia Gildersleeve, Dean of Barnard College, some of the most prominent members of the profession, to address the audience (Phillips, 1953).

The meeting was a distinct success. Throughout the evening, McLean recalled that "unmistakable enthusiasm and interest grew," [and] "when the meeting was over there was a great feeling of confidence and hope in the future of our association" (Phillips, 1964, p. 67). Following the formal addresses, the women established the National Association of Deans of Women (NADW) and elected Kathryn McLean president (Phillips, 1953).

NADW leadership and membership demonstrated dramatically the geographic orientation of the association. For the first 20 years of its existence, women from the Northeast and the Midwest dominated NADW leadership. Between 1916 and 1936, of the ten women who held the presidency, seven served in an administrative capacity at northeastern or midwestern institutions. Not surprisingly, during that same period, approximately 70% of the membership came from the Northeast and the Midwest. Clearly Marion Talbot at Chicago and the Sturtevant-Strang group at Teachers College encouraged that kind of participation.

Meanwhile, NADW members from White southern colleges and universities represented only about 14% of the total. Deans of women from Black institutions in the South joined in even more modest numbers, comprising only .4% of NADW membership. Such figures are not inconsistent with the region's reluctance to embrace coeducation for women of any color, hire deans of women, and pay them adequate salaries. In fact, the complete establishment of coeducation in the region spanned nearly a century, from 1871, when the University of Arkansas became the first public institution to accept White women students, to 1970, when the University of Virginia finally opened its doors to women (Ihle, 1976).

FOUR DEANS OF WOMEN IN THE SOUTH

Despite the initial unwillingness of the region to accept coeducation, deans of women across the South, albeit in modest numbers, joined the NADW in search of professional development. Among those pioneers, four merit special attention: Katherine S. Bowersox (Berea College, 1907–1939), Agnes Ellen Harris

(University of Alabama, 1927–1945), Adele H. Stamp (University of Maryland, 1922–1960), and Sarah Gibson Blanding (University of Kentucky, 1923–1941). Anomalies in a conservative environment, Bowersox, Harris, Stamp, and Blanding could easily have taken the path of least resistance, content to function in a purely supervisory capacity.

They chose instead to function as aggressive advocates on their home campuses for both women students and faculty members. Furthermore, within their profession, they rose to positions of regional leadership and were among the first women from the institutions in the South to assume major responsibilities in the NADW. Despite cultural and institutional challenges, these four strong-minded women nevertheless not only achieved meaningful careers for themselves but also claimed for academic women access to the full range of college life and professional opportunity. Such a course of action brought almost continual conflict, greater risk, and fewer, but often more precious, rewards. To better appreciate such conflict, risk, and reward, it is instructive to introduce these four deans at the end of their careers, after decades of service to college women.

Why introduce these women through their retirement? Does not this culture consider the old, particularly women, to be useless? What possible relevance has this to their contributions as deans of women?

Such a question cuts to the heart of Carolyn Heilbrun's (1988) analysis of the perennial dilemma of the biographer of women. Where does the story begin? What should it include? These questions sufficiently complicate stories of women whose lives follow the traditional scenario of marriage, motherhood, and domestication. Biographers of single women, Heilbrun contends, face more perplexing obstacles. What are the benchmarks of an unmarried woman's life? What roles do career, family, and friends assume? In large measure, the "unnarrated lives" (p. 28) of single women remain largely uncharted terrain.

Heilbrun's (1988) comments concerning the "active old age" (p. 28) of women, from 60 to 75, offer an instructive framework for beginning the stories of Bowersox, Harris, Stamp, and Blanding. With the exception of Agnes Ellen Harris, who died at the relatively young age of 62, these women enjoyed long lives by any standards. Adele Stamp and Sarah Blanding lived into their 80s, while Katherine Bowersox died at 92.

Active old age accurately describes their retirement, which, in essence, reinforces the quality of their lives of professional activity and economic independence dating from their collegiate days. Examination of their old age reveals both bitter loss and rich rewards for lifetimes of achievement. Beginning their stories from this relatively neglected vantage point encapsulates lives of impressive professional achievement, intense strength, and indomitable spirit.

Katherine S. Bowersox

Katherine Bowersox prepared for her retirement by presenting herself with a long-awaited gift. In 1938, accompanied by her great friend Mary E. Welsh, the dean purchased her first and only home, in St. Petersburg, Florida. If Bowersox was the driver for their many peregrinations, then Welsh was the conscientious chronicler of their adventures. Over the years, she kept a number of notebooks recording their activities.[2] On February 25, 1938, the two left Berea and drove 234 miles. Three days later, they "arrived in St. Petersburg 6PM . . . Roll waiting for us. Found good room at the 'Earlene' . . . $8.75 each week." Welsh proudly recorded that on March 3, "Kassie bought her home," for $6,450.

For the next 8 years, the two, often accompanied by Rollin Bowersox, the dean's brother, established an annual routine, which Welsh recounted to her former Wellesley classmates. "My long-time friend and co-worker . . . Miss Bowersox bought this house at St. Petersburg where we have spent the winters since 1939; our summers are spent in Maine, a very happy arrangement for us both" (*Annals of the Class of 1885*, 1945, pp. 53–54).

In 1946, the familiar and comfortable pattern changed somewhat as both women confronted the reality of aging. Welsh recorded in her notebook: "1946—my last trip to Florida and Berea." Still, the two friends corresponded regularly and, from June until October, Bowersox visited Welsh's family home in Boothbay, Maine, now traveling by train. Welsh faithfully recorded the celebration of her friend's birthday, August 24, which included luncheon and tea parties. Despite their infirmities, the two did not remain cloistered on Sawyer's Island, the site of the Welsh home. They attended church services and musical concerts, visited friends, picked berries, and enjoyed the beauty of the harbor. Age did not diminish their sense of family responsibility. Welsh noted that Rollin Bowersox was a part of many of their summers on the island.

Unfortunately, few letters from Katherine Bowersox to her dear friend survive. However, the two methodically remembered anniversaries of significant events. Among Mary Welsh's private papers, a one-page note, handwritten in the unmistakable, confident scrawl, probably dating from 1947, indicates the normally matter-of-fact Bowersox's dedication and affection. "Forty years ago, we met on the Berea campus and thru [*sic*] all these years we have shared . . . joys and sorrow. Your faith and friendship have [been] . . . a sense of deep happiness and inspiration. I know that these last sunset years will be full of radiance for you."

The sunset year of 1950 included a surprise for Bowersox and Welsh. In April, Francis Hutchins, President of Berea College, informed the two that "at this mid-century Commencement we . . . take particular notice of those whose services have gone into . . . the foundations of this college,"[3] through the conferring of honorary degrees. Unfortunately, only Bowersox attended the ceremony. In her reply to Hutchins, she indicated that although her friend was "quite well physically and mentally *alert*, her eyes are failing rapidly and she feels helpless." Bowersox consequently hoped that "the college would confer the degree [on Welsh] in absentia."[4]

In June 1950, Katherine S. Bowersox, who long regretted her lack of a college degree, accepted the honorary doctorate from the institution she had served long and faithfully. Julia F. Allen, her successor as dean of women, read the citation: "In the minds of many Bereans, Katherine Bowersox and Berea College are almost synonymous. Her interest and affection extended to all the women of the campus."[5] Ever the self-effacing soul, Bowersox expressed her deepest feelings to Charlotte Ludlum, a colleague at Berea. "The excitement and the beautiful service . . . upset my emotional balance a bit—It took me about a month to get back to normal!"[6]

The next year, Bowersox received yet another special recognition. The Wellesley Club of St. Petersburg invited her to join, a particular honor in view of her sustained service to women and of Wellesley College's unique heritage. Francis Hutchins heartily supported her selection. "Over a long period," he indicated to the club president, "she guided with extraordinary good common sense the women of the College."[7] Mary Elizabeth Welsh, Class of 1885, enthusiastically concurred. "Letter from Wellesley Club," her notebook from March of 1951 reads. "Kassie has been honored by Club. Glad to hear."[8]

In April 1955, Mary Elizabeth Welsh died. Bowersox made the long journey to Boothbay to collect her belongings. Writing to Charlotte Ludlum of this irreplaceable loss, she remarked that "the Cottage at Sawyer's Island was 'Home' to me for many summers." Finding it too painful to contemplate ever returning, she termed this visit "my last trip to Maine."[9]

Katherine S. Bowersox survived her friend by 6 years. She died on Christmas Eve 1961, fittingly in St. Petersburg, where she had established her hardwon "bit of freedom and privacy." Describing Bowersox's contributions to Berea College, her obituary observed, "As dean of women her enthusiasm seemed boundless" (*St. Petersburg Times*, December 1961). Such energy, enthusiasm, and dedication—to her family, to Native American and Appalachian youth, to Mary Elizabeth Welsh, and to the beauty of service—characterized the whole of her 92 years.

Agnes Ellen Harris

Agnes Ellen Harris, like Bowersox, received many well-deserved tributes late in her career as dean of women. At the 1944 commencement exercises, which marked the 50th anniversary of coeducation at the University of Alabama, the Alumnae Association, which Harris was instrumental in founding, presented the university with her portrait. Friends, former students, and university officials unanimously praised the dean. In congratulating Harris, Lillian Storms, a professional colleague, offered the most practical observation: "I'm glad they didn't wait until you were under the sod five years before doing this."[10]

Inevitably, many considered her contributions to equal, if not exceed, those of Julia Tutwiler, the moving force behind coeducation of the University of Alabama. "The mantle of Julia Tutwiler is upon her," wrote Dixie Bibb Graves, a close friend. "The lives of many thousands of Alabama women have been enriched by contact with her high qualities of mind and heart."[11] Mary Robertson, a former student and great admirer, agreed. "You and Julia Tutwiler have been the two great women in coeducation at the University of Alabama."[12]

Former President George Denney, who brought Harris to Tuscaloosa, paid her the highest compliment one administrator can offer another. "If anybody at the University has achieved success, Dean Harris had done so in notable degree. . . . When she came to the University, there was for young women . . . an uncertain future. She has seen the woman's campus expand . . . until it is today one of the finest in the country."[13]

Harris's success, reflecting that of the profession itself, was short-lived. On July 1, 1945, she resigned as dean of women after 18 years of exemplary service. Harris hastened to explain her actions to her closest friends, an explanation almost identical to that other deans of women would offer in the future. Raymond Paty, the new president of the university, "came in with a . . . plan of organization which included . . . a Dean of Students . . . under which the work of the Dean of Women and Dean of Men would be coordinated." After nearly 20 years during which she enjoyed relative autonomy, reporting only to the president, Harris found the prospect of subordination, in effect demotion, to be "unworkable."[14]

Of course, the dean maintained a brave public stance, indicating that she would continue as Dean of the School of Home Economics, sufficient responsibility for any individual. To her closest friends, however, she minced no words. "I did not discontinue work as Dean of Women on account of health," she reported to Eleanor Livingston, a colleague in Washington, D.C. "The break has given me many heartaches . . . I wanted you to know that I did not resign."[15] Astonished, yet supportive, Livingston assured her friend that "you *are* the University, without you there won't be any. No one is comparable to you. . . . No one can ever take your place."[16]

Health problems continued to plague Harris for her last years at the university. In addition to her chronic heart ailment, the dean discovered, in 1949, "a cyst in my right breast." Her response was typical. Rather than miss any of the fall semester, she confided to her colleague and close friend Henrietta Thompson, "I thought I could wait until December for its removal but Dr. Pack says I must not."[17] Fortunately, the cyst was benign.

The university community did not forget Harris's accomplishments as dean of women. In 1952, commemorating her 25th year in Tuscaloosa, the *Alumni Bulletin* evocatively captured her generosity and her achievement. "The first [women] to enter [the University] fed on crumbs that fell from tables set for men. Agnes Ellen Harris provided places for them at the head table of the feast" ("Tribute to a Great Woman Educator," 1952).

On December 18, 1952, Harris, at the end of a long day, collapsed and died, while taking a taxi across town to join a supper party of women. Henrietta Thompson preserved notes reconstructing her friend's final days. As usual, the dean maintained a full schedule, attending a number of holiday parties. Two days before her death, Harris delivered her last public remarks. Thompson noted, "Dean was in her finest form—keen wit—alert—great talk."[18]

Women at the University of Alabama commemorated the life of this great-hearted woman. In May 1953, on Alumnae Day, of which the dean was the founder, her friend and colleague in the School of Home Economics, Neige Todhunter, paid tribute to Harris's life and career. Although "Julia Tutwiler opened the doors of the University to women," Todhunter proclaimed, "it was Agnes Ellen Harris who brought women into the University." She portrayed the dean not merely as an administrator but also as an evangel for women's education and a genuine friend to women students. "Never a meeting she attended . . . but she would talk with the women about sending their daughters to the University. . . . She wanted every Alabama girl to have the opportunity to come to the University" (Todhunter, 1953, p. 9).

Once these daughters enrolled, the dean did her best to make them feel welcome. Despite the fact that she held two demanding administrative jobs, "her office door was always open, so was the door to her home" (Todhunter, 1953, p. 9). Throughout her distinguished career as a dean of women, Agnes Ellen Harris drew on her faith in the Progressive tradition, long ago pledged among the farm women of rural Florida, believing that the university could change women and that women could change the university.

Adele H. Stamp

Students, alumnae, and friends honored Adele Stamp, the University of Maryland's first Dean of Women, as she approached her retirement, after nearly 40 years of service. In May 1956, as the dean completed her 35th year in College Park, nearly 400 of her former students attended a testimonial dinner in her honor and presented her portrait to the university. Mrs. John Whitehurst, the vice-chair of the Board of Regents, presented the official citation to "a daughter of Maryland who by her vision and faith in the potential power of women has been an inspiration to them to achieve their best in the service of others" ("Prominent Guests," 1956).

The Adele Stamp Papers contain many, many letters of heartfelt thanks from the dean to the many alumnae who attended. Overwhelmed by both the official honor and the response of so many former students, Stamp confessed that "with difficulty I kept the happy tears under control." Reflecting on her long career, she observed, "I am the one to be thankful that I have the privilege of working with the fine young [women]. Who could ask for a happier life?"[19]

In December 1960, Adele Stamp retired as Dean of Women at the University of Maryland. The Board of Regents unanimously voted to confer on her the title Dean of Women Emerita, the first woman in the institution's history to be honored with emeritus status ("University of Maryland Honors," 1960). In a lengthy article ("Girls Her Hobby for 38 years"), the *Baltimore Sun* of December 4, 1960, enumerated her many accomplishments, the first being sheer longevity. "She had held the position for thirty-eight years . . . probably the longest record of continuous service at a single school of any dean of women in the United States."

Her other contributions were equally impressive. During her tenure in College Park, the number of women students grew from 93 in 1922 to 4,000 in 1960. Not content with merely bringing them to campus and confining them to the classroom, the dean "originated almost every women's organization now in existence" ("Girls Her Hobby," 1960).

Adele H. Stamp enjoyed 14 years of retirement prior to her death in October 1974. Befitting her prominence in the life of the university and in the state of Maryland, Joseph D. Tydings delivered the eulogy, in which he saluted the dean as "a pioneer in women's rights in Maryland."[20] In 1983, the University of Maryland reaffirmed the achievements of Adele H. Stamp by naming the university student center in her honor (Grabiner, 1983). Surely there could be no more fitting monument to the woman who claimed for women students at the University of Maryland the space to conduct and the right to pursue a full collegiate life.

Sarah Gibson Blanding

During her 18 years as Dean of Women at the University of Kentucky, Sarah Blanding developed the administrative skills, professional reputation, and personal network that contributed significantly to her career as a figure of national prominence in higher education in the United States in the postwar period. A number of institutions, including Oberlin College, Case Western Reserve University, and Bryn Mawr College, recognized the young dean's ability and considered her for administrative jobs. Blanding also enhanced her reputation during her tenure as president of the NADW. "Her opening speech was splendid," reported Blanding's assistant, Sarah B. Holmes, to Frank and Frances McVey, Blanding's benefactors at the University of Kentucky, after the NADW convention in 1940. "She presided with a great deal of ease and charm. . . . There was an air of informality and cordiality about the convention which has never existed before."[21]

Sarah Blanding's friendship with the McVeys deepened through the years, and this fact, more than any other, contributed to her reluctance to leave Lexington. In 1940, however, Frank McVey retired as president of the University of Kentucky, and Blanding reconsidered her options. Officials from Cornell University approached her about applying for the position of Dean of the College of Home Economics. With few personal ties to hold her, Blanding reported to Thomas P. Cooper, Acting President of the University of Kentucky, "I have had to take the bull by the horns and say that it will be possible for me to come to Cornell for an interview with the president."[22] Blanding impressed both him and other university officials, and despite her lack of formal training in home economics, the university offered and she accepted the deanship, thus becoming the first woman to hold that office in the history of Cornell University (University of Kentucky Press Release, 1946, p. 2).

Five years later, Sarah Blanding reached the peak of her career when, out of more than 200 candidates, she was selected to become the sixth person and first woman to serve as president of Vassar College. Kentuckians took great pride in a daughter of the South achieving such a distinction. Frank McVey led the delegation that represented the University of Kentucky at the inaugural ceremonies (University of Kentucky Press Release, 1946, p. 1). Doubtless, Blanding must have been honored to lead the institution from which her late friend and mentor, Frances Jewell McVey, graduated in 1913.

In the spring of 1964, Sarah Blanding retired as president of Vassar College. After 41 years as a university administrator, the 66-year-old president embraced her well-earned rest. In typical Blanding style, she commented to the press, "I'm going to be free for a year. . . . I'm not going to make a speech or be on a board . . . I'm just going to cut my own grass" ("Former University Dean," 1964).

Sarah Blanding lived for 21 years after her retirement from Vassar. In 1968, the University of Kentucky honored this native of the Bluegrass state by naming a four-building dormitory complex in her honor. Nothing could have been a more appropriate tribute to this woman who saved funds and solicited support so diligently for women's housing at the university (University of Kentucky Press Release, 1968, p. 1).

In March 1985, Sarah Blanding died, at the age of 86. University of Kentucky alumnae, many of whom, like Blanding, had to be self-supporting as college students, remembered her generosity in the midst of the Great Depression. "She made every effort to help us stay in school. She took money . . . for our tuition, books, and fees out of her own pocket while telling us we must stay in school" ("Memories of Blanding," 1985).

From childhood, Sarah Blanding met and mastered challenges with good grace. Unable to pursue a career in medicine, she nevertheless earned the best education she could with the resources available to her. Fortunately, the three strong women in her life—her mother, Sally Anderson Blanding, the woman physician who loaned her the money to attend New Haven Normal, and the elegant Frances Jewell McVey—convinced her that if she took risks, she could accomplish great works. Never losing her basic sense of self, despite her obvious administrative acumen and growing professional reputation, Blanding, while under consideration for the presidency of Bryn Mawr, joked with Frank McVey about "how far a graduate of a state university can get with the committee."[23] She need not have worried, for in the end, she forged a distinguished career dedicated to the cause of women's education and advancement.

RATIONALE FOR *"STALWART WOMEN"*

Deans of women encountered an additional, unexpected challenge from women students themselves. Increasing numbers of young women, responding to the civil rights, antiwar, and feminist movements of the 1960s, resented what they considered to be the unwarranted intrusion of the office of dean of women into their personal lives. To many of these students, the dean of women represented not their advocate within the administrative structure but rather their adversary, enforcing regulations that violated their rights not only as citizens but also as women. Such vocal response, accompanied by the administrative mania for reorganization, proved fatal to this innovative profession.

Why study the lives and careers of members of a profession that no longer exists? There are at least four reasons to do so. First, for over 70 years, the dean of women determined the quality of women's experience at coeducational institutions across the United States. Women such as the four on whom I focus in this book not only helped to increase the number of facilities, extracurricular opportunities, and honoraries open to women students but also worked to improve the campus environment for women faculty members.

Although the number of undergraduate women continues to grow, Mary S. Hartman, Dean of Douglass College of Rutgers University, contends that "the state of women's education at the end of the 20th century . . . is not a reassuring one" (Hartman, 1990, p. 1940). Moreover, Anne Firor Scott maintains that although the number of women attending institutions of higher education has increased, "another factor worked at cross purposes with educational goals" (Scott, 1984, p. 310). Both she and Hartman identify the basic problem as one of expectations. Quite simply, most administrators, while perfectly willing to grant women access to higher education, consign them to traditional female roles.

Most deans of women, however, possessed a different set of expectations for women and acted on their conviction. More than anything else, Bowersox, Harris, Stamp, and Blanding wanted college women to have meaningful choices after graduation. They knew, from personal experience, that crucial to achieving this goal was the ability of women to claim economic independence. Consequently, these deans struggled to provide women students with both the space and the opportunities to cultivate judgment, to exercise leadership abilities, and to maintain robust health. They knew that these skills, coupled with academic credentials, better prepared college women to live independent adult lives.

Second, although the profession survived for nearly a century, and scholarship concerning the profession has increased, confusion over the nature of the office and the women who occupied it continues. For many, the dean of women remains a vaguely comic, virginal figure. In one of the earliest studies of the office, Kathryn Sisson Phillips (1920) notes that, despite the obvious administrative character of the position, college and university administrators considered the dean of women "primarily responsible for the social atmosphere of the institution" (p. 34). Reflecting on the profession 50 years after the founding of the NADW, Mildred Bunce Sayre (1950) lamented the almost universal lack of understanding of the nature of the dean of women and her work. In addition, Margaret W. Rossiter (1982) has questioned the legitimacy of the profession.

An increasing number of historians of higher education suggest revised interpretation. Indeed, this growing body of work spans the entire history of the profession. The office, Paula Treichler (1985) claims, offered bright, capable women one of the few opportunities to demonstrate leadership skills on the coeducational campus. Further, Geraldine Clifford (1989) emphasizes the scope of the profession, which provided large numbers of women academic employment. For well over 50 years, virtually all coeducational institutions of higher learning in the United States employed a dean of women.

Jana Nidiffer (1994) evaluates the achievements of the founders of the National Association of Deans of Women, while Robert Schwartz (1990) contends that deans of women also established the student personnel profession. Joyce Antler (1987), Ruth Bordin (1993), and Ellen Fitzpatrick (1990) explore the lives of three prominent deans of women, respectively, Lucy Sprague Mitchell, Alice Freeman Palmer, and Marion Talbot. Patricia Bell-Scott (1979) identifies the contributions and concerns of Black deans of women, while Karen Anderson (1989) recounts the distinguished career of Lucy Slowe, the preeminent Black dean of women in the United States. Finally, Kathryn Tuttle (1996) evaluates the impact of the student and women's movements of the 1960s and 1970s on the profession.

Through their extensive annual reports, and personal and professional correspondence, Bowersox, Harris, Stamp, and Blanding present a compelling picture of determined professionals. Consistently rejecting a restrictive definition of their work, these women used their considerable administrative acumen to further the interests of women students, faculty, and professional peers. Their story dispels much of the confusion concerning the profession.

Third, although the office of the dean of women disappeared in the 1970s, and despite the continued increase in the number of women undergraduates at coeducational institutions, only a few women administrators have replaced the dean of women. Penina M. Glazer and Miriam Slater (1987) conclude that women's relationship to the professions has actually changed very little throughout this century. Although women employed a number of strategies in their effort to achieve professional acceptance, these authors contend that, because of cultural attitudes toward women and power, none of these approaches has been terribly successful. Of the four strategies, Glazer and Slater maintain, innovation is particularly problematic. In innovative professions, such as the dean of women, "career patterns were not clear" (p. 217) and the rewards remain problematic.

Contemporary statistics concerning women faculty and administrators in higher education in the United States confirm the conclusions of Glazer and Slater (1987). Women comprise scarcely 30% of the full-time faculty members and only about 12% of the faculty holding the rank of professor at colleges and universities in the United States. Women serve as president of barely 8% of the public institutions in the United States. Not surprisingly, 80% of women's colleges boast a woman chief executive (Anderson, 1989). Nevertheless, high-ranking women administrators and faculty members continue to be few and far between. To date, no woman administrative officer with the comparable visibility, influence, and access of the dean of women has emerged. Clearly, deans such as Bowersox, Harris, Stamp, and Blanding functioned as unique and powerful role models and advocates in coeducational institutions.

Finally, despite the impressive number of studies of women in higher education, the story of academic women remains far from complete. In their agendas for research, Patricia A. Graham (1981) and Sally Schwager (1987) advise scholars to identify women in nonelite institutions, for "that is where nearly all the women have been" (Graham, 1981, p. 428). Only recently have historians turned to a particularly rich pool of such institutions—the public, coeducational colleges. "The silence about early women in coeducational institutions," observes Geraldine Clifford (1989), "remains especially pronounced" (p. xi). Furthermore, the story of women faculty and students at White or Black southern coeducational institutions is largely unknown (Scott, 1984, p. 254). According to Jacquelyn Hall and Anne F. Scott (1987), "the whole subject [of Southern women's higher education] waits for an imaginative historian" (p. 469).

Patricia Palmieri (1981) encourages scholars to explore "the richly pluralistic history of the academic profession in the United States" (p. 548). This study represents a contribution to that history. Born in modest circumstances, economically independent from an early age, Katherine S. Bowersox, Agnes Ellen Harris, Adele H. Stamp, and Sarah Gibson Blanding present a striking variation on the "conventional plot" of academic women.

As dean of women at nonelite institutions across the South, they fashioned a new, not always welcome, variety of professionalism. Unwilling to give unquestioning support to either institution presidents and their goals or to the NADW and its traditional leadership, these four women combined a sensitivity to marginal groups with an unfailing belief in the potentially redemptive power of institutions to integrate women students, female faculty members, and their female peers more fully into the community of higher education. Furthermore, they rose to positions of regional and national leadership within the profession. Their compelling stories provide not only an unknown chapter in the history of American higher education but also a deeper understanding of academic women and the professional experience.

OVERVIEW OF THE BOOK

Chapter 1 of this study examines the education and early work experiences of Bowersox, Harris, Stamp, and Blanding. Following graduation from college, these women obtained jobs involving marginal groups in American society. Such experiences made them particularly effective advocates for academic women. Chapter 2 details their struggle with the issue of space on the male-dominated campus. These deans sought simultaneously to claim for women students greater access to campus space and to claim for themselves and their unmarried women colleagues freedom from the onerous task of living in the dormitory in constant proximity to their charges. Chapter 3 evaluates their response to the financial challenges that both students and deans of women encountered, particularly during the Great Depression.

Chapter 4 analyzes the particularly pragmatic perspective from which these deans sought to combine academic societies and ritual for college women. Chapter 5 reveals their efforts to enhance athletic opportunity for women students. This campaign encompassed not only the value of personal health for young women but also the campus politics involved in claiming and retaining precious campus space for women's athletics.

Chapter 6 centers on their strategy to foster professional outlets for themselves and for their colleagues, a vital and lasting component of the mission of the dean of women. Chapter 7 provides a much-needed consideration of how single academic women in coeducational institutions fulfilled family responsibilities and forged close personal friendships despite the demands of their profession. The Epilogue not only assesses the achievements of Bowersox, Harris,

Stamp, and Blanding, but also discusses the demise of the profession and suggests avenues for additional research.

CONCLUSION

What quality most clearly defined Katherine S. Bowersox, Agnes Ellen Harris, Adele H. Stamp, and Sarah Gibson Blanding? How should they be remembered? An incident in the life of Bowersox provides the most instructive answer. After receiving her honorary degree at the Berea College commencement of 1950, she triumphantly brought to Boothbay her dear friend Mary Welsh's degree and citation. Anxious that this be received with proper ceremony, Welsh, in full academic regalia, stood in the garden of the cottage on Sawyer's Island, while Bowersox, similarly attired, conferred on her this great honor. In order to preserve the day, the two recorded the event through photographs, one of which they sent to Francis Hutchins.

"This morning I received a beautiful . . . photograph of you and Miss Bowersox in your garden," the president wrote to Welsh. "I will cherish it for the two stalwart women who served so valiantly and successfully the students of this campus . . . and in later years have blessed us with . . . their friendship."[24] Such an assessment might well apply to all of these women. Throughout their personal and professional lives, they met challenge with fortitude, humor, and gumption. They did not always win. In the end, their chosen profession disappeared. But their spirit and their achievements endured in the hearts of generations of academic women—students, faculty members, and professional colleagues—throughout the South and the nation.

A formidable presence on the Berea campus for 20 years, Katherine Bowersox worked to enhance the experience of women students and faculty. (Archives and Special Collections, Berea College)

CHAPTER 1

"The Alternative Story"

Early Life and Challenging Careers

In her discussion of contemporary biography, Carolyn G. Heilbrun (1988) marvels at "the ease of male lives" (p. 38) and the variety of possible plot lines. Scripts of women's lives, however, she observes, follow one of two predictable scenarios, of which the first is the conventional plot, including courtship, marriage, family, and fulfillment. The second is the "unnarrated lives" of single women of all ages. Seldom, concludes Heilbrun, do scholars of women's lives search out and evaluate the many "alternative stories" (pp. 38–39).

Susan Ware (1992) identifies a component essential to understanding women's lives, especially those "alternative stories" of single professional women. "One of the most important contributions of women's history to the craft of biography may be its emphasis on personal lives and their impact on public accomplishment" (p. 61). Women's status as daughters, potential mothers, and caregivers colors their decisions, particularly those concerning professional careers, in ways unknown to most men.

Thus, to evaluate the careers of Bowersox, Harris, Stamp, and Blanding, one must examine the personal circumstances that shaped their lives. What, if any, role did their parents and siblings assume? Why and where did they attend college? What did they study? Did they marry? Why did they work? What work did they choose? Why did they finally become deans of women?

Katherine S. Bowersox, Agnes Ellen Harris, Adele H. Stamp, and Sarah Gibson Blanding represent alternative stories on three levels. Most obviously, they were women professional leaders in higher education, which men have traditionally dominated. However, because of the common tendency to consider women professionals as a relatively homogeneous group, historians often overlook the multiple textures the lives of these four women suggest. Bowersox, Harris, Stamp, and Blanding differ in significant ways not only from their women contemporaries in higher education but also among themselves.

Most studies of academic women, including those few of deans of women, highlight the "conventional plot" of early professional women, focusing on privileged circumstances, elite education, employment at prestigious institutions, and northeastern connections. Two of the best-known women to hold the office of dean of women, Marion Talbot and Lucy Sprague Mitchell, dominate the literature and thus reinforce this standard image of the professional woman. Raised in comfortable circumstances, these women attended either prominent public research institutions or elite women's colleges. Although both held the deanship at institutions outside the Northeast, Talbot at the University of Chicago and Mitchell at the University of California at Berkeley, each maintained close connections with the northeastern women's network.

Katherine S. Bowersox, Agnes Ellen Harris, Adele H. Stamp, and Sarah Gibson Blanding, on the other hand, illustrate the "unnarrated lives" of a woman's profession. Furthermore, these deans share certain characteristics that suggest an alternative profile for women in the professions. Their educational and vocational experiences reveal lives of rugged independence and persistent involvement with marginal groups.

Born in modest circumstances, Bowersox, Harris, Stamp, and Blanding eschewed the luxury of either the old-time southern woman's college, whose graduates reinforced the status of their families, or the elite northeastern woman's college, which, in the postbellum era, offered peerless, but occasionally impractical, liberal arts training. These women attended college for neither cultural polish nor training for unremunerated community service, but rather to prepare themselves for economic self-sufficiency. When they became deans of women, the four worked at nonelite institutions in a poor section of the country. Their professional networks, which included a wide variety of women professionals—deans of women, YWCA workers, U.S. Department of Agriculture (USDA) employees, and political figures, reflected neither regional, educational, nor occupational bias.

The most obvious difference among Bowersox, Harris, Stamp, and Blanding was chronological. Nearly 30 years separated Bowersox and Blanding, respectively, the oldest and the youngest. In fact, the four can be divided into two cohorts: Bowersox, born in 1869, and Harris, in 1883; and Stamp, in 1893, and Blanding, in 1898. Such a difference may well have influenced both their collegiate training and their initial attitudes toward becoming deans of women.

The variety of institutions of higher education the four attended, between approximately 1890 and 1920, reflected the range of choice available to women, particularly to those living in the South. Bowersox and Harris enrolled in public institutions designed to train women, respectively, a teachers college and a single-sex college for women. Both majored in feminized fields—Bowersox in education and Harris in home economics. In contrast, Stamp and Blanding attended institutions that offered women students a wider curricular choice. As students, respectively, in a private women's college and in a public, coeducational state university, Stamp and Blanding embraced liberal arts majors—the former, sociology, and the latter, political science. Betraying a shared practicality as well, however, both women also sought credentials in physical education, the field in which each found her first job.

The four women also differed dramatically in their initial response to being a dean of women. Again, the age difference appears to be significant. Bowersox and Harris, at 38 and 44, respectively, assumed the deanship as mid-career professionals, with impressive credentials in administration. Katherine S. Bowersox brought 14 years of teaching and administrative experience to the office, while Agnes Ellen Harris, for the preceding 20 years, held administrative posts both in higher education and in government service. Each woman actively sought not just a deanship, but those particular deanships, at Berea College and at the University of Alabama. For each, the position represented the fulfillment of her career.

Stamp and Blanding, by contrast, became deans of women while still in their twenties. Sarah Blanding, at 25, numbered among the youngest deans of women in the country. Neither woman actively applied for the deanship. In fact, each took the job on a temporary basis. Only after some experience in the office did they appreciate the work.

Shared economic reality and social commitment, however, connected Bowersox, Harris, Stamp, and Blanding across the years. All four worked their way through college at the height of the Progressive period. On their respective campuses, these bright young women could not ignore the enthusiasm that surrounded various reform initiatives.

These women enrolled in college first and foremost to prepare themselves for necessary economic independence. Unlike many of their classmates, Bowersox, Harris, Stamp, and Blanding combined their need to be self-supporting with their commitment to social Progressivism. Like the pioneering first generation of college women, none of the four married, and all entered the work force immediately upon, if not before, graduation.

Bowersox, Harris, Stamp, and Blanding embraced work that addressed family, neighborhood, and community concerns. Here they encountered the framework that defined the course of their professional lives as deans of women. Through their service to children—Native American and Irish, and to women, industrial workers, and farm wives, the four discerned the concerns of marginal groups. Through their work within local and federal government agencies and private charities, the four recognized the potentially redemptive power of rightly directed institutions. Bowersox, Harris, Stamp, and Blanding maintained and nurtured their concerns for marginal populations through their first jobs and subsequently brought this to campus in the service of women's educational, personal, and professional needs.

KATHERINE S. BOWERSOX

The daughter of a country minister, Katherine Sophia Bowersox was born in 1869, in Paxtonville, Pennsylvania, a small community in the central portion of the state. Her lifelong love of nature, especially arduous hikes and simple picnics, might well be traced to her rural childhood. So might her maturity and sense of purpose, for Bowersox's early years did not remain free of tragedy.

Following her father's death in 1879, the 9-year-old girl, her mother, and two brothers struggled to survive as a family. Despite severe economic problems, however, the young Bowersox displayed an active intellectual curiosity, which served her well at the Indian Industrial School in Carlisle, Pennsylvania, and at Berea College. Turning to her late father's modest collection of books, she read them all, "including a five volume History of the Reformation and a two volume Ancient History" ("Some of the People," 1919, p. 2).

Determined to improve her circumstances, and those of her family for whom she took responsibility, Bowersox sought collegiate training. Like many other ambitious but penniless young women, she took advantage of the closest state-supported institution that would prepare her for economic independence and enrolled in Bloomsburg Literary Institute and State Normal School, which provided inexpensive training for both women and men seeking careers in public school work in nearby Bloomsburg, Pennsylvania (Edwards, 1982).

Bowersox enrolled in the elementary teachers course, an almost infallible path to employment (*Alumni List*, n.d.). She did not, however, earn a degree from Bloomsburg. Although she subsequently attended summer school at a variety of institutions and Berea College awarded her two honorary degrees, Bowersox considered her lack of a college degree her "lifelong regret." Reflecting on the matter, she confessed to William J. Hutchins, President of Berea College, that "like so many of our Berea students, I went to school during the summer and worked the rest of the year to support my mother and semi-invalid brother."[1] For four years, Bowersox taught in the public schools of Middleburg, Pennsylvania, a rural village close to Paxtonville.[2]

Perhaps in search of a larger salary, perhaps in search of a greater challenge than public school work, in 1893 Bowersox joined the faculty of the Indian Industrial School in Carlisle, Pennsylvania. For 8 years, she served as supervisor of the Normal-Training class. In 1902, she assumed an administrative post as the Principal of the Academy Department.

The Indian Industrial School became a reality because of the dedication of one man. In 1875, Second Lieutenant Richard Henry Pratt, USA, a cavalry officer serving the Plains Territory, transferred 75 Plains Indians to Fort Marion in Florida (Morton, 1962). Rather than incarcerate them, the lieutenant advocated not only productive work but also education for the Native Americans, who he believed could function as responsible American citizens (Prucha, 1984).

Pratt subsequently approached Secretary of the Interior Carl Schurz in 1879, in hope of founding a government-supported school for Indians (Morton, 1962). He had selected Carlisle Barracks, Pennsylvania, a military post since 1801, as the site for the proposed school. The federal government agreed to support him. On November 1, 1879, Pratt officially opened the Indian Industrial School in Carlisle.

In accepting employment at Carlisle, Bowersox unwittingly became part of one of the most controversial experiments in the acculturation of Indians in the United States. Although Carlisle's founder, Richard Henry Pratt, proceeded from a genuine desire to help Indians become responsible citizens, in the end, his work at Carlisle, and indeed the entire boarding school experiment, yielded at best ambiguous results. Anthropologists and others respectful of the value of indigenous cultures opposed the severing of Indians from their traditions. Furthermore, many graduates of the boarding schools considered themselves to be alienated from both White and Indian culture.

How did Katherine Bowersox contribute to the mission of the Indian Industrial School? She worked devotedly to enrich the religious, intellectual, and social experiences of her students. Pratt considered religious training a vital component of education for citizenship. Each Thursday evening, students attended prayer meeting, which Bowersox often conducted (*Red Man and Helper*, February 2, 1902, p. 3). Of course, religious activities dominated Sundays, with Bowersox taking her turn as superintendent of the Sunday School (*Red Man and Helper*, November 11, 1901, p. 3).

The lifelong pleasure she derived from reading, fueled by her natural curiosity, served Bowersox well at Carlisle. In addition to her teaching and administrative responsibilities, Bowersox delivered numerous speeches to groups large and small. The array of subjects is somewhat astounding—both that she would be familiar with them and that they might be of interest to the students. She spoke on such diverse topics as Charles Lamb, Alfred the Great, Chinese literature, Greek civilization, and Japanese education (*Indian Helper*, February 23, 1894, p. 3).

Katherine S. Bowersox loved life and loved her students, as an examination of her social activities, both on and off the campus, suggests. She participated in the activities of both the Invincibles, a men's debate society, and the Susans, or Susan Longstreet Literary Society for women (*Red Man and Helper*, February 22, 1901, p. 3). Bowersox also hosted parties for student groups, including the senior women and "the senior pupil-teachers and their young gentlemen guests" (*Red Man and Helper*, December 19, 1902, p. 3).

How could the fair-minded Bowersox work within a repressive institution such as the Indian Industrial School? Critics now maintain that the mission of these schools contributed as significantly as did any military campaign or tribal relocation to the devaluation and destruction of Indian culture. Doubtless it is a fanciful hope indeed to expect her to reflect this sort of criticism of the boarding school experiment. Bowersox's papers and correspondence offer no direct response, other than to indicate her enjoyment of the work and her fondness for the students. Like many reformers of her generation, Bowersox apparently considered the cultural uplift of Western Christianity and literature, vigorous athletics, and spirited debate of value to all cultural groups in the United States.

Despite her hectic schedule, Bowersox neglected neither family nor professional connections. Both of her brothers visited Carlisle. The exact nature of these relationships, concerning which little correspondence survives, remains somewhat resistant to full disclosure. It is obvious, however, that Katherine Bowersox was not the only energetic person in her family. In 1904, her brother F. C. Bowersox, a former school superintendent and incumbent member of the Pennsylvania state legislature, traveled to the school (*Arrow*, December 8, 1904, p. 3). He appears nowhere in Bowersox's correspondence and seems to have played little or no role in the life of this independent woman. Her other brother, Rollin, however, not only visited Carlisle but remained an intermittent responsibility for her entire life (*Indian Helper*, June 22, 1894, p. 3).

Bowersox also retained ties to her alma mater. She frequently visited Bloomsburg, including her 10th reunion in 1903 (*Red Man and Helper*, June 26, 1893, p. 3). More important, however, she also maintained close contact with O. H. Bakeless, her predecessor as principal of the Academy Department, who subsequently held a faculty appointment at Bloomsburg Literary and Normal. While at Carlisle, she visited him and his wife on numerous occasions. Bakeless's enthusiastic recommendation of his former colleague was essential to her success in obtaining the much-desired post at Berea College (*Red Man and Helper*, June 3, 1904, p. 3).

By 1907, Bowersox, ready for a new challenge, energetically pursued a position at Berea College. That she chose Berea is not surprising, considering its similarity to Carlisle. Both institutions took as their mission the uplift and education of neglected, if not forgotten, segments of American society. Founded in 1855, Berea College was dedicated to fostering free inquiry and to meeting the educational needs of both Blacks and mountain youth of Appalachia (Peck, 1982). Berea's founders and its early faculty shared a proud heritage of dedication to racial equality and to other reform initiatives. The institution attracted a unique sort of person to its faculty. Katherine S. Bowersox fit the mold.

"I learn," she wrote President W. G. Frost, "that the position of Lady Principal is vacant at Berea and I respectfully ask to be considered." Concerned with her lack of a college degree, she hastened to cite her continual efforts at self-improvement. "I have . . . [attended] the leading summer schools and the NEA almost annually. Have also visited Hampton and Tuskegee this year."[3] Not wanting Frost to think that Berea was her only employment option, Bowersox also indicated that she had other employment prospects. In 1906, the Pittsburgh chapter of the YWCA asked her to become its general secretary, and in 1907, federal government officials, obviously pleased with her work at Carlisle, offered her the principalship of the Indian school in Lawrence, Kansas.[4]

Despite those offers, Bowersox assured Frost that Berea was "just the atmosphere I would seek for my work." She clearly wanted to serve in an institution where "the building of character and higher ideals are of first importance."[5] Reflecting a deep sense of duty and personal honor, Bowersox assured the president that "if I feel that I cannot do the work satisfactorily, I will not undertake it."[6]

Bowersox's experience at Carlisle prepared her well to serve as Dean of Women at Berea College. As the principal of the Academy Department, she moved beyond the traditional woman's work of teaching into a supervisory role, in which she developed valuable administrative skills that assured her that she had a variety of career options. She understood and appreciated the potential power of educational institutions to foster a more just society. Most important, however, Bowersox's work with Native Americans reinforced her affinity with marginal groups, enhancing her ability to understand the problems that Appalachian Americans faced.

AGNES ELLEN HARRIS

Agnes Ellen Harris, like Bowersox, grew up in a family that valued sacrifice and service. Born in 1883 in Cedartown, Georgia, a small community near the Alabama border, Harris was the second child and first daughter of Ellen Simmons Harris and James Coffee Harris. James Harris relinquished his own dream of becoming a physician and turned instead to teaching in order to educate his eight siblings. Successful in this profession, he served for over 40 years as superintendent in the public schools of Cedartown, Marietta, and Rome, Georgia, and as director of the Georgia School for the Deaf.

James Harris's sacrifices for his siblings and his offspring bore fruit. His brothers and sons enjoyed successful careers in politics, medicine, industry, and the military. His daughters, as well, took their places in the public sphere. Agnes Ellen Harris and her sister, Margaret, held faculty and administrative positions in higher education (S. Harris, 1935).

Throughout her life, Agnes Ellen Harris remained especially devoted to her father. Their close relationship may well have been a consequence of her mother's untimely death in 1895, when Harris was only 12. James Harris cared for his children as conscientiously as he did for his siblings. Recalling his sacrifices for her education, nearly 40 years later, Harris characterized her father as possessing "high ideals but a limited purse."[7]

In 1900, despite that lean purse and resistance from her late mother's family, Agnes Ellen Harris, at the insistence of her father, attended a one-year course at Oread Institute of Domestic Science in Worcester, Massachusetts. Founded in 1849 as Oread Collegiate Institute, to offer higher education to New England women, the school remained in operation until 1881, when it became Oread Institute of Domestic Science, designed "to provide practical teachers of a practical domestic science" (Wright, 1905, pp. 450–451). The institution accepted approximately 50 students each year for its one-year course of study.

A naive 17-year-old who had never traveled outside Georgia, Harris embarked for Massachusetts with "my Mother's seal skin coat" and much admonition from her family. Reflecting nearly 35 years later on her time at Oread, she said that she cherished that "glorious year" in New England. Harris recognized that she would not have gone at all had it not been for "a very wise father who had led me to believe that Massachusetts had a great deal to give in the education of young people."[8] She also acknowledged her own reticence to leave familiar surroundings and her father's farsightedness in "[making] me realize that all life did not center in Rome, Georgia."[9]

Harris soon forgot her homesickness and relished her "glorious year" in New England. In addition to academic work, she enjoyed the social life, including the traditional New England Thanksgiving and clam bake. Most importantly, however, Harris maintained that the experience at Oread "gave me the inspiration for my life work in home economics, and I cherish it."[10]

On her return to Georgia, Harris found her father insisting, "very much to my chagrin,"[11] that she attend Georgia Normal and Industrial College for Women, a two-year public institution in Milledgeville, Georgia. Armed with a two-year diploma, Harris embarked on a public school career. After one year as an elementary school teacher, she spent the next 6 years as a teacher of home economics throughout Georgia. Between 1903 and 1907, Harris worked at Lanier High School in Macon, Georgia. She then accepted a position at the State Agricultural School in Douglas, Georgia. There she first worked with adult students, which provided a valuable experience for her subsequent involvement in home demonstration work.[12]

Determined to earn a college degree, however, Harris again left the South to attend summer sessions at Teachers College, Columbia University. Founded in 1880 as the Kitchen Garden Club and designed to train young women in domestic skills, Teachers College became an official unit of Columbia University in 1889 (Coon, 1947). The following year, college officials, mindful of the need to make teacher training as accessible as possible, initiated the Columbia Summer Session. In this way the institution exerted a profound influence on a significant majority of American teachers, including Harris, who earned her degree in home economics in 1910.

Throughout her lengthy career, which spanned over half a century, Agnes Ellen Harris served women's interests first as a home economist and subsequently as a dean of women. She acquired her initial administrative training between 1910 and 1919, as Dean of the School of Home Economics at the Florida State College for Women (FSCW).[13] In addition to that position, between 1910 and 1919, Harris also put her home economics skills to more immediately practical service with the U.S. Department of Agriculture, first as the director of canning clubs in Leon County, Florida, of which Tallahassee is the county seat, and later as Assistant State Agent in Charge of Home Demonstration Work.

Home Demonstration in the South

The home demonstration movement attracted national attention as a consequence of the work of Seaman A. Knapp, noted agriculturist, former college president, and USDA Agent for the Promotion of Agriculture in the South. To alleviate the persistent agricultural problems in the region, Knapp realized that he must not only instruct the farmer but also attempt to "reach the farm wife and . . . the children of the South" (Scott, 1970, p. 237). In 1907, he approached farm boys through the establishment of corn clubs, which combined social interaction with agricultural innovation. Six years later, 91,000 southern boys participated in the program (Dabney, 1981).

Beyond farmers and their sons, however, Knapp also hoped, through farm daughters, to reach the farm wives, essential to a productive and orderly agrarian life. With this end in view, he advocated the establishment of tomato clubs, the first of which appeared in 1911 in Aiken County, South Carolina. Like the corn clubs, these agencies, which fostered social contact while teaching the best ways to grow and can tomatoes, expanded dramatically. By 1913, 30,000 girls were participating in tomato clubs established in fourteen states (Dabney, 1981).

Harris's initial involvement with home demonstration work came when a USDA official visited the University of Florida in Gainesville, and encouraged J. J. Vernon, Dean of the College of Agriculture, to identify women to organize tomato clubs throughout the state. Vernon contacted the Leon County farm demonstration agent, who was unable to locate a candidate. Finally T. B. Byrd, a prominent Tallahassee merchant, contacted Dean Harris. Years later, she recalled that Byrd, in a rather cryptic conversation, advised her that "a man was in his store and wanted a woman to do some demonstrating for the Government" (Moore, 1929, p. 131).

In her account of the first meeting with Dean Vernon in Dade City, Florida,

Harris acknowledged her understandable confusion. "I had visions of making bread with oleomargarine, or using flour of some particular kind, because at that time, demonstrating meant standing before an audience and preparing some kind of food." Nevertheless, she proceeded to Dade City "with a suitcase full of utensils . . . thinking I would give demonstrations if necessary" (Moore, 1929, p. 132).

On learning the actual purpose of the meeting and of the work—the establishment of canning clubs in Leon County—Harris eagerly accepted the position. Devoting her one free day each week to the work, she hired a horse and buggy and visited each of the county schools. Despite her own enthusiasm for the job, she noted that "some members of the faculty . . . looked askance at one of their colleagues going out to teach the process of canning tomatoes." Nevertheless, she persisted, and she discovered "the wonderful service this work could be to Florida" (Moore, 1929, pp. 131–132).

Convinced of the value of extension work, Harris moved decisively to make it a part of the dual mission of the School of Home Economics at FSCW. In addition to the regular collegiate curriculum, designed for home economics majors and other interested students, the School of Home Economics, during Harris's tenure, developed a diverse extension program that included four major activities: on-campus short courses, publication of bulletins, extension school, and club work (*Bulletin 1912–1913*, p. 110). Each year, FSCW offered a 2-week on-campus course "open to housekeepers, and to all women over 16 years of age." Designed to enhance domestic skills, the short course included sessions devoted to "Care of Milk, Poultry Raising, Care of the Sick, Sanitation and Hygiene, and Training of Children" (*Bulletin 1912–1913*, pp. 65–66). Also charged with the preparation of county home demonstration agents, Harris conducted an annual training conference at FSCW. To disseminate material to the widest possible audience, the extension program also published a series of bulletins devoted to efficient domestic practice.

Mobility and accessibility defined the home demonstration movement. Designed neither for college students nor for urban housewives, the program could work only with a dedicated cadre of agents, primarily women, who could infiltrate the farmhouses of the entire South like an army, bearing the gospel of modernization. More than a mere footsoldier in that army, Agnes Ellen Harris instituted a statewide network of extension schools and canning clubs.

She quickly moved beyond her initial work with the Leon County canning clubs to become the second-highest-ranking extension worker in the state. The USDA divided the work into the farm and home demonstration divisions, with the Stage Agent in Charge of Farm Demonstration Work at the University of Florida and Harris, the Assistant State Agent in Charge of Home Demonstration Work, at FSCW. The Florida home demonstration program grew dramatically under Harris's leadership, from 13 counties in 1912 to 41 counties in 1919. In addition, agents conducted extension work in four urban areas, and African American home demonstration agents worked in 17 counties.

Did Agnes Ellen Harris's work for FSCW and for the USDA prepare her in any way to become a dean of women? These experiences, without doubt, provided her with varied and intensive opportunities to develop oratorical and organizational skills, both of which served her well during 18 years in Tuscaloosa. Harris spoke extensively in her capacity as dean and field agent, not only to farm women but also to a wide variety of social, educational, and political groups. Among the varied audiences to which she preached the gospel of home demonstration, domestic modernization, and food conservation were the Tampa Woman's Club, the students and faculty of Winthrop College, and the wartime meetings of the Florida Food Commission (*Florida Flambeau*, April 7, 1917, p. 3).

The Florida Flambeau, FSCW's student newspaper, closely and enthusiastically chronicled the peripatetic dean's activities. Neither the class nor the race nor the gender of her audience prevented Harris from delivering her message, no insignificant feat in the socially conservative South of the early 20th century. Oblivious to the heat of May and to the curiosity of the crowd, in 1915, she, and other women as well, invaded a predominantly male domain in small southern towns to conduct canning and cooking demonstrations "on the courthouse grounds in Kissimmee" (*Florida Flambeau*, May 8, 1915, p. 3). In October 1917, speaking on behalf of the federal government, Harris visited Ft. Myers, where she addressed 2,000 farmers concerning the necessity of food conservation (*Florida Flambeau*, November 3, 1917, p. 4).

Food Conservation and World War I

World War I offered Harris a valuable, if not entirely welcome, challenge to her administrative skills. In 1917, she became the USDA field agent responsible for food conservation work in the urban areas of the 15 southern states. As a consequence, her schedule became even more hectic. Harris relocated to Washington, D.C., and although she took a leave of absence from FSCW, she nevertheless returned to Tallahassee each month to monitor activities at the college (*Florida Flambeau*, November 24, 1917).

The growth of agricultural extension work, whether in wartime or in peacetime, like the dramatic increase in the number of collegiate women, created a new profession for women—home demonstration work. Both Harris's correspondence and reports of various agents across the South suggest the dedication these women brought to the work, despite difficult circumstances and minimal compensation (Kett, 1985). At a conference commemorating the 25th anniversary of cooperative demonstration work, Maud Wallace, State Home Demonstration Agent for Virginia, exhorted her audience to

> pay tribute to those pioneer county home demonstration agents . . . [who] received
> the tremendous salary of $50 to $75 a month . . . fed themselves, paid their own
> transportation, wrote their own letters and sent in their own reports when they could.
> (Wallace, 1929, p. 123)

Harris was clearly one of these pioneers, dedicated to the value of home demonstration and the larger cause of southern economic and domestic modernization. Nearly 20 years after leaving Florida, she reminisced fondly with several friends concerning the work in all its aspects. "I shall never forget," she observed, "those trips [to] some of those places in Florida where I could pay only 50 cents a day and lived accordingly."[14]

Despite these hardships, however, Harris, nearly 2 decades after leaving Tallahassee, retained a proprietary interest in the program she built at FSCW, insisting that she felt "quite like a woman must feel who divorces a fine husband and then sees him marry a fine woman and have her rear the children."[15] The Florida years, from the tomato club work to the direction of the entire statewide program in home demonstration, represented for the dean "ten of the happiest years of my professional life . . . as happy as any professional woman ever had."[16] These experiences, in which she left the classroom and carried the Progressive message of the value of community ties directly to southern farm women, provided the foundation for Harris's subsequent work with women faculty and students, who shared with these farm women a pervasive sense of genuine marginality.

Educational Administration

Before beginning her work as a dean of women at Alabama Polytechnic Institute in 1922, Harris made one last foray into public education, this time not as a teacher but as an administrator. In 1919, she left FSCW for Texas, to become State Supervisor for Home Economics. Harris's assumption of this post coincided with a veritable political revolution in Texas. The year before, Texans elected Annie Webb Blanton State Superintendent of Public Instruction, making her the first woman to hold that post and the first woman to capture statewide elective office in the history of the Lone Star State. Thus Harris, a seasoned administrator herself, enjoyed the rare opportunity to work at the state level with another dedicated woman leader. In addition to their professional relationship, the two began a friendship that stretched across the decades of two remarkable careers (*Florida Flambeau*, May 24, 1919, p. 5).

Although Harris initially accepted the position at FSCW in order to pursue her career as a home economist, after a decade of daily contact with women students, she developed a strong sensitivity to their problems and potential.

Never one to resist a challenge, Harris decided that she could best serve college women on a coeducational campus. She believed that this often-unwelcome minority needed a forceful advocate with proven administrative skills to protect and advance their interests. Consequently, in 1922, Harris resigned as USDA Field Agent for the midwestern and eastern states and returned to campus in a different capacity, as the Dean of Women at Alabama Polytechnic Institute, in Auburn, Alabama. In addition to her work as dean of women, she also served as State Home Demonstration Agent for Alabama and earned a master's degree in home economics by attending summer sessions at Columbia University.[17]

These were productive but not totally satisfying years for Harris. Despite her devotion to home demonstration work, she enthusiastically embraced her new vocation as dean of women and developed an abiding commitment to securing for women access to the full range of college life. However, after 5 years at Alabama Polytechnic Institute, Harris had come to doubt the likelihood of success, for the number of women students had increased only from 65 to 125.[18]

Meanwhile, Harris also recognized that prospects for women at Alabama Polytechnic Institute compared unfavorably with those at the University of Alabama. Central to the success of coeducation at that institution were Julia Tutwiler and George H. Denny, who assumed the institution's presidency in 1912. Dedicated to the value of women's education and their full participation in campus life, Denny not only encouraged the admission of women students but also made suitable provision for their on-campus housing and supervision. As a consequence, the number of women students increased dramatically, from 52 in 1912 to nearly 500 in 1926 ("Capstone to Mark," 1943).

It was such sustained growth, coupled with President Denny's aggressive support for women's education, that attracted Harris to Tuscaloosa in 1927. This institution, she maintained, provided the atmosphere in which she could accomplish what she believed to be her life's work, namely "to develop a program in the education of women."[19] Even before assuming her duties in the fall of 1927, Harris assured Henrietta M. Thompson, her close friend and colleague at Alabama Polytechnic, that she left that institution without regret and relished the new challenges before her.

ADELE H. STAMP

Born in Catonsville, Maryland, a suburb of Baltimore, Adele Hagner Stamp, like Sarah Blanding, spent her childhood and adolescence in a predominantly urban setting. A highly motivated and energetic young woman, Stamp held almost continuous employment before graduating from Sophie Newcomb College, with a major in sociology, in 1921. Her natural athletic ability coincided fortu-

itously with an increased interest in recreational opportunities for women of all
ages to provide Stamp with a variety of employment options both before and
during her college years.

Between 1913 and 1915, she worked as a physical education instructor in
the Catonsville High School. For the subsequent 2 years, Stamp went to Alfred
University in western New York, where she taught in the recreation program of
that institution's summer school. In 1917, Stamp returned to Maryland to work
with the summer school recreation program of the University of Maryland, in
College Park. Little did the young woman realize the role that institution would
assume in her professional life only 5 years later ("Adele Stamp," *Who Was
Who*, 1976, v. 1).

The United States entry into World War I provided Stamp, like Agnes Ellen
Harris, with employment that prepared her well for her career as a dean of
women. Adele Stamp used her collegiate expertise in sociology and recreation
in the service of yet another marginal group—women industrial workers. An
employee of the War Work Council of the YWCA, she held two positions of
responsibility. Between 1918 and 1919, Stamp served as director of recreation
at the Old Hickory Munitions Plant, in Jacksonville, Tennessee. The following
year she worked as director of the YWCA's Industrial Service Center for
women workers in New Orleans ("Maryland's Woman Dean," 1939).

YWCA leaders considered the organization's work among women industrial workers one of its most significant missions. Attracting these workers to
the YWCA and its services, however, proved to be no simple task (Simms,
1950). Central to that effort was Florence Simms, the YWCA's first Industrial
Secretary. In 1904, while working with women industrial workers at the YWCA
of Chicago, she began fundamental revisions of programs for women industrial
workers (Robinson, 1960).

To accomplish this goal, Simms first modernized the Industrial Department
staff. No longer content with well-meaning but inadequately trained workers,
she hired college-trained women who, like Stamp, were familiar with the new
social sciences (Frederickson, 1984). Simms then sent these women into factory
towns to establish chapters that would directly address the needs of women
industrial workers.

When the United States entered World War I in April 1917, the YWCA
soon established its War Work Council, charged with meeting the needs of
women defense workers. It did so primarily through the establishment of approximately 300 War Service Centers, which "provided rooms, food, recreation,
and fellowship to women employed in defense industries" (Frederickson, 1984,
p. 78). As more women joined the industrial work force, the YWCA also encouraged greater public support for adequate health and safety regulations in the
war industries.

Stamp began her work at the Old Hickory Munitions Plant in Jacksonville,

Tennessee, while both the facility and "the impassable roads" ("Maryland's Woman Dean," 1939) connecting it to nearby Nashville were still under construction. The complex, designed to be one of the largest producers of smokeless gun powder in the world, employed approximately 5,000 women. These workers represented every class and region of the country, "from the daughters of Tennessee mountaineers . . . to the debutantes from the West Coast who wanted to do their bit for their country" ("Maryland's Woman Dean," 1939). Equally diverse in their recreational needs, some requested French classes so that they might better understand letters from their soldier-companions, while others favored organized athletic events. Stamp's work consisted of developing recreational programs that addressed these varied needs ("Maryland's Woman Dean," 1939).

Stamp continued her association with the YWCA after the war. Between 1919 and 1920, while a student at Newcomb, she worked as director of the YWCA Industrial Service Center in New Orleans. Such facilities, the YWCA maintained, provided "an opportunity to serve an industrial community to an extent that it has never been able to before" (Industrial Committee, 1918, p. 15). There women workers, professionals, and YWCA officials could come together to devise strategies for the improvement of working conditions in industry (Frederickson, 1984).

Industrial service centers included women industrial workers, along with women professionals and reformers, on their governing boards. Each center offered a variety of programs, including "housing, cafeteria service, education, and recreation" (Industrial Committee, 1918, p. 17). Most important, however, was the psychological role these facilities assumed. The overarching goal of the service centers, concluded the YWCA, was to engender within women industrial workers "the realization of the power of a woman . . . the realization of her worth, of the necessity of all women standing together . . . and a realization of the dignity of all women" (Industrial Committee, 1918, p. 19). Such a message served Adele H. Stamp well both in her own life and in her role as the principal advocate for the interests of college women.

Adele H. Stamp's association with the YWCA played an essential role in her subsequent career as a dean of women. Like Bowersox and Harris, she acquired substantial administrative experience. Like Harris, she also relished the liberating power of working within institutions in which women assumed major responsibilities. Having developed a recreation program for 5,000 women industrial workers, Stamp was confident of her ability to implement a comprehensive women's program at the University of Maryland. Furthermore, the variation among those women industrial workers prepared the young dean well for the growing diversity she encountered among women on the college campus.

Adele H. Stamp's collegiate experience at Newcomb merits special attention. Not only was she a different sort of southern woman, she attended a different sort of southern women's college. Like Bowersox, Blanding, and Harris, Stamp was not a student in the traditional sense of that term. Employed before and during her collegiate career, this young woman brought an unusual maturity to her educational experience. Furthermore, on graduation, the 28-year-old Stamp became the oldest of the four to earn a degree.

Unlike Bowersox, Blanding, and Harris, however, only Adele H. Stamp attended a private school, H. Sophie Newcomb Memorial College of Tulane University, in New Orleans, endowed in 1886 by Josephine LeMonnier Newcomb in memory of her daughter. The college differed dramatically from its sister institutions in the South, both in its expectations of its students and in their expectations of themselves. The institution defined women as actors—in their own educational process, in their careers, and in their communities.

Although Newcomb attracted young women of wealth, most of its students came from families impoverished by the Civil War. Lynn Gordon (1990), in her study of the institution, suggests that both the principal benefactor of the college and the parents who sent their daughters there concurred on its primary mission. Josephine Newcomb desired that the school "provide a practical as well as a cultural and intellectual education" (p. 167). The mothers and fathers of many Newcomb students agreed and sent their daughters to college to enhance "their capacities for self-support" (p. 173).

Adele Stamp numbered among those Newcomb students who responded favorably to such expectations. Building on her extensive experience in recreation, with a variety of populations, she chose for her major the immediately applicable field of sociology. Unlike the traditional college student of the era, Stamp continued her employment with the YWCA while attending Newcomb.

Through her major in sociology and her work with the YWCA, Adele Stamp managed to combine these goals of practicality and service. The caption accompanying her senior photograph in the 1921 edition of *The Jambalaya* (1921) suggests this happy combination:

A—means Ability,
    'Twas never known to shirk her.
S—Stamps her right away
    As a peachy Social Worker.

In 1922, Adele Stamp left YWCA work and had already accepted a position with the American Red Cross, as field representative in the southern states, when Albert F. Woods, president of the University of Maryland, asked her to come to College Park as the institution's first dean of women. Only in 1916 had the university opened its doors to women. By 1922, however, 93 women had enrolled, enough to warrant the appointment of a dean of women ("Girls Her Hobby," 1960).

Recalling the event nearly 40 years later, Stamp acknowledged her reluctance to accept the position. "I had really promised Harry Hopkins that I would take a post with the American Red Cross." She discussed her dilemma with Hopkins, director of the organization's Gulf Division in New Orleans, who insisted that she would "never like being dean of women." Despite her reservations, Stamp accepted a one-year contract, which she renewed for another year. At the end of that trial period, the young dean harbored no further doubt, realizing "that I wanted to make this my life's work" ("Girls Her Hobby," 1960).

SARAH GIBSON BLANDING

The youngest of the four deans of women discussed here, Sarah Gibson Blanding was born November 22, 1898, on a farm near Lexington, Kentucky, to Sally Anderson Blanding and William de Saussure Blanding. Despite their modest economic resources, Sarah Blanding's parents came from prominent southern families. Sally and William Blanding, an attorney, lived in Sumter, South Carolina, for a number of years before relocating to Kentucky in 1889, hoping "Mr. Blanding would benefit from a change in climate" ("How the 'Little Reb,'" pp. 6–7). In Kentucky, he worked at a number of jobs before becoming a collector of internal revenue. As a consequence, the family moved several more times before settling in "an old brick house on the Richmond Pike" ("How the 'Little Reb,'" pp. 6–7), where Sarah Blanding was born.

Sally Anderson Blanding influenced her daughter in many ways, and the two remained devoted to each other throughout their lives. Sarah Gibson Blanding's athletic prowess, independent spirit, and irreverent sense of fun can doubtless be traced to her irrepressible mother. Determined that his daughter be no fragile flower, Sally Anderson's father "insisted that [she] be taught three things—how to ride a horse, how to shoot a pistol, and [how to] swim with fair proficiency."[20] Recalling her mother's energy, Sarah Blanding observed that "after the War, because everybody in the South was ruined my mother had to learn to do many things."[21]

When her husband's health declined, Sally Blanding willingly moved to Kentucky, although "it meant a new kind of pioneering."[22] Sarah Blanding recalled that in addition to raising three children and managing a farm, her mother also "did social work in Lexington working in the slums . . . at a time before social work as a profession had come into being" (Interview with Blanding, 1964, p. 5). As a consequence of that work, Sally Blanding met Madeline McDowell Breckinridge, a major force in the Progressive movement in Kentucky. Both her mother's example and her friendship with Breckinridge served Sarah Blanding well in the subsequent years.

Sally Blanding and Madeline McDowell Breckinridge were but two of the strong-minded women who assumed a pivotal role in Sarah Gibson Blanding's life. As an adolescent, Blanding dreamed of becoming a physician. In preparation for this, she would often accompany her uncle, Dr. A. L. Blanding, as he made his house calls, occasionally driving the horse and buggy herself ("Sarah Gibson Blanding," 1963). Unlike most young women interested in a medical career, however, Blanding possessed a woman role model as well, the family physician, who earned her degree at Johns Hopkins University.

The young woman's dream of becoming a physician ended in 1912, with the death of her father. Blanding realized that she lacked the financial resources necessary for medical training and that she was unwilling to pursue the more accessible alternative of nursing. Unafraid to face reality, Blanding concluded that "I had to get out and make my own living" (Interview with Blanding, 1964, p. 2).

Both Adele H. Stamp and Sarah Gibson Blanding recognized the economic value of their natural athletic ability. Years later, Blanding recalled that "I was a good tennis player and a good swimmer, could hit a basketball from forty or fifty feet away." Without hesitation, she subsequently turned to her role model, the woman physician, who loaned her the necessary funds to enroll in the New Haven Normal School of Gymnastics, in New Haven, Connecticut, which offered a two-year training program in physical education.[23]

Like Bowersox, Harris, and Stamp, Sarah Gibson Blanding combined education and employment. She soon found that a 2-year degree was at best of limited value. Although several high schools offered her jobs following her graduation in 1919, Blanding refused them all in order to pursue a college degree. Short on funds, but brimming with resourcefulness and self-confidence, this young woman negotiated a unique contract with the University of Kentucky. She agreed to accept an instructorship in physical education if she could enroll in undergraduate courses in the mornings and teach physical education in the afternoons. University authorities concurred, and, in 1919, Blanding became instructor of physical education, at an annual salary of $800.[24]

The young instructor combined teaching responsibilities with a full collegiate life. Active in athletics and campus politics, Blanding demonstrated her academic skills as well. Majoring in both history and political science, she earned induction into Mortar Board, the national senior women's honor society. University of Kentucky students also recognized her versatility, as the *Kentuckian* suggested in 1923: "Speaking of all-round good girls, just gaze upon 'Sally.' She can do anything from putting down 'A's' to dropping the ball in the basket. [She] not only succeeded in becoming established in the Physical Education Department, but in landing her A.B. as well" (*Kentuckian*, 1923).

Between 1915 and 1921, in addition to her work at New Haven and subsequently at the University of Kentucky, Blanding worked with the public park system in Lexington, Kentucky ("Dean Blanding," 1941). In doing so, she was involved in one of the most significant Progressive reform efforts in the state. Melba Porter Hay (1980) maintains that the women of Lexington and Louisville created a strong social reform movement. The Lexington Civic League, founded in 1900, was the moving force in the Bluegrass state and owed much of its success to Madeline McDowell Breckinridge, one of the organization's founders, member of a prominent Kentucky family and friend of the Blandings.

Breckinridge maintained that adolescent hooliganism was the result of inadequate recreational outlets for children. Public parks, with their supervised play activities, taught children the rudiments of cooperation, a necessary component of responsible citizenship (Hay, 1980). She insisted that "if we can free the play instinct common to all humanity . . . we shall need to bother far less about the question of public morals" (*Lexington Herald Leader*, July 23, 1916).

On June 17, 1901, the league opened the West End Playground, Lexington's first public recreational facility for children. By 1920, the system included five playgrounds and employed a staff of 12 (Breckinridge, 1921, pp. 49–50). The Civic League remained actively involved with the Lexington playgrounds until 1927, when they became a fully supported municipal department (Hay, 1988).

Sarah Gibson Blanding worked with two of Lexington's recreational facilities, Woodland Park and the Lincoln School Playground. Founded in 1902 on an eighteen-acre tract, Woodland Park was serving approximately 350 children each day by 1918 (Pherigo, n.d.). The program, dedicated to providing "the best and the most healthful recreation possible," was a varied one, including folk dancing, storytelling, volleyball, and soccer. The park also sponsored an "'inventing match,' where each boy and girl was given the opportunity of making a boat . . . and launching it on the pool" (Ingels, 1918, p. 1).

In the summer of 1921, Blanding served as director of the Lincoln School Playground ("City Playground," 1921). Consistent with her resourceful nature, she made an agreement with the school that benefitted both the women students at the University of Kentucky and the pupils of the Lincoln School. In return for the use of the school's swimming pool for a physical education class from the university, Blanding agreed to teach swimming to pupils at the Lincoln School (Miner, 1921, p. 1).

Sarah Gibson Blanding did not actively seek to become Dean of Women at the University of Kentucky. Here, however, she encountered yet another independent southern woman, Frances Jewell, a Vassar alumna who returned to her native Kentucky to accept a faculty position in the English Department and to serve as the Dean of Women at the University of Kentucky. As a first-year student, Blanding took a course from her, and the energetic Jewell recognized a kindred spirit. Little did Blanding realize, however, the importance of either Jewell or Vassar College to her subsequent professional career. In 1923 Frances Jewell resigned to marry the University of Kentucky's widowed president, Frank

L. McVey. In that same year, Blanding graduated. Convinced of her friend's ability and potential, Frances Jewell McVey encouraged Blanding to assume the deanship. Initially, Blanding "couldn't think of anything worse" than assuming such a responsibility (Interview with Blanding, 1976, p. 5). Nevertheless, she finally agreed to take the job on a temporary basis, at least until the McVeys returned from their wedding trip.

After only a few months in office, however, Blanding found the work enjoyable and challenging and subsequently confessed that had any other candidate applied for the permanent position, she "would have had to go over my dead body to get it."[25] She retained this temporary assignment until 1925, when she formally accepted the position. Only 27 years old at the time, Blanding became one of the youngest women administrators in higher education in the United States.

Sarah Gibson Blanding's work both on the campus and in the parks enhanced her effectiveness as a dean of women. As a student who, unlike wealthy women at the university, earned her degree while holding continuous employment, she understood the reality of life on the economic margins. As a recreation worker in the Progressive tradition, she encountered both skepticism toward a public program many considered to be a luxury and satisfaction in being part of a reform movement in which women played a major role. Finally, as an instructor in physical education, Blanding discovered the difficulty of making a place for women students in this most masculine of collegiate domains.

CONCLUSION

The lives of these four women present rich stories that contribute significantly to the history of women, higher education, and professionalization. In their early careers, Bowersox, Harris, Stamp, and Blanding managed to combine economic practicality with a dedication to social service. As deans of women they retained their practicality and commitment to reform, while carving out distinguished professional careers.

The case of Sarah Gibson Blanding provides a particularly persuasive example. In 1940, representatives from Bryn Mawr College asked her to apply for the institution's presidency.[26] In support of her application, University of Kentucky President Frank L. McVey assured the search committee of Blanding's versatility as an administrator.[27] Although obviously interested in the position, Blanding also possessed a realistic sense of the competition for such an opportunity. Commenting on her prospects, she informed McVey, "I am not losing sleep over this job but I shall take a good deal of pleasure in seeing how far a graduate of a state university can get with the committee."[28]

Although Blanding did not get the job, her offhand remark to McVey does reflect a perception she shared with Bowersox, Stamp, and Harris. Each of these women, who faced economic challenge from their youth, saw herself as an outsider among academic women. Economic circumstances determined both their employment and their educational options. Necessity demanded that they not only be self-supporting but that, in some instances, they supplement family income as well. Necessity demanded that they attend colleges and universities not to form social or professional networks but to obtain practical training for immediate employment. Necessity demanded that they work where they could obtain employment—in a woman's profession in coeducational institutions in a poor section of the country. Despite such exigencies, however, Bowersox, Harris, Stamp, and Blanding fashioned careers of substantial achievement, attaining regional and, in some cases, national prominence.

The economic circumstances, education, and initial work experiences of Bowersox, Harris, Stamp, and Blanding thus represent an alternative professional profile to that of most graduates of prestigious northeastern women's colleges. From modest backgrounds, these four held jobs before, during, and immediately following their college careers. Although they became deans of women under diverse circumstances, their early employment in service to marginal groups, more than any other factor, defined their concerns, tactics, and goals as the principal advocate for and advisor to women on the coeducational campus. The task for each of them was not simple, and none of them achieved immediate success. However, as a consequence of their work with children and women, the four brought to campus not only a sensitivity to marginal groups but also an appreciation of the power of well-directed institutions to foster a more inclusive society. These, combined with their strong sense of independence and administrative experience, made Bowersox, Harris, Stamp, and Blanding formidable agents of change.

Adele Stamp, who served as the first Dean of Women at the University of Maryland, inspired the affection and respect of generations of women students. (Special Collections, University of Maryland at College Park Libraries)

CHAPTER 2

"A Legitimate Place on Campus"

Academic Women
and Space on the Coeducational Campus

On December 1, 1931, the University of Maryland opened the first dormitory for women students, Margaret Brent Hall. Determined to showcase Maryland women's dedication to higher education, Adele H. Stamp invited prominent members of religious, political, and civic organizations. The Federation of Jewish Women's Organizations, the International Federation of Catholic Alumnae, and the General Federation of Women's Clubs numbered among those groups sending representatives. Deans of women from George Washington and American universities also attended.

Stamp asked Mrs. Charles E. Elliott, President of the Maryland League of Women Voters, to deliver the dedication speech. Her remarks best expressed the significance of this achievement for women's higher education at the University of Maryland. The facility, Elliott maintained, not only provides women students a much-needed home but also gives them "a legitimate place on campus and is an aggressive recognition of them as an integral part of the University."[1]

Elliott's ostensibly judicious phrase, "a legitimate place on campus," suggests an issue essential to understanding the experience of women students, faculty members, and administrators on coeducational campuses. Although women comprised nearly one-third of the student population in coeducational institutions and occupied a growing number of faculty and administrative appointments in the 1930s, the nature of their relationship to the college campus remained unresolved. Activist deans of women such as Bowersox, Harris, Stamp, and Blanding challenged their superiors to address a number of questions concerning academic women and campus space.

Should women students occupy anything beyond purely academic spaces? If they live on campus, where should dormitories be located? Should they have particular spaces reserved for extracurricular and athletic activities? What relationship should the dean of women and other women faculty members, virtually all of whom were single, maintain with the campus?

WOMEN AND PUBLIC SPACES

Although Bowersox, Harris, Stamp, and Blanding confronted administrators who were often ambivalent concerning women students' place on the coeducational campus, these four women experienced no such confusion. They maintained that access to the classroom alone failed to prepare students of either gender to function as autonomous adults. In attempting to bring college women out of the classroom and into the living accommodations, playing fields, meeting rooms, and ceremonial spaces of the campus, Bowersox, Harris, Stamp, and Blanding challenged the conventional relationship between women and public spaces in higher education and the larger society.

In her study of women and the public sphere in the 19th-century United States, Mary P. Ryan (1990) discovered this same conflict between municipal authorities and women attempting to enter public spaces. She found that often-confused city fathers alternatively identified such women as "dangerous and endangered" (p. 6). On the one hand, women threatened the traditional cultural equilibrium by their participation in public ceremonies or political events. Yet, on the other hand, men had learned since childhood that they must protect women from the rudeness of public life.

These images of dangerous and endangered women not only describe the ambiguous relationship between college and university administrators and women students but also suggest a rather complex role for the dean of women. By placing young men and women in such close academic and social proximity on the college and university campus, administrators confronted an unprecedented circumstance. How would these young people react to each other? Would women be a civilizing influence or a sexual distraction? In this context, most skeptical administrators harbored fears: first, that women would distract men from their work, and second, that a disproportionate number of women, enrolling in certain subjects such as literature, would detract from the traditional prestige of those disciplines, and thus decrease male enrollment (Solomon, 1985). On the other hand, they believed that "endangered" women students, beyond parental control for the first time in their lives, clearly needed protection from impetuous male undergraduates.

Coeducational institutions, then, hired deans of women ostensibly to monitor and to protect women students. Dedicated professionals such as Bowersox, Harris, Stamp, and Blanding, however, discovered that these women faced an additional, far more insidious danger. Consequently, to these deans, protection assumed greater nuance. Women students needed to be defended not only from unwarranted sexual advances, but also, more importantly, from administrators who were insensitive to their needs.

To appreciate their work one must first understand how Bowersox, Harris,

Stamp, and Blanding envisioned the job, with its potential rewards and persistent difficulties. For each, the office functioned not as an agency dedicated to the mindless enforcement of institutional regulations and skirt lengths, but rather as an agency dedicated to a vision of what a full collegiate experience could mean to young women, both as college students and as independent adults. Furthermore, as the highest ranking women on campus, they also championed the rights of their women colleagues. Devotion to such goals, however, blinded none of these women to the indifference and outright hostility they encountered. Katherine S. Bowersox also recognized the cultural limitations against which women of all ages struggled. Because of his "greater freedom and larger opportunity," she observed, "no boy ever wishes he were a girl, but a great many girls wish they were boys."[2] These observations aptly summarize the feelings of all four women concerning academic women. As deans of women, they sought to claim a full share of educational opportunities for women students, including campus space, financial support, and a greater range of extracurricular opportunities. They also claimed for themselves, and for their unmarried women colleagues, a professional, autonomous relationship to that same campus space.

The first step in this process, Bowersox and Stamp agreed, was "the development of independent action and thought"[3] among women students. Stamp maintained that to achieve this, institutions must provide women students with opportunity for "training in leadership."[4] The development of such skills would not only enhance their college experience but also prepare women more fully for independence.

To achieve such full educational opportunity, Bowersox, Harris, Stamp, and Blanding maintained that women students needed access not only to the classroom but also to dormitories, athletic fields, and meeting rooms. Consequently, on their respective campuses, these deans tirelessly asserted the claim of women students to a larger portion of campus space in which they, like their male counterparts, could enjoy the full range of college life. Conversely, they repudiated the traditional conception of single academic women's relationship to the campus, which, dating from the earliest women's seminaries in the 1830s, no longer reflected the contours of modern professionalism.

These deans defined the campus as a public space in its most inclusive form. For them, the campus functioned not only as a setting for supervised study or play, but also as an arena for open debate. Here students or faculty members, regardless of gender or size of the contingent, could discuss their grievances and express them to the administration.[5]

Bowersox, Harris, Stamp, and Blanding recognized that attracting and retaining a growing number of women students would be difficult without also making it possible for them to participate in all of the activities on campus. In attempting to achieve this, these four deans challenged what Linda Kerber

(1988) has identified as the formidable relationship between space, gender, and power. Throughout history, argues Kerber, space has remained "complexly structured by an ideology of gender" (p. 39). As a provocative example, she identifies universities as traditionally "male spaces . . . that women enter only at male invitation" (p. 39).

In their struggle for adequate space for women students, however, the deans enjoyed at least one hard-won victory. Bowersox, Stamp, and Blanding led campaigns that resulted in the construction of the Woman's Building—a space devoted entirely to women students' extracurricular and athletic activities. Helen Horowitz (1984) identifies a similar process at the northeastern women's colleges, which by the late 1920s all boasted buildings dedicated entirely to student activities. At both single-sex and coeducational institutions, notes Horowitz, the growing number of women students fashioned "an increasingly elaborate college life unanticipated by the authorities" (pp. 169–170). This variety of college life, however, could not develop fully without adequate campus space. Bowersox, Stamp, and Blanding were instrumental in acquiring for women spaces in which to participate in extracurricular activities and to establish unique campus traditions.

For nearly 10 years, Bowersox encouraged both President Frost and his successor, William J. Hutchins, to secure funds for the construction of a Woman's Building at Berea College. The women, both faculty and students, needed space other than the dormitories and classroom buildings. Bowersox envisioned a multipurpose structure, including a gymnasium, recreation rooms, meeting rooms, a faculty women's dining room, and apartments for the dean of women and the director of physical education for women. Such a building, she believed, would become "the social center for college women,"[6] by providing organizations such as the YWCA and various literary societies with permanent meeting rooms. In addition, faculty women would enjoy access to a private sitting room for a respite from dormitory life.

In October 1926, Berea College celebrated the opening of the Woods-Penniman Building, which included social and meeting rooms and a women's gymnasium.[7] Bowersox soon learned, however, that acquiring space for women was but half the battle, for she had to defend the building "sacred to the interests of girls and women"[8] from encroachment by the male faculty, who wanted access to the women faculty members' social room. The dean protested such a measure, reminding the president that allowing men faculty access to the Woman's Building "would be like the camel getting his head in the tent—once the men were invited to use the social room, they should take possession of the whole first floor." Moreover, she noted that women faculty relished the freedom and privacy of the social room after a long day in class. Furthermore, Bowersox realized that such a policy would entail the enforcement of certain regulations—yet another responsibility for her.[9]

DORMITORIES FOR WOMEN

In 1922, approximately 800 students attended the University of Maryland. Of that figure, 93 were women. Dean Stamp soon discovered that the only on-campus housing for women was the Y-Hut, "a tongue-and-groove structure used as a Y.M.C.A. hut during [World War I]" (Jacobs, 1977, p. 354), which could accommodate 50 women. Initially, the young dean lived in this crowded facility with her students. Privacy was a rare commodity in that cramped structure. The dean later surmised that if any of the women wished to voice objections to her policies, "they just had to go out into the cornfields" (*Baltimore Sun*, December 4, 1960).

In addition to the lack of adequate housing, women at the University of Maryland, Stamp insisted, were in "acute need" of athletic facilities for their exclusive use. During her first 9 years in College Park, she observed that women students "shared the use of the men's gymnasium with the R.O.T.C., band, track, lacrosse, and basketball teams," a situation she deemed "highly unsatisfactory and undesirable."[10]

Nearly 10 years elapsed before the legislature appropriated funds to build the first women's dormitory, Margaret Brent Hall. Using her election as president of the NADW University Section in 1930 as an opportunity to publicize the persisting problem, Stamp publicly stated that although over 300 women attended the University of Maryland, the institution still could house only 50 in the woefully inadequate Y-Hut. Stamp thus concluded that "proper supervision" was impossible, and with the women scattered all over the College Park area, "a great deal of college spirit and morale is lost" (*Baltimore American*, May 30, 1930).

In 1930, the dean celebrated the results of a long campaign when the Maryland state legislature appropriated funds for the construction of both a women's dormitory and a field house (*Baltimore Evening Sun*, November 22, 1930). Involved with construction plans from the outset, Stamp argued vigorously with President R. A. Pearson over the specifications for this facility. When she learned that the architects were taking as their model a woman's prison, she tartly reminded Pearson that "Montrose is a penal institution and I see no reason why the dormitories at the University of Maryland should be compared to that." Protective of the women students and their well-being, Stamp insisted that this dormitory, "the first one for women . . . set an example as far as good housing is concerned."[11]

In November 1931, one month before the dedication of the new facility, Dean Stamp expressed concern to University of Maryland Board member E. Brooke Lee about the fate of the Y-Hut. So long as it remained standing, she feared that administrators would be tempted to reactivate it as a dormitory, should the need arise. "Once we are out," she concluded, "I think we ought to stay out."[12]

Women students, particularly the seniors, shared Stamp's joy. On learning that the cornerstone for the Women's Field House would be laid at the 1931 commencement, the senior women petitioned the dean for the right to participate in the ceremony and to place certain articles of significance in the cornerstone. In her formal request to the Board of Regents, Stamp emphasized the women's excitement and desire "to make an event of it."[13] The board concurred, and on June 8, 1931, the senior women contributed various items commemorating the women's athletic tradition at the University of Maryland.[14]

In the fall of 1932, Stamp reported that Margaret Brent Hall was "filled to overflowing" and had a "waiting list."[15] Throughout the 1930s, women's enrollment at the University of Maryland steadily increased, but the institution proved reluctant to provide additional dormitory space. In her budget request for 1933, Dean Stamp observed that although 500 women attended the university, only 120 could live on campus.[16] Despite her best efforts, however, the problem persisted throughout her tenure.

Sarah Blanding achieved no greater success than did Stamp in providing adequate on-campus living space for women students. Although by 1939 she could point with pride to the increase in the number of women attending the University of Kentucky, Blanding failed to obtain adequate on-campus living space for her charges. While the number of women had more than doubled, the percentage living in dormitories remained constant, approximately 30%.[17] An additional 30% lived with parents or other relatives, while the rest lived in boarding houses, sorority houses, or the homes of relatives.

Central to Blanding's campaign to secure campus living space for women students was her conviction that dormitory life promoted academic success. To persuade the administration, Blanding and her staff compiled statistical data concerning the enrollment, academic achievement, and living accommodations of the women students. In her annual reports to McVey, Blanding persistently maintained that "the women over whom we have the least supervision rank lowest in scholarship."[18] In contrast, the office of the dean of men contains no comparable annual reports. Clearly the dean had to justify, year by year, the continuing and increasing presence of women students.

Blanding's annual reports to the president grew in length and complexity over the years. A consistent theme of these documents was the lack of on-campus housing for women. At the beginning of her second year as acting dean of women, she advised the president that because "applications have been pouring in,"[19] she had been unable to satisfy requests for dormitory space, directing women instead to boarding houses in Lexington. This alternative satisfied neither the dean, the women students, nor their parents. Thirteen years later, conditions remained unchanged. In 1937, Blanding informed McVey that "100 students were turned away because their parents were unwilling for them to board in town."[20]

She did succeed, however, in obtaining the establishment of a Woman's Building at the University of Kentucky. Blanding maintained that the establishment of such a facility would serve the institution's women students, most of whom neither lived on campus nor joined sororities. For several years, she encouraged President McVey to approve the project. The dean insisted that all of the university's women, whether living in dormitories or not, would benefit from the facility. In addition to the obvious problems of off-campus women, Blanding reminded the president that dormitory women had already sacrificed precious privacy, since women's organizations normally met in dormitory lounges or parlors.[21]

In 1932, the Patterson House, a potential site for the Woman's Building, became available. Built in 1880, it had been the home of University of Kentucky President James K. Patterson, until his death in 1922. His brother, Walter K. Patterson, continued to occupy the property until his death in 1933.[22] Blanding immediately surveyed the building, obtained an estimate of the renovation costs, and assured McVey that the women's student government possessed the necessary funds to prepare the building for use.[23] McVey consulted the Executive Committee of the Board of Trustees, which, in the fall of 1932, agreed to Blanding's request. Nevertheless, the president cautioned her that the university could afford no renovations, only basic cleaning of the facility.[24]

Despite limited funds, Blanding assured the McVeys that "I am bubbling over with plans for a woman's building."[25] As chair of the committee to prepare the Patterson House for women students, the dean turned to a wide range of women, including students, faculty, and faculty wives. In little over six months, they prepared the facility for occupation. The former residence now included reception rooms, committee rooms, and office space.[26]

Following the formal opening in April 1933, Blanding observed that the Woman's Building quickly became "the center of women's activities."[27] She reported to the president that each year an increasing number of women used the facility, with "as many as five group meetings going on at once." Furthermore, the building served as a valuable social space for those women who did not pledge sororities. Blanding assured McVey that the Woman's Building "has served a group of students who might not otherwise have been provided for."[28]

But, like Stamp, Blanding failed in her determined campaign to secure adequate campus living facilities for the University of Kentucky's women students. By 1940, although the number of women enrolled increased dramatically, only one-third lived on campus. Despite their diverse working environments, both Stamp and Blanding discovered the unwillingness of institutional authorities to offer the same opportunities to women that they provided for men. The majority of the women students at both institutions remained largely segregated from the life of the campus community.

HOUSING FOR WOMEN FACULTY

Ironically, single academic women—deans of women and their faculty colleagues—desired greater segregation from the campus. They challenged their superiors to accord them the autonomy characteristic of the modern professions, especially the unmistakable demarcation between private and public space. Long an issue at many women's colleges, the right relation between academic women and campus space remained a chronic dilemma at private, coeducational institutions such as Berea College.

Within this context, Katherine S. Bowersox emerged as an especially visible advocate of Berea's women faculty members. A woman of forceful personality and extensive administrative experience, she never hesitated to voice the concerns of her female colleagues. Throughout her years at Berea, the dean sought to secure certain basic rights for faculty women, such as suitable working conditions during their years of active service and provisions for a secure retirement.

College authorities expected Bowersox, along with other single women faculty members, to live in the women's dormitories and to supervise their residents. Both she and her colleagues continually questioned this policy, but they had little success. Recent research indicates that this problem troubled many faculty women, in both single-sex and coeducational institutions.

In her study of the Seven Sisters campuses, Helen Horowitz (1984) outlines the ways that women faculty members as a group redefined their relationship to the campus in order to attain greater personal autonomy. Northeastern women's colleges, following the seminary tradition established at Mt. Holyoke in 1837, required women faculty members to live in the dormitories with the students. Institutional authorities assumed that single women faculty would without objection sacrifice their privacy to "provide proper role models for students" (p. 180). In the 1880s, however, Horowitz claims that many women became restless living under such a regime. Aspiring scholars such as Lucy Salmon at Vassar and Alice Freeman at Wellesley found that dormitory life "robbed them of time for scholarship and allowed them no privacy" (p. 182).

Women students and faculty members at these institutions, Horowitz maintains, shaped the college to their own needs. Once on the campus as students, women collegians moved beyond the confines of the dormitory to claim campus space for a whole range of activities—social, athletic, and academic. Women faculty, however, shaped the campus by leaving it. By 1920 they had defeated the seminary ideal and established independent residences apart from the campus. No longer responsible for the daily supervision of women students, these academic women created private lives as independent professionals. College became for them, like their male counterparts, simply the workplace.

The relationship of women faculty members to the physical space of the coeducational campus, however, remains complex and largely unexamined. Unlike their counterparts in single-sex institutions, these women struggled initially to establish a substantial presence on the coeducational campus. Although most of them held the lowest faculty ranks and worked primarily in feminized fields, nevertheless these women demanded the same respect accorded their male colleagues. This included the right to live off campus as independent professionals.

Dean Bowersox repeatedly requested improved living accommodations and fewer supervisory duties for herself and for other overburdened single women faculty members. Her residence in the dormitory, she informed President William G. Frost, detracted from "the larger influence which the Dean of Women should command."[29] To do her work effectively, the dean insisted that she needed regular periods of privacy and solitude to bring a "balanced and sane judgment"[30] to the job. Other administrators, mostly male and married, lived in town and enjoyed a dignified respite from campus duties. Bowersox believed that, as the highest ranking woman administrator on the campus, she too should enjoy this privilege.

Throughout her years at Berea, Dean Bowersox vigorously defended the right of single faculty women to privacy and dignity. After "twenty-five years in institutional living," the dean considered herself unusually sensitive to the personal needs of single women faculty. Presenting her case to Frost, she estimated that women faculty members living in the dormitories spent 9 months a year, 7 days a week, attending the needs of their charges. Seldom would a woman be "really free until after ten o'clock at night."[31] In addition to supervising the women students, listening to their problems, and tending to them when they were ill, dormitory supervisors had to supervise laundry service and report maintenance problems. Furthermore, single women faculty members also taught a full load of courses and served on various college committees.[32]

Bowersox advocated a number of innovations that she believed would enhance college life for single faculty women. Among them were higher salaries for workers living in the dormitories[33] and no supervising of students at mealtime. Moreover, she urged that Berea establish a private faculty dining room, which would provide single faculty women with "relief from noise and confusion . . . [and] board at a price they could afford."[34]

Bowersox realized that single women faculty, especially the younger ones, needed—in addition to a teachers' dining room—a place for social gatherings, apart from their rooms and from the students. Such a space, she suggested, would serve the interests of both the college and the workers, engendering "personal health, a more cheerful attitude and more efficient work."[35] Bowersox succeeded in this campaign when, in 1925, the administration designated the Log House as a faculty social center.[36]

Because of her age, single status, and extensive experience in institutional living, Dean Bowersox understood that retirement presented serious problems for some single faculty women. Although Berea established a retirement program for its faculty in 1923, some of the older workers nevertheless found themselves in such a precarious financial position that they could not afford adequate living facilities (Peck, 1982). Salaries for single women, despite dormitory living, left little for future security. As a consequence, Bowersox frequently approached President Hutchins with proposals to enhance retirement benefits for single faculty women. In addition, she urged him to establish a "sunset cottage," on or near the campus, where retired faculty women could live. Many of these women, after 20 or 30 years at Berea, had established deep friendships and were quite reluctant to break their ties with the locale and the people. Bowersox declared that both the women and the college could benefit from such a facility. She also informed Hutchins that "some of us unmarried women have never realized the desire to keep house for ourselves and have . . . a bit of freedom and privacy—impossible in an institution." In return for this opportunity, she added, the retired women could lend a hand during faculty illnesses or any other college emergency.[37]

CONCLUSION

Despite their previous administrative experience in a variety of jobs involving marginal groups, once on campus, Bowersox, Harris, Stamp, and Blanding soon learned the complexity of their new responsibilities. Pioneers in an entirely new administrative post, these independent women brought a wealth of skill, understanding, and gumption to the task of serving the interests of all the academic women of the campus. Skeptical presidents, however, sensitive to both advocates and critics of coeducation, considered the primary tasks of the dean of women to be those of protecting and disciplining the women students.

Bowersox, Harris, Stamp, and Blanding nevertheless refused to accept such a limited conception of the work or of the relationship between academic women and campus space. Unwilling to operate exclusively as disciplinarians for women students, they sought instead to function as advocates for the academic women of their institutions. Central to this mission was redefining the relationship of academic women to campus space, a goal characterized by paradox. Determined that women students claim access to the entire campus for academic, extracurricular, and athletic purposes, they were equally dedicated to claiming for women faculty and administrators the right to an autonomous professional relationship to their workplace.

In challenging traditional attitudes toward the relationship of academic women to campus space, Bowersox, Harris, Stamp, and Blanding dramatically reconfigured their role as deans of women. This choice often resulted in conflicts with institutional authorities, frustrations over inadequate revenues, and failures to achieve cherished goals. Nevertheless, these deans believed that their goal of providing their women students with a well-rounded collegiate experience that would aid them in developing as independent adults and their women colleagues with enhanced professional autonomy more than justified the struggle.

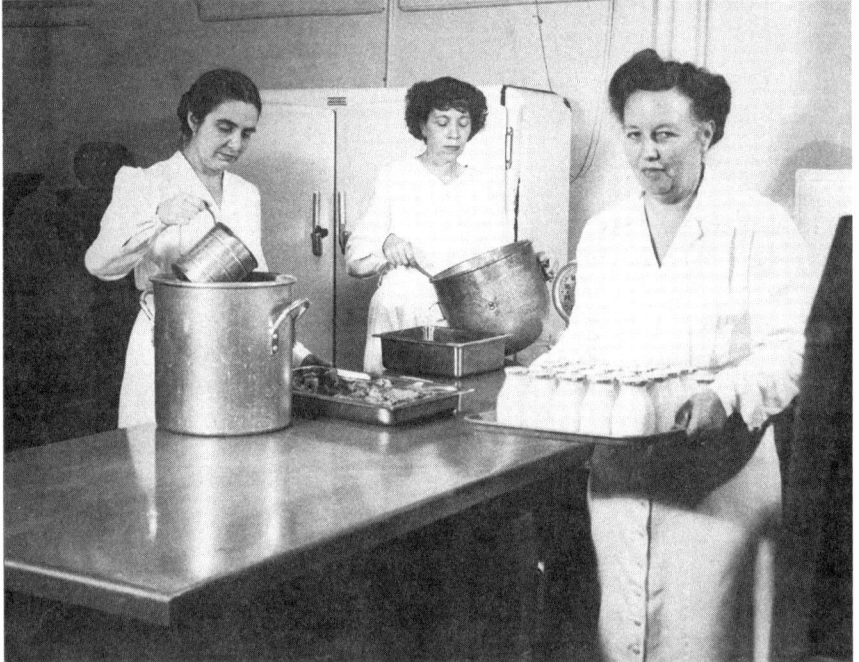

Unique among academic women, Agnes Ellen Harris (left) served simultaneously as Dean of Women and Dean of the School of Home Economics at the University of Alabama. (William Stanley Hoole Special Collections Library, The University of Alabama)

CHAPTER 3

"A Bright Mind and a Lean Purse"

Academic Women and Financial Challenge

The Great Depression seriously jeopardized the college career of first-generation women students across the United States. College women in the South, however, suffered even more acutely because the region had not universally shared in the prosperity of the 1920s. Desperate for assistance, these young women often turned to the dean of women. Katherine S. Bowersox had long received many such entreaties. She responded forcefully to the young women's plight, reminding the administration that although the typical young woman arrived at Berea "with a bright mind and a lean purse,"[1] she merited, equally with her male counterpart, access to higher education.

Although women comprised nearly one-third of the student population and a growing number of the administrative and faculty populations in coeducational institutions, the Great Depression intensified the unresolved debate over their relationship to higher education. Should their numbers increase on the college campus? Should they be trained to compete with men for all-too-scarce jobs? Should they receive financial aid equal to that of men? Could most women administrators and faculty sustain larger reductions in salary because, after all, they were single?

Bowersox, Harris, Stamp, and Blanding took a rather expansive view of their job. They considered themselves to be the principal advocates for the rights of academic women. Central to the challenge of attaining and retaining access and fair treatment was adequate financial support for women. Throughout the Great Depression, the four addressed the financial needs of a wide spectrum of women on campus—students, professional colleagues, and nonprofessional support staff.

Consideration of the response of Bowersox, Harris, Stamp, and Blanding to this crisis is valuable because, although studies of women in the South during the Great Depression abound, most historians concentrate on the admittedly dramatic circumstances of rural women. For example, although in her broad-ranging history of women in the South, Margaret R. Wolfe (1995) examines the effects of the Great Depression, nowhere does she consider the plight of those largely, and sometimes just barely, middle-class academic women and the financial challenges they faced. While the evocative photographs of rural women in the South seared the conscience of the nation in the 1930s and retain their power to this day, the actions of Bowersox, Harris, Stamp, and Blanding in the face of the acute widespread financial emergency of many women on campus dramatically expands historical understanding of women on the margins and of those who championed their cause.

FINANCIAL SUPPORT FOR WOMEN

By the 1930s Bowersox, Harris, Stamp, and Blanding faced a more variegated student population than ever before. No longer were college women a self-conscious minority, dedicated solely to academic success and career achievement. Furthermore, not all academic women in the South suffered during the Great Depression, but those who did suffered severely indeed. In the face of such diversity, these deans sought to maintain a balanced program, which, while it did not dismiss the needs of economically secure women, responded to the economic challenge a significant number of women on campus encountered.

Neither women students nor faculty members could escape the effects of the Great Depression. Despite a sustained increase across the decade in the number of women attending institutions of higher education, they represented scarcely 12% of the total population of college-age women in the United States (Newcomer, 1959). When parents decided to send their children to college, they often chose to send their sons rather than their daughters.

College and university administrators adopted much the same attitude toward women faculty members, including deans of women. Although across-the-board salary reductions were the rule on most campuses, women faculty members suffered doubly because of their already inadequate compensation. Administrators and state legislatures had traditionally assumed, of course, that the women, most of whom were single, simply did not merit the same pay as their male counterparts, whether single or married. In addition to this, on many smaller campuses, harried presidents, desperate to cut costs, questioned the need for a dean of women. As a consequence of both circumstances, deans of women in the 1930s were in a very genuine sense fighting for their professional lives.

Within this context, the problems Bowersox, Stamp, Harris, and Blanding faced became abundantly clear. In times of economic stress, authorities naturally question the newest programs and personnel. On college and university campuses, this often meant the feminized disciplines and institutional services for women students. For over 30 years, deans of women had conducted a two-pronged campaign to secure academic and extracurricular recognition for women students and professional recognition for themselves. Through the founding of the National Association of Deans of Women (NADW) and the development of graduate training programs, they directly confronted the vexing issue of perception that plagued many feminized fields.

By the 1930s, deans of women across the country found that the Great Depression was seriously threatening their best efforts on behalf of women. "The economic instability of the 1930s," maintains Erin Brisbay (1990), "created an atmosphere hostile to [women's] advancement" (p. 34). Indeed, many male administrators and students began to question the wisdom of allowing large numbers of women to enroll in institutions of higher education.

Harassed college and university presidents experienced sufficient difficulty in obtaining adequate funding for men's education, let alone for programs that attracted primarily women. Quite simply, housing, meeting, and athletic facilities for women cost money, and many college administrators dismissed those as frivolous compared with the needs of men. Furthermore, as Brisbay (1990) notes, anxious college men objected to competing with college-educated women in an already strained job market. As a result of these trends, observes Brisbay, a tendency to regard career-oriented college women as "usurpers of the jobs of men who had families to support grew" (p. 34). Consequently, many college women believed that they were under tremendous pressure to renounce their personal ambitions in favor of marriage and family.

Unwilling to see deserving women students unfairly deprived of collegiate and career opportunities, the four deans acknowledged the problem and worked energetically to secure the necessary funds to bring women to, and keep them on, campus. Reflecting on the decrease in women's enrollment for the 1933–1934 academic year, Blanding clearly identified the problem that many aspiring young women faced: "In times of economic stress, if there are two children in a home to be educated, the boy . . . is given preference for a college education."[2]

Harris also encountered reluctance to increase support for women's education during the Great Depression. In a memorandum in 1932, she alerted women faculty members to the growing unwillingness on the part of the Alabama legislature to appropriate funds for women students. In response, she sought support not only from academic women on campus but also from the university's growing number of alumnae. Harris thus urged women faculty members to identify promising women students and to encourage them to remain in school.[3] Furthermore, she reminded alumnae of the need to inform talented women throughout the state of the opportunities for women at the University of Alabama. Always emphasizing women's need for economic independence, Harris insisted that "in these troubled times higher education becomes more difficult for girls to secure but at the same time more necessary to the success of women."[4]

As Brisbay (1990) notes, securing adequate funds remained "one of the biggest obstacles to women seeking college degrees" (p. 39). Throughout the troubled 1930s, then, the deans of women struggled not only to get women to the campus but also to locate the financial resources to keep them there. In her annual report to President McVey in 1933, Blanding described the academic year as "the most strenuous one since my appointment." Eager young women, many "without adequate means of support," enrolled at the University of Kentucky, only to run short of funds. These students, in particular, often had trouble locating employment because "there are always fewer work opportunities for college women than for men."[5]

New Deal agencies such as the Federal Emergency Relief Agency and especially the National Youth Administration (NYA) supplied valuable work opportunities for college women. At the University of Kentucky, for example, Blanding's assistant, Sarah B. Holmes, directed both programs, which provided employment for hundreds of women students who worked at a variety of jobs, including office assistant, waitress, and child-care provider, both on campus and in town. Despite the unenviable volume of paperwork these programs required, Blanding confided to McVey that "I do not even let myself think of the day when the government ceases this program [the NYA] because it has been such a boon . . . to the students."[6] (On the NYA see Blakey, 1986; Lindley & Lindley, 1938.)

Central to Berea's ability to offer a high-quality education at a modest price was its student-labor program. But, as Bowersox observed, women students faced inequities in hours, compensation, and labor assignments. Bowersox persistently requested that President W. G. Frost and his successor, William J. Hutchins, make necessary adjustments, arguing that the typical woman who enrolled at Berea had to work long hours for low pay at primarily domestic labor. In an effort to address these problems, she recommended that the 20-hour work week be reduced by at least 25%. Without some relief, Bowersox warned President Hutchins, "either [their] health or scholarship is bound to suffer."[7]

Bowersox also protested that men students earned higher wages and had a larger range of jobs available to them. The latter, in particular, was a major source of discontent among the women students, a substantial number of whom, unlike their male counterparts, worked almost exclusively in domestic jobs. Many resented their perpetual assignment to the laundry and dining hall at lower wages than the men students. In her annual report for 1917, Bowersox suggested that cafeteria work provided a vivid example of these inequities. Men students, working as waiters, earned $1.25 each week, while women students, confined to dishwashing, earned only 60 cents, although they worked virtually the same number of hours.[8]

The women students also objected to this policy, and one clever poet summarized their discontent in the "Dishgirl's Soliloquy," which appeared in Berea's student newspaper.

Three times a day
We stop to say
"We thank thee for this food"
And 'tis quite true;
Sit down we do
In very thankful mood.

We eat the food,
Forget the mood
And sigh with longing wishes—
"The boys may go."
Dish girls not so!

We stay to do the dishes.
(*The Pinnacle*, March 21, 1932)

Sympathetic to that complaint, Bowersox continually protested not only the disparity in pay but also the nature of work opportunities that did nothing to help women gain employment upon graduation.[9] Berea women, she maintained, were not "snobs," but "bright mountain girls," who had done more than their fair share of domestic work at home. The dean reminded President Frost that these young women will view "the injustice of this [policy] as long as their school bills are exactly the same." While conceding that perhaps first-year women might be assigned to some domestic duties, Bowersox insisted that all Berea's women students "have labor that is educational as well as remunerative."[10]

Bowersox considered her major task as dean of women to be the preservation of Berea's "simplicity and democracy."[11] To do so more effectively, she enforced, despite persistent opposition, a dress code for women students. The Office of the Dean of Women sent all freshman women information concerning this policy, informing them that Berea women did not wear "silk dresses or silk waists or silk stockings,"[12] but rather simple cotton or woolen dresses. Such regulations, the dean believed, enhanced the democratic spirit of the institution,[13] and allowed Berea to provide "a first-class education at a very low price."[14]

This concern with student attire was entirely consistent with Bowersox's sensitivity to marginal groups. Since her arrival in Berea in 1907, the dean had visited schools and homes in some of the most depressed areas of eastern Kentucky,[15] and, as a consequence of those expeditions, she became all the more convinced of the value of the dress code, without which "the poorest girl would silently disappear from our campus."[16] Furthermore, Bowersox insisted, obvious variation in student attire would engender "class feeling on our campus."[17]

Maintaining the dress code, however, brought Bowersox into conflict with the younger faculty members and some women students. Frequently insensitive to Berea's traditions, the young faculty members, anxious to be popular among the students, refused to support such college regulations.[18] Such opposition, Bowersox believed, undermined her proper role as "friend and advisor" to students and forced her to become "simply a proctor or law enforcement official."[19] To avoid this, she reminded members of the Dress Committee that without their support of the policy, many women students would lose the opportunity for an education.[20]

Reflecting on her long career at Berea in 1939, Bowersox acknowledged the difficulty of the task, when the dress code often became "the 'storm center'"[21] of campus life. Although she believed that a direct link existed between simple dress and Berea's larger mission to mountain youth,[22] she understood why women students consistently opposed what they considered a repressive policy. In fact, hardly a year passed at Berea without some controversy concerning dress fabric, shoe style, or heel height.

Although the dress code appears inconsistent with Bowersox's other actions on behalf of women students, the ensuing furor illustrates what William A. Link (1992) considers to be the heart of southern Progressivism—conflict between paternalism and localism. Seeking to install "an outward-directed standard of conduct," Progressive reformers instead intensified persistent, local adherence to "precepts of personal honor [and] individualism" (Link, 1991, p. 63). While Bowersox's ultimate goal—to improve life for Berea's women students—never varied, she soon discovered a fundamental internal dissonance between the economic and cultural preoccupations of the women students. Grateful for her support for higher wages and nongendered student employment, a vocal contingent nevertheless hotly opposed a dress code that they believed set college women apart as a distinct class of students and as people who were unable to make independent decisions concerning their clothing.

VOCATIONAL COUNSELING

Cognizant of the necessity of adequate financial resources to bring women students to campus and to keep them there until graduation, these deans—themselves self-supporting since their early twenties—deemed it essential that these young women acquire the ability to be economically independent. Within this context, Blanding and Harris served not only as effective advocates for their women students but also as perceptive advisors, addressing their needs both as workers and as women. Determined that they know the strength of economic independence, Blanding presented women students at the University of Kentucky with a variety of vocational counseling opportunities. Concerned that young women did indeed benefit from strong role models, Harris brought many successful women to the University of Alabama.

Since she had been self-supporting from an early age, Blanding knew the importance of a marketable skill. Consequently, she dedicated herself to providing women students with access to information concerning an array of occupations.[23] To achieve this end, the dean experimented with several types of vocational programs during her 18 years at the University of Kentucky. Initially, she instituted an annual speakers' series, which included a number of women, prominent at both the regional and national levels.[24] To provide more sustained, personal vocational counseling, Blanding also began an extensive individual advisement program. In the fall, each woman student, after indicating her career preference, met, at various times during the academic year, with an appropriate faculty advisor.[25]

Finding neither the speakers' series nor the faculty advisement program entirely satisfactory, Blanding advocated instead one- or two-day programs, at which women from numerous fields addressed the students. During her first year as acting dean of women, she arranged such a meeting, with only six prominent women speakers.[26] In 1939, however, the Association of Women Students, with her support, sponsored a noteworthy two-day conference, at which "twenty-one leaders of different professions"[27] discussed their work. In addition to the traditional fields of education, home economics, and social work, students learned about opportunities in such diverse professions as publishing, advertising, business, and government.[28]

Harris's far-reaching network of social, political, and professional connections dramatically enhanced her ability to encourage Alabama women to consider many professional options. In addition to extensive Alabama and regional connections, she was also able to bring to the university several internationally known women from academia, the arts, and government. These programs enriched the education of women students, the vast majority of whom were Alabama natives from rural communities.

Women students at the University of Alabama not only profited from Dean Harris's example as administrator and academic, but also met world-renowned scholars such as Margaret Mead and Vera Brittain.[29] Furthermore, the dean used her dual professional connections with home economics professors and student personnel directors to bring prominent women administrators to campus. Strongly dedicated to enhancing the reputation of the University of Alabama College of Home Economics and its graduates, the dean invited Martha Van Rensselaer, Dean of the New York State College of Home Economics at Cornell University and a leader in the profession, to address Alabama women in 1931.[30] Drawing also on her NADW ties, Harris brought Bernice Brown Cronkhite, Dean of the Graduate School, Radcliffe College, to Tuscaloosa.[31]

Along with her extensive social and professional networks and as a result of both family relationships and her own work with the U.S. Department of Agriculture (USDA), Harris also enjoyed extensive political connections. Through her uncles, Seale Harris, a successful physician, and William Julius

Harris, U.S. Senator from Georgia, the dean knew many southern political figures. Because of her long association with the USDA as a Home Demonstration
Agent, she was also part of the unique network of women working in government service during the New Deal years (see Ware, 1981). Anxious that her
students be aware of women's achievements in public service, Harris used these
connections to bring well-known public servants, including Ruth Bryan Owen,
ambassador to Denmark, and Judge Florence Allen, member of the Sixth Circuit
Court of Appeals, to the university.[32]

PROFESSIONAL DEVELOPMENT

Despite their primary involvement with women students, Bowersox, Harris,
Stamp, and Blanding also embraced the struggle for equal benefits for their
female faculty colleagues. Cognizant of their low numbers and academic rank
as well as their usual departmental segregation, these deans lobbied energetically
to secure institutional commitment to equal treatment for women and men faculty members. In this endeavor, they tackled the especially troubling challenges
of securing institutional support for their professional activities.

Central to membership in the larger professional community is attendance
at national conferences. For academic women in general, and southern academic
women in particular, such connections assumed special significance. Often
working at marginal institutions in small towns or in rural communities, these
women craved opportunities for professional growth and fellowship. Blanding
and Harris especially recognized this need, both for themselves and for their
colleagues, and they persistently encouraged their presidents to promote such
activities.

From the earliest years of the NADW, the organization's leaders also acknowledged the need for adequate professional support for deans of women.
Addressing the annual meeting in 1918, Dean Florence L. Richards (1918) reminded her colleagues that women and their institutions benefitted from such a
policy. Professional involvement, she continued, enhanced both the dean's and
the institution's reputation. Perceptive college and university presidents, she asserted, will be aware of this and of the "information and inspiration" (p. 400)
such meetings provided. Thus, without hesitation, they must not only encourage
deans of women to attend but also underwrite their expenses.

Not all chief executives responded favorably to such requests, however, as
Blanding and Harris soon learned. Despite cordial relationships with their presidents, these deans struggled repeatedly, and not always successfully, to obtain
adequate funds for their colleagues and for their own professional activities.
Committed to enhancing the prestige of the Office of the Dean of Women and
the professional prospects of Assistant Dean Sarah B. Holmes, Blanding encour-

aged President McVey to allocate funds for Holmes so that she could attend both NADW and AAUW (American Association of University Women) national meetings.[33]

Equally concerned that Henrietta M. Thompson, her close friend and one of the University of Alabama's four women holding the rank of professor, obtain recognition for her work, Harris insisted that the institution assume all expenses for her presentation at the annual meeting of the American Home Economics Association (AHEA) in 1938. Dean Harris reminded the executive secretary to the Board of Trustees, Ralph E. Adams, that Thompson, a prominent home economist who enjoyed a national reputation, had made numerous presentations at AHEA meetings, including an address to "an audience of around five hundred home economists from all over the country."[34]

Even her own growing regional and national reputation did not guarantee Sarah Blanding adequate institutional support to attend NADW conferences. By 1936, she was among the most prominent southern members of the NADW. Between 1933 and 1935, Blanding served as chair of the organization's influential University Section. She also held various committee appointments, participated on panels at annual meetings, and was already mentioned as potential presidential timber. Nevertheless, the University of Kentucky was not readily prepared to meet her full travel expenses.[35]

That these deans achieved at best minimal success in obtaining support for professional activities is not surprising. College presidents, particularly at less prestigious southern institutions, had limited funds to support any faculty professional activities. Naturally, then, citing the economic exigencies of the Great Depression, they could easily dismiss the requests of a relatively small number of faculty women, especially since they were in primarily feminized fields.

AGNES ELLEN HARRIS AND HOUSEMOTHERS

In addition to Agnes Ellen Harris's initiatives to obtain financial assistance for women students and faculty, she also received a staggering number of applications for another campus employment opportunity for women in the 1930s—the position of housemother. In fact, alone among the papers of these four deans, the Agnes Ellen Harris Collection includes nearly 1,000 applications from women seeking work as housemothers between 1927 and 1942. Most of these contain correspondence between Dean Harris and the applicant, a formal letter of application, and letters of reference. This rich source, which reveals a cadre of women on the furthermost margins of academic life, broadens historical understanding of the plight of women on coeducational campuses in the South during the Great Depression.

Since the admission of the first women to coeducational institutions, chief among the obstacles administrators cited concerning this new student population were the problems of adequate housing and supervision. The women's colleges in the East initially solved this problem by requiring their women faculty members to live in the dormitories alongside the students. Because of the extremely small number of women faculty, however, coeducational institutions, almost from the outset, employed nonacademic support personnel: the housemother, a neglected yet essential figure in the expansion of coeducation and in the enhancement of professional dignity for women faculty members.

As more women of sufficient means matriculated at coeducational institutions, they too wanted to share in college life, particularly the Greek letter societies. At the University of Alabama, there were 16 sororities in the 1930s, each of which employed a housemother. Competition for the positions was intense.

Because of the public pressure, Harris considered only candidates from Alabama. Throughout the period, applications arrived almost daily, with often more than 200 on file for only two or three vacancies. Because of the Great Depression, few women relinquished their positions. Those who successfully obtained employment often remained on a waiting list for nearly 2 years.

Who were these women? In age, education, location, and marital status, they represented a diverse group indeed. Applicants ranged from 20 to 60 years of age. Not only high school graduates but also normal school and university alumnae and even women with graduate degrees sought employment as housemothers. Women from virtually all regions of the country were willing to relocate to the largely rural community of Tuscaloosa to secure work. Finally, while a number of married women submitted materials to Dean Harris, not surprisingly, widows comprised the largest contingent of applicants.

What drove these white middle-class women to seek service employment in the conservative South? A small number of applications ranged from the frivolous or unique to the pathetic and the tragic. A very few widows of prosperous men sought work primarily as a diversion.[36] A college-educated woman whose husband was pursuing medical training needed the employment for only a year.[37] One woman did not even submit her own application. Rather, her son contacted Dean Harris in her behalf, and, one hopes, with her consent.[38] Finally, some of the applications suggest that a small contingent of women sought employment because their husbands deserted them during the economic crisis of the 1930s.[39]

Most women, however, needed the position to support themselves or various family members. A few enterprising women hoped to enhance their subsequent employment prospects by combining the job of housemother with that of student. Normal school alumnae, armed with the standard two-year degree, wanted to work at the university while completing their collegiate course work.[40]

A number of women required the income to help them care for a family member—in one case a blind sister, in another a disabled husband.[41]

The majority of widows, however, sought employment to educate their children, especially their daughters. Although one does, of course, find much concern for sons, it is this urgency to educate daughters that dominated the sources. Several of these women were willing to work for the lowest of salaries so that their daughters could attend the university. So determined was one woman to obtain college education for her daughter that she assured Dean Harris that she wanted "no money, just our board and Ellen's tuition."[42]

Verbal desperation equaling, if not surpassing, the visual desperation mirrored in the unforgettable photographic record of the rural South during the Great Depression permeated all too many of the letters Agnes Ellen Harris received from these middle-class white women. One applicant, who had met Dean Harris at a woman's club meeting in happier days, reflected on her altered circumstances. "Since then, how the tables have turned. All things . . . must give way to wondering what the future holds for one not trained in business, yet faced with the reasonability of educating three boys."[43]

An Alabama native who had not yet lost her sense of humor assured Harris that she understood the competition for the posts was keen. "I am so anxious for a place but it seems to me it is just about as easy to be elected president of the United States."[44] Another woman forthrightly assured the dean that "I am willing to do anything that is honest and honorable."[45]

What do Harris's responses reveal concerning the troubled relationship between women, cultural proscription, and economic independence? Although Harris had been economically autonomous since her 20s, her correspondence suggests that she sympathized deeply with the many women who had "given their lives to home-making"[46] but sought remunerative employment during the 1930s. Such sympathy, however, did not prevent her from enumerating the realities she faced in hiring housemothers.

Harris made it clear that applicants needed "deep, deep roots in Alabama soil."[47] Because a number of Alabama families relied on the income their women relatives earned from these jobs, Harris felt enormous public pressure to hire for a public institution from within the state. But, as a consequence of the volume of applications, even Alabama women stood little chance of securing a post. Although applications for housemother arrived "almost daily" in 1931, the dean informed an applicant that "not a single chaperone . . . has resigned." In fact, she contends, women with such jobs "are holding on to them with grim determination." Furthermore, those few women who actually acquired a housemother's job had been on a waiting list "for one or two years."[48]

In January 1932, Harris reported to an applicant that she currently had "more than three hundred applications on file."[49] So beleaguered was the dean that she could not even help her own niece, who sought a job. In fact, the situation of most of the applicants was so extreme that "we are able to get women for no more compensation than room rent."[50]

CONCLUSION

Bowersox, Harris, Stamp, and Blanding soon learned that obtaining access to the full range of campus space for academic women meant little indeed if these same women lacked equitable financial support to keep them on the campus long enough to earn their degrees. They also discovered that tackling the issue of access to equitable financial support, like access to campus space, entailed not only securing administrative acquiescence but also discerning and addressing the often conflicting needs of a variety of women, including students, administrators, faculty, and nonprofessional staff. Cognizant of the nature of this challenge, the four nevertheless served as vocal advocates for the financial interests of women on campus. Whether seeking additional federal monies for women students' on-campus employment or enforcing a dress code that worked to students' indirect financial and psychological advantage, Bowersox and Blanding—ever aware of their own monetary struggles as young women—continually lobbied the administration on behalf of women students to provide the programs to keep them on campus.

Mindful of women's need for economic independence after college, Harris and Blanding provided students with access to comprehensive vocational counseling and to outstanding women role models in a variety of professions, a rather remarkable feat in the conservative South of the 1930s. Equally determined that they and their faculty maintain regional and national ties to their particular discipline, Harris and Blanding also functioned as tireless, if not always successful, advocates of continued financial support for academic women's professional development. Finally, although she could do little for the vast majority of women who applied for those few housemother posts at the University of Alabama, Harris, in her responses and in her retaining of those valuable primary sources, not only articulates the dilemma of the traditional woman in the South in the 1930s but also expands historical perception of the rather startling variety of women who sought access to the college campus during the Great Depression.

Essential to the establishment of a chapter of Mortar Board at the University of Maryland, Dean Stamp accepts a certificate of merit for its contribution to the war effort in 1942. (Special Collections, University of Maryland at College Park Libraries)

CHAPTER 4

"The Academic Dignity of the Campus"

Collegiate Women, Academic Societies, and Campus Ritual

Because the Office of Dean of Women developed in a rather haphazard fashion and remained closely associated with women's maternal qualities, National Association of Deans of Women (NADW) officers not surprisingly inherited the problem of public perception, which plagued the profession from its earliest days. In her analysis of the development of women's professions, Nancy Cott (1987) draws a clear distinction between professional women as individuals and women as members of a professional society representing a feminized occupation. Such organizations, Cott maintains, suffer from "a problematic identity and an ambiguous mandate." She concludes that the associations, although dedicated to "fostering professional standards which discouraged women from any sex-based loyalty," nevertheless, by their very nature, spoke "uniquely for women" (p. 230). Joan Jacobs Brumberg and Nancy Tomes (1982) maintain that because women professionals generally assume tasks that men traditionally ignore, feminized fields suffer from a distinct lack of prestige.

Although an increasing number of deans earned graduate degrees and participated in other scholarly pursuits, the general public remained reluctant to discard its stereotypical view of the position. Speakers at NADW conventions enumerated a catalog of common descriptions of the position: "glorified chaperone," "innocuous housekeeper," and "gracious and charming lady who 'loves girls'" (Simrall, 1925, p. 554; see also Kunkel, 1926; Lee, 1927). In response to such uninformed generalizations, NADW leadership sought to define the office, its qualifications and significance, through the association's programs and publications.

Deans of women since the founding of the profession recognized the need to explain precisely the major duties of the position. Lois Kimball Mathews established the modern foundation for the profession in her study *The Dean of*

Women, published in 1915. Ten years later, the NADW commissioned Ruth Merrill and Helen Bragdon (1926) of the Harvard Graduate School of Education to write an additional analysis of the position. These, along with various dissertations and presentations at NADW annual conventions, provide a precise catalog of the dean of women's primary responsibilities, which fell into four categories: academic, administrative, advisory, and social[1] (see also Jones, 1928; Sturtevant & Strang, 1928; Sturtevant, Strang, & McKim, 1940). Many deans of women, including Bowersox, Harris, Stamp, and Blanding considered the fostering of women's academic success and reward to be one of their primary goals.

From the establishment of the republic, critics of higher education for women based their attack on the presumed unsuitability of women's mental and physical resources for serious, sustained academic endeavor. Cognizant of this recurring charge, perceptive deans of women wasted no time identifying the primary challenge they faced as women's advocates on coeducational campuses. Indeed, several years before the establishment of the NADW, Mary Bidwell Breed (1908), Dean of Women at the University of Missouri and a future leader in the profession, exhorted her colleagues to prove these critics wrong by identifying and enhancing women students' role in maintaining "*the academic dignity of the campus*" (p. 63, emphasis in original; see also Herrick, 1927; Priddy, 1922).

Responsive to her challenge, Breed's colleagues initiated a lively scholarly discussion of the academic component of this profession. As chief academic officer for women, the dean of women was responsible for duties that extended beyond the stereotypical reprimanding of students for poor academic performance. In fact, many deans considered their primary obligation in this area to be the collection of a variety of statistical data concerning women students' academic achievement. Armed with such information, the administrators would encourage institution presidents either to admit more women students or to approve the founding of campus chapters of national academic honor societies for women. Especially ambitious deans apprised promising young women of graduate fellowship competitions, a rare commodity for collegiate women.

Despite the undisputed value of classroom achievement and of academic societies in women's collegiate experience, these alone do not bind women students to the physical spaces of the campus, either as students or as alumnae. Equally essential to this process of belonging to the institution is the fostering of ritual, yet another variant of women students' relationship to the campus landscape. In her evaluation of ritual in elite women's colleges, Helen Horowitz (1984) found that through a variety of ceremonial activities, "students symbolically claimed college ground" (p. 178).

Bowersox, Harris, Stamp, and Blanding perceived women students' need for both academic achievement and recognition and inclusive ritualistic activities. Intertwining the two, these deans devised rituals for their campuses that tied the claiming of public spaces to the larger academic fortunes of women. Cognizant that need for such campus activity transcends gender, Bowersox, Harris, Stamp, and Blanding nevertheless perceived their particular value for women students, who often considered themselves outsiders on the coeducational campus in the conservative South.

Nancy Fraser's (1989) discussion of the "needs claims" of the powerless provides an instructive framework for understanding these women's conception of their role as deans of women. College and university presidents often felt that in granting women students, faculty members, and administrators legal access to previously all-male institutions, they had met women's basic, or "thin" need. However, as Fraser suggests, most needs claims "tend to be nested" (p. 163). Bowersox, Harris, Stamp, and Blanding quickly perceived this distinction on campus and dedicated their careers to meeting these "nested needs."

At issue for women students were neither skirt lengths nor Sunday afternoon teas, but rather the extent of their opportunities on the coeducational campus. Aggressive advocates for their charges, these deans believed that if women students were to enjoy the full range of college life, they must claim not only the classroom, but also the campus—its honorary, extracurricular, and athletic spaces—as their proper domain. In their role as advocates for women, Bowersox, Harris, Stamp, and Blanding considered the founding of academic societies and the establishment of meaningful campus ritual to be among their greatest achievements.

COEDUCATION IN HIGHER EDUCATION

To appreciate the accomplishment of these deans of women on the problematic terrain of the public coeducational campus, it is necessary to examine the development of coeducation in higher education and the growth of higher education for women in the South. At the heart of the debate over coeducation in colleges and universities was the relationship between women, academic ability, and traditional gender expectations. Could women attain academic success? Would they attain such success in undue proportion to their male counterparts? How might such success affect their future husbands, their children, and, indeed, the entire social order?

Throughout the last decades of the 19th century, the debate over coeducation dominated both the scholarly and popular presses. The major arguments on both sides concerned the academic and social effects of educating women and men together. Woody (1929) found that opponents of coeducation charged that women in college classrooms would lower academic standards. Furthermore, they insisted that the growing feminization of particular academic areas, especially in the humanities, devalued segments of the traditional curriculum. Increasingly, men students refused to enroll in classes containing a disproportionate number of what they considered to be socially and academically inferior women (Olin, 1909; see also Solomon, 1985).

Opponents also maintained that coeducation was socially detrimental to both sexes. They argued that continual contact with women students, in academic and social settings, would distract young men from their serious purpose. In his comprehensive study of adolescence, psychologist G. Stanley Hall (1904) formulated a "sex attraction" theory, which mitigated against close proximity between the sexes during this crucial period in their development.

The most provocative argument against coeducation, however, was that it produced sickly women, incapable of fulfilling their primary task as mothers. Dr. Edward Hammond Clarke concisely outlined the problem in his treatise *Sex in Education: Or a Fair Chance for Girls*, published in 1873. In adolescent girls, argued Clarke, both the brain and the reproductive organs developed simultaneously. The unremitting brain activity characteristic of coeducation, Clarke maintained, retarded the development of the reproductive organs, producing adult women unable to bear healthy children (see also Douglass, 1992; Maudsley, 1874).

Advocates of coeducation, on the other hand, maintained that far from distracting male students or devaluing certain subject areas, women students actually exerted a positive influence on men, enhancing the academic performance of both sexes. In fact, Thomas Woody (1929) claimed that women and men benefitted academically and socially from coeducation, which, in replicating the family relation of the sexes, "was in accord with nature" (Vol. 2, p. 264). Furthermore, numerous studies of the effects of academic and physical activity on women's health continually disproved Clarke's supposition (Howes, 1885; see also Jacobi, 1876; Rosenberg, 1982).

Despite the lively debate that the question of coeducation generated, between 1870 and 1910, the number of women attending coeducational institutions grew over 23-fold, from approximately 4,600 to 106,500. Those 106,500 women represented over 75% of the total number of women attending institutions of higher learning in the United States. Furthermore, Mabel Newcomer (1959) found that in 1910, women students comprised nearly one-third of the student population at coeducational institutions, an increase of over threefold since 1870.

While historians of women and higher education have finally commenced evaluation of their experiences in coeducational institutions, the lives of academic women in the South remains largely uncharted territory. Paradoxically, the postbellum South offered White women access to a wider variety of institutions of higher education than did any other region of the country. Prospective students could choose among three options: private, denominational, single-sex colleges for women; public single-sex colleges for women; or a slowly increasing number of coeducational land grant and private colleges and universities. In each case, however, historians have barely begun to uncover the story of women students—Black or White—much less women faculty members and administrators working in these institutions.

In the postbellum era, an increasing number of women in the South, as indeed all across the country, demanded access to previously all-male public and private colleges and universities. Those coeducational experiments in higher education that predated the Civil War occurred primarily in private denominational colleges in the Midwest, such as Oberlin and Antioch. Subsequently, in response to both a decline in the number of male students and a need for revenue, public land grant institutions in the Midwest and Far West admitted women.

Although coeducation challenged gender relations throughout the country, it remained an especially unsettling prospect in the South, which increasingly emphasized the purity, self-sacrifice, and status of White women. Not surprisingly, then, some private and public institutions in the region established innovative, if not widely emulated, alternatives to educating women and men together: the coordinate college, or women's annex, and the public single-sex college for women. As noted earlier, Tulane University, unwilling to admit women students, yet in possession of a generous bequest for that very purpose, established Sophie Newcomb Memorial College, the first coordinate college in the United States.

Economic and cultural considerations again conspired to produce an additional, more widespread, innovation in higher education in the South—the public single-sex institution for women. Most private denominational women's colleges suffered two calamities in this period: severe funding shortages and inability to meet newly established national standards of accreditation. Simultaneously, more southern women than ever before needed to be self-supporting and demanded financially feasible educational opportunities. Reluctant to open public men's colleges to women, as was increasingly the case in the Midwest, eight southern states—Georgia, Florida, Mississippi, North Carolina, Oklahoma, South Carolina, Texas, and Virginia—established public single-sex colleges for White women (see Dean, 1991; Letson, 1994; McCandless, 1984, 1993; Orr, 1930; Solomon, 1985). Although these institutions included a liberal arts curriculum, their primary goal was to train women in the feminized professions of teaching and home economics.

Increasingly, southern economic reality made alternatives such as these less acceptable to legislators, educators, and women. Few private institutions in the South possessed the financial resources to establish coordinate colleges for women. Despite the success of the public single-sex colleges, most state governments could not afford a dual system of higher education for White women and men. An increasing number of middle-class women in the region needed to attend college, but could not afford the fees at private schools. Furthermore, these women recognized that land grant institutions offered a practical curriculum, designed to prepare them more readily for economic independence. Thus, in the South, as in other areas of the country, women attended coeducational private and public institutions in dramatically increasing numbers. Nevertheless, the experience of women students, faculty members, and administrators—Black or White—in coeducational institutions across the country remains relatively unexplored ground, nowhere more so than in the South.

To appreciate the work of Bowersox, Harris, Stamp, and Blanding in establishing academic societies and college rituals, it is essential to discern yet another facet of this largely untold story of the fortunes of academic women on coeducational campuses. During the tenure of these four women, a dramatic change occurred not only in the numbers but also in the motivation of college women. These deans, like many of their professional colleagues, saw a sharp contrast between their own experiences as undergraduates and those of their charges during the 1920s and 1930s. Such change rendered their efforts to foster academic recognition and campus rituals for women all the more problematic because they often faced challenges not only from the administration but also from the women students.

While the first generation of women students at coeducational institutions was highly dedicated, conscious of its unique status, and devoted to the pursuit of serious careers, by the time Bowersox, Harris, Stamp, and Blanding became deans of women, a larger number of women with increasingly diverse goals enrolled in coeducational institutions. Nevertheless, as Helen Horowitz (1987) maintains, a variant of those first-generation pioneers, "the strong minded women" (p. 200), still attended coeducational institutions, albeit as a smaller proportion of the total number of women enrolled.

ACADEMIC SOCIETIES FOR WOMEN

During these same years, NADW members from a variety of institutions expressed concern over the role of the dean of women in fostering academic excellence among women students. This often proved a large order, because at many colleges and universities, not only clubs and athletic teams but also many honor fraternities excluded women. Furthermore, college ritual on many campuses bore no academic stamp whatsoever, reflecting instead the frivolous, often stereotypically gender-based character of college life.

On their respective campuses, Bowersox, Harris, Stamp, and Blanding resisted such discrimination and consistently encouraged and honored that crucial core of strong-minded women. Determined that women be formally rewarded for their academic achievements, these deans actively supported the establishment of a wide variety of honor societies, combining them in some cases with more meaningful college rituals.

Adele H. Stamp's 10-year campaign to bring a chapter of Mortar Board, the national senior women's honorary, to the University of Maryland exemplifies this commitment to the recognition of scholarly excellence among women. It also reflects her own experience at Sophie Newcomb College, which, unique among private women's colleges in the South, perceived the need for many of its students to become economically independent. Undoubtedly Stamp understood the value of formal academic recognition in enhancing women's employment prospects.

Anxious to acknowledge outstanding women students, the dean founded the Women's Senior Honor Society in 1925. The new organization recognized a select group of women distinguished by their "standards of scholarship and leadership," service activities, and "loyal spirit toward college authorities."[2] The society soon became a valued part of campus life, and, as Stamp observed, "membership is deemed one of the greatest honors that can come to a student."[3]

Determined that the larger campus community appreciate the purpose of the Women's Senior Honor Society, the earliest members of that group sought to define the organization as one of service. Among their service activities, Honor Society members acted as pages at the annual conventions of the AAUW (American Association of University Women) and the PTA (Parents–Teachers Association).[4] More importantly, however, they recognized that service activities alone could not make the organization unique among campus societies.

After "a very lengthy discussion," members decided that the Women's Senior Honor Society needed to establish rituals "that will make ourselves 'known on the campus' and yet not appear ridiculous."[5] The women students acted decisively and, in 1926, they obtained permission from President Albert F. Woods to present "the woman student of the three upper classes having the highest scholastic average for the year" with a cup commemorating her achievements at the annual commencement exercises.[6] Thus, only 4 years after Stamp's arrival, university authorities recognized women's academic achievements in a ceremony that had traditionally bound its male graduates to the institution.

Stamp soon sought to affiliate the Women's Senior Honor Society with Mortar Board,[7] for she was eager to make women students a part of a wider honorary network and thus to enhance their career prospects. Unfortunately, she soon discovered that acceptance by Mortar Board was no simple task. In answer to her initial inquiries, the national secretary of Mortar Board advised Stamp of the organization's "very conservative" admissions policy.[8] Although the University of Maryland met the basic requirement for consideration, that is, membership in the Association of American Universities, Mortar Board's Director of Expansion would not allow the Women's Senior Honor Society to apply for membership until 1933.[9] Stamp repeatedly assured Mortar Board officials that the University of Maryland, through its admission policy, its construction of on-campus dormitories, and its athletic program, which "will surpass any in the vicinity,"[10] had indeed made a substantial and dedicated commitment to women's education.

In October 1934, Mortar Board recognized that commitment when it agreed to establish a chapter at the University of Maryland.[11] Overjoyed at the news, Stamp reveled in the success of "our ten year endeavor,"[12] and, along with the women students and alumnae, planned an elaborate initiation ceremony to commemorate the occasion. For all these women, this national recognition of their academic achievements represented a major victory that would strengthen their presence in the larger network of academic women.

Eager to ensure that as many eligible women as possible shared in this honor, Stamp contacted numerous alumnae and invited them to participate in the first initiation ceremony. Not surprisingly, most of these women were pursuing careers, and many were attending graduate school. Clearly, these academic achievers discerned both the economic and the emotional value of their employment and relished their independence and productivity. Although most worked in traditionally feminized fields, such as teaching and home economics, these women nonetheless took pride in their intellectual skills and wished that they be formally recognized.[13]

In addition to information concerning Mortar Board, this correspondence between the dean and her former students indicates the lasting respect and devotion with which they regarded each other, years after their graduation. For many, the cramped conditions of the Y-Hut only served to bring them closer to the young dean. "It doesn't seem so long ago," one recalled, "that we all gathered in your sitting room in the 'Y-hut' to discuss our chances, and ways and means of increasing them."[14] These women, pioneers themselves at the University of Maryland, recognized the pivotal role that Stamp played in claiming for them the right not only to membership in a women's national honor fraternity but also to a full collegiate experience.

CAMPUS RITUAL

Women students at coeducational institutions valued not only social and intellectual but also emotional ties to their alma mater. Since the founding of the earliest institutions of higher education, class rituals, or traditions, along with athletic activities and honor societies, constituted a central feature of college life for men students. Helen Horowitz (1984) discovered that women students at elite northeastern women's colleges, eager to enjoy these same connections, established a variety of campus rituals. Just as they claimed campus space for their extracurricular and athletic events, so too did their class traditions "cast a special aura over the landscape" (p. 172) and soon became irreplaceable components of college life.

The earliest women students in coeducational institutions, few in number, living in local boarding houses with little or no institutional supervision, had few ties with the campus beyond their classwork. Without this daily connection to the institutions' athletic and social spaces, they remained unlikely to establish those close bonds, both to the campus and to their classmates, from which rituals could develop. Consequently, women students at coeducational institutions continued to be not only social and academic but also emotional outsiders.

Deans of women played a crucial role in assuring that women students forged emotional ties to their classmates and to their alma mater. Despite the increasing number of women who gained access to campus living space, they still needed an administrative advocate to support their requests and to encourage their efforts. As a consequence of their experience in single-sex institutions, Harris and Stamp understood the abiding significance of class rituals for women students. Furthermore, as self-supporting women immediately following their graduation, the two also recognized the importance of academic achievement for women students. These rituals, however, while reflecting traditional gender bonding, also incorporated a significant academic component, specifically confounding cultural stereotypes of southern women.

Within their first year as deans of women, Harris and Stamp established, respectively, the Woman's Convocation and May Day, which became central features of student life. Spanning the academic year, these events accomplished two goals. In addition to publicizing women's activities and skills to both the university and the larger community, these rituals also bound women students more closely to their peers, the dean of women, and their alma mater.

In 1927, Harris, along with the Women's Student Government Association, established the Woman's Convocation, a part of the annual homecoming festivities.[15] The dean considered the ceremony, dedicated to honoring women's academic and professional achievements, to be the highlight of the academic year for women students. "It is the only time," she reminded her colleagues, "during the year when the women faculty appear as a body before the women students."[16] During the Harris years, this special ceremony extended formal recognition to outstanding Alabama women—alumnae, students, and faculty members.

For each convocation, the dean drew on her extensive social, political, and professional connections to bring impressive women to the campus, both as guests and as participants. Concerned that women students enjoy access to strong female role models, she ensured that a variety of prominent women addressed the audience. In an effort to bind alumnae more closely to the institution, she also included several presidents of the alumnae association on the programs.[17]

Harris sensed that women students needed role models on the university campus as well. At the Woman's Convocation in 1944, faculty members and students honored Septima C. Smith for her promotion to the rank of professor.[18] A closer look at the status of women on the University of Alabama faculty suggests the significance of this event. In 1944, the few women faculty members at the University of Alabama continued to hold the lowest ranks and to work in primarily feminized fields. Of the 77 faculty members who held the rank of professor on campus, only 7 were women. Predictably, most worked in departments that women tended to dominate: one in physical education, one in education, and four in home economics.[19] Within this context, Smith's promotion to Professor of Zoology indeed merited recognition. Because Harris wanted women students to have access to a wide variety of career options, she believed it important that they realize women could succeed in traditionally male fields.

In addition to promoting the establishment of campus rituals such as the Woman's Convocation, Harris also retained strong connections with her students long after their years in Tuscaloosa and she took special pride in their professional accomplishments. Deeply committed to her advancing home economics and student personnel work, she derived great satisfaction from students who entered either field. In 1938, Mary Boniske wrote to Harris from Edinburgh University, where she was pursuing doctoral study in nutrition, informing her that "much of the credit for my work is due to the most adequate background that I received from the University of Alabama Home Economics department in nutrition."[20] Boniske also assured Harris that her network of friends spread far and wide. "Although Scotland is about four thousand miles away from Alabama," she wrote, "two friends of yours met in Aberdeen and discussed their sincere admiration for you. One was Miss Sybil Smith from Washington [USDA employee] and the other was . . . me."[21] In her reply, Harris indicated her great pride in "our first Ph.D." and assured Boniske of abiding interest "in every step you take."[22]

In 1923, Stamp established the May Day festival, a ceremony that, unlike the traditional celebrations of female beauty, recognized women students' artistic and academic accomplishments (*Baltimore Evening Sun*, June 1, 1923; see also Farnham, 1994). The program, which occurred annually on the university's Gerneaux Green, cemented ties between the junior and senior classes. Junior women presented a play for the departing seniors, while graduating Mortar Board members tapped the next year's initiates.[23]

During Stamp's tenure at the University of Maryland, two programs in particular suggest both the close ties among students and alumnae and their love for the dean. The May Day celebration in 1937, "Famous Women Past and Present," celebrated the achievements of a number of women in various occupations. In addition to tableaux honoring luminaries such as Catherine the Great and Queen Elizabeth, the women students also recognized notable contemporary

Maryland alumnae and faculty members for their achievements. To highlight the women's contributions to the university, they invited a number of women "firsts": the first woman member of the Board of Regents, the first women graduates of the University of Maryland, the first May Queen, the first president of the Women's Student Government Association, and, of course, the university's first and only dean of women. In their presentation to Stamp, the women students acknowledged their "greatest debt of gratitude for [her] advancement of the University of Maryland as a coeducational institution."[24]

At the May Day celebration in 1956, held in conjunction with the university's Centennial Celebration, both the women students and Governor Theodore R. McKeldin honored Stamp for her 34 years of devoted service to women's higher education.[25] Both women students and the dean's professional colleagues heartily approved of this honor. In its assessment of the ceremony, the student newspaper, the *Diamondback*, concluded that "if there is anything or anyone who is more symbolic of Maryland than May Day, that person would be Dean of Women Adele Stamp."[26] In her letter of congratulations, M. Eunice Hilton, director of the Student Dean Program at Syracuse University and president of the NADW, reminded her friend that she was a role model for both young women and seasoned professionals. "Bless you, my dear," she concluded, "for all you have done over the years for the women of Maryland and for bringing to all of us professional women distinction through your contributions."[27]

CONCLUSION

The dedication of Stamp and Harris to the establishment of academic societies and significant campus ritual was among their most valuable achievements. Expanding the definition of the Office of Dean of Women beyond that of duenna and disciplinarian, they fearlessly confronted the perennial issue at the heart of the lingering suspicion of, if not outright antipathy to, the presence of women students on the coeducational campus—their problematic relationship to the academic life of the institution. Resourceful and independent from their early adulthood, Stamp and Harris appreciated the persistent and indeed rightful need of serious women students, despite the troubling influx of more frivolous classmates, for recognition of their academic skills, of their desire, and often need, to be self-supporting, and of their wish to be connected in some meaningful way to the physical spaces of their alma mater. Shrewdly, skillfully, and sensitively, these deans devised rituals that tied the claiming of public campus space to the larger academic fortunes of women.

Athletic since childhood, Sarah Blanding was a standout on the 1923 women's basketball squad at the University of Kentucky. The coach of the Kittennettes, Albert B. ("Happy") Chandler (back row center), subsequently served as Governor of Kentucky and as Commissioner of Baseball. (University of Kentucky Archives)

CHAPTER 5

"That Physique Which Is So Essential"

College Women and Athletic Opportunity

On May 10, 1922, the Berea College student newspaper, the *Pinnacle*, published a lengthy article entitled "Attention, Girls!" in which a woman student acknowledged the growing enthusiasm of her peers for organized athletic activities. Like many traditional college women, "we had [considered] all sports . . . the rightful property of the male sex and . . . had accepted this state of affairs without a murmur." No longer willing to brook such subordination either on the playing field or in the marketplace, Berea women asserted that they wanted to be "capable of carrying on a nation's work . . . whether it be doctor, lawyer, teacher, or mother . . . successfully." The perceptive student author articulated the direct relationship between academic achievement, physical health, and economic independence. She concluded that, to do their work competently, women must have the opportunity in college "to acquire that physique which is so essential" (p. 4).

Deans of women played a central role in the establishment, maintenance, expansion, and control of women's physical education programs. Early on, they realized that athletics, like academic rituals and honor societies, intersects with larger issues of campus space, institutional finance, and cultural expectations of women. Skeptics, both on and off the campus, concluded that the entire issue of women's physical fitness—its maintenance and control—was as much, if not more, troubling than their academic achievement on the campus.

Consequently, Barbara Solomon (1985) found that athletic programs, staff members, and facilities for women in coeducational institutions appeared more slowly. Plagued by limited funds, particularly in the 1930s, college presidents often remained reluctant to invest precious monies in women's athletic activities. Only after years of lobbying did Katherine S. Bowersox and Adele H. Stamp secure the construction of facilities such as the Woods-Penniman Building or the Women's Field House. In most cases, as both deans discerned, the best women could expect before then was restricted access to men's athletic facilities.

The establishment, format, and control of women's athletics on campus remained an especially provocative challenge for Bowersox, Harris, Stamp, and Blanding. However, undergirding the administrative acumen necessary to obtain and retain a physical education program for women were the strong views that Stamp, Blanding, and Bowersox held concerning the fundamental purpose of those programs. Physically active themselves, they reflected an unusually modern preoccupation with both the desirability of the broadest possible student participation and the value of lifelong physical fitness.[1] As a consequence of her training in physical education and her work with women industrial workers, Stamp believed that college women, too, would perform better in the classroom as a consequence of a comprehensive physical education program.

Throughout their careers, Bowersox, Harris, Stamp, and Blanding maintained that the widest range of women must have access to athletic opportunity. Thus, if the conferring of academic honors is a fundamentally exclusionary process, then the establishment of physical education programs, like many college rituals, reflects a more inclusive, democratic vision of college life. Sources reveal that Bowersox, Harris, and Blanding, convinced that personal health was an essential component in the lives of educated women, sought to control the establishment, maintenance, configuration, and administration of athletic opportunities for women students on the coeducational campus.

To appreciate the role of Bowersox, Harris, and Blanding in the achievement of these goals on the coeducational campus requires that historians address four questions. How will women obtain access to physical education programs? Will administrators allocate adequate portions of campus space to such programs? What sorts of activities will these programs include? Who will control women's physical education programs?

Ironically, the Berea College woman who, in 1922, voiced her desire for a formal physical education program did so in the midst of a national crisis confronting women physical educators in the United States. At a private institution, far from the heart of the growing profession of women's physical education, this young woman, in her request for organized athletic opportunities for women, on one level reflected the unambiguous concern for the majority of college women across the country. On another level, however, she unknowingly raised an issue that increasingly placed women physical educators and their wholehearted allies, deans of women, at odds with male administrators, male coaches, and, occasionally, women students.

Accounts of the efforts of Bowersox, Harris, and Blanding to foster women's athletic opportunity on campus converge to reflect two major trends that Patricia A. Vertinsky (1994) identifies in her survey of women and sport history, 1983–1993. Vertinsky discovered that most historians focused on the dramatic stories and achievements of individual women. Significantly, however, she also found that a growing contingent of scholars had begun to address more comprehensive questions concerning women, sport, and the dominant culture.

Vertinsky (1994) concluded that, dissatisfied with "simply writing women into sport history" (p. 23), perceptive historians of women and sport discerned that women's increasing involvement in sport, in the public arena and on the college campus, provided a context perhaps even more elemental than politics or professions for either reinforcing or reconfiguring traditional conceptions of gender. These scholars, Vertinsky concludes, have produced perceptive analyses of "the historical relationship between sport and the social construction of gender" (p. 23). Recovery of the stories of conflicts concerning women's participation in sport reflects, at least as dramatically as do conflicts over women's access to the ballot box or to the professions, the historically "unequal power relatives between women and men" (p. 23).

Examination of the efforts of Bowersox, Harris, and Blanding to expand athletic opportunity for college women encompasses both of these historical perspectives. However, one cannot appreciate this aspect of their work as deans of women without recognizing the importance of nature and athletics in the lives of these independent women. Neither can one fully appreciate the significance of class and ambition in their lives without examining the ways in which they sought to configure and control the conduct of women's sport on campus.

ACADEMIC WOMEN AND THE LOVE OF NATURE

Because historians have devoted almost exclusive attention to the experiences of academic women in single-sex institutions, stories of their relationship to the outdoors and athletic activities dominate the literature. However, numerous academic women in coeducational institutions, including Katherine S. Bowersox and Sarah Gibson Blanding, harbored an intense, lifelong love of nature. Outdoor activity dominated Bowersox's childhood in rural Pennsylvania. As a student at Bloomsburg Normal School and as a faculty member at the Carlisle Indian Industrial School, she enjoyed picnics, hikes, and sporting events with her colleagues and students.

During her 30 years at Berea, Bowersox's appreciation of the outdoors intensified as a consequence of her encounters with one of the last relatively wild landscapes east of the Mississippi River. The foothills of Appalachia, the home of Berea College, remained essentially untouched wilderness when she joined the faculty in 1907. Pristine rivers and virgin timber still abounded in eastern Kentucky.

Because of its unique mission, Berea College encouraged its faculty to cultivate an understanding, if not outright appreciation, of the unique Appalachian landscape, which so decisively shaped its students. Fortunately, Bowersox, along with Mary Welsh, forged strong bonds with this challenging yet beautiful terrain through a variety of activities with mountain folk, professional colleagues, and Berea students. Through her series of summer expeditions with Welsh into the mountains to meet parents and prospective students, the dean came to appreciate the untamed character of Appalachia and the strength of its people.

Berea's academic women, including Bowersox and Welsh, frequently took hikes and had picnics in the mountains. A favorite location was the home of Anna Ernberg, head of the Fireside Weavers, a college industry. Located at the foot of Indian Fort Mountain, this cottage bordered on the wilderness area not too far from the college. Photographs taken here reveal a healthy, forthright contingent of women faculty and administrators, among whom was Katherine Bowersox, dressed in plus fours, enjoying the friendship, the activity, and the landscape.

The central college holiday, Mountain Day, a fall celebration of the region's natural beauty, provided for Bowersox, her faculty colleagues, and her students a cherished college ritual that combined devotion to Berea with respect for nature and for bracing athletic endeavor. Begun in 1875, this event served multiple purposes (*Berea Citizen*, October 4, 1990). It provided one of the few times alumni could visit Berea and socialize with students and professors. It provided the students, all of whom performed some variety of useful labor, a holiday. Most important, however, it afforded the entire college community the opportunity to enjoy, as a group, the natural beauty surrounding Berea. According to a college directive of September 1916, at 8:00 in the morning, on "the third Monday of the fall term," students would depart from Ladies Hall, where the dean of women lived. Groups left the campus in "walking parties and wagons," with "members of the faculty as conductors." Activities, including "a substantial meal," which the college provided, lasted until 2:00 in the afternoon, at which time groups would gather "at the foot of Indian Fort Mountain" for the return to campus.[2]

During Mountain Day activities, Bowersox, while enjoying the fellowship and the surroundings, not surprisingly played a supervisory role. Determined that the day be devoted to "the enjoyment of scenery and good company," the college demanded that students "not wander in small groups by themselves." Bowersox had to ensure that if students took independent "excursions" they did so "in definite parties with members of the faculty."[3] Even with these essentially reasonable restrictions, Bowersox, her colleagues, and students counted Mountain Day as a much-beloved college ritual celebrating physical activity and nature.

Like Katherine S. Bowersox, Sarah Gibson Blanding had enjoyed nature and athletic activities since her childhood in the Bluegrass region of Kentucky. Whether serving as the church bellringer or the local swimming instructor, she lived a life of rigorous physical activity. Subsequently, Blanding capitalized on those athletic skills and enrolled in the 2-year course at the New Haven Normal School of Gymnastics, thus becoming involved in physical education in a formal, professional manner. Furthermore, she did so at a time when the relatively new profession of women's physical education experienced the arduous process of self-definition. Appreciation of her training as a professional women's physical educator is essential to understanding Blanding's subsequent role in the configuration and control of women's sport at the University of Kentucky.

It is instructive to evaluate Blanding's various early work experiences with the Lexington public park system and the Department of Physical Education at the University of Kentucky from two perspectives. First, these jobs reflect a concern for social-reform initiatives to aid marginal groups. An activist dean of women such as Blanding could easily place such concern and energy at the service of women on the coeducational campus. Second, however, less immediately obvious but surely more provocative, through these jobs Blanding accepted a distinct, class-based professional perspective that dramatically influenced her actions on behalf of women and sport on the University of Kentucky campus. Thus, what on one level appears to be fairly innocent forms of employment in fact reflects an unmistakable professional agenda, which subsequently set Blanding, the dean of women, at cross purposes with a contingent of women students and with the male athletic structure on campus.

ACADEMIC WOMEN AND SPORT ON CAMPUS

However enthusiastically either the dean of women or the women students supported the establishment of women's sport on the coeducational campus, they encountered far more formidable opposition than did their counterparts in women's colleges. Unquestionably, coeducational campuses were thoroughly male-dominated spaces, bolstered by a male-dominated culture. Determined to secure access to the full range of college life, deans of women, their students, and assorted supporters raised sufficiently troubling issues of finance, space, and extracurricular life.

So long as these issues remained confined to the securing of largely female, nonthreatening ends, such as access to gender-oriented fields, limited portions of the campus, and exclusively female clubs and societies, administrators could defend the granting of these requests. However, in asking to establish, maintain, configure, and control sport programs for women, deans of women raised a provocative subject that combined issues of finance, space, and extracurricular life to serve explicitly nontraditional ends. Having secured access to the essentially male space of the college campus, these women sought to lay claim to that most masculine of activities—physical athletic competition.

Such requests often pitted deans of women against male administrators and other cultural conservatives concerning the very bedrock of culture—the social construction of gender. Women's potential success in sport, it seems, represented a far more upsetting prospect than did their academic achievement. Thus, the struggle to establish programs, let alone the issues of maintenance, configuration, and control, constituted one of the greatest challenges deans of women faced.

ESTABLISHING AND MAINTAINING
ATHLETIC PROGRAMS

Dedicated to serving the economically poorest of students, Berea College officials did not consider a sport program for women to be a necessity. Furthermore, during the early decades of the college, administrators, who struggled merely to maintain an institution of higher education for Appalachian Americans, had little inclination to consider the addition of expensive curricular amenities. Indeed, Berea students, virtually all of whom were accustomed to arduous physical labor from their childhood in rural Appalachia, continued that labor on campus, performing the majority of the college's maintenance work in exchange for their education. Women and men, campus authorities assumed, derived sufficient physical exercise from the college's labor program.

Katherine S. Bowersox disagreed. However essential and rewarding the occasionally monotonous work of the college labor program, she contended that it could not replace organized physical education for women on the campus. Indeed, after only a few years at Berea, Bowersox discovered that "mountain girls do not know how to play."[4] Accustomed to hard work at home, when these young women had free time on campus, the dean observed that they would "sew and iron or 'just sit' [and had to be] cajoled and pushed into regular physical training."[5]

A comprehensive physical education program, complete with a women's gymnasium and physical education director, Bowersox insisted, would benefit Berea women in a number of ways. The dean claimed that there would be fewer "petty cases of discipline . . . if there were greater opportunity for wholesome, legitimate play."[6] Most important, however, a 4-year physical education program would produce more women graduates devoted to the long-term physiological and emotional benefits of physical fitness for themselves and their families.[7]

The eventual establishment of sport programs for women on coeducational campuses afforded deans of women and their students at best minimal security. However difficult the struggle to establish such programs, the maintenance remained at least equally problematic. Following closely on the establishment of women's sport programs was the issue of campus space. Should women share facilities with men? Should institutions build for them a separate, entirely new plant? Cost-conscious administrators usually answered both questions negatively, relegating women instead to men's cast off, and usually shabby, facilities.

Within this context, Agnes Ellen Harris's success, along with the essential support of President George Denny, in establishing and maintaining the Woman's Campus at the University of Alabama remains a unique achievement in the economically deprived South of the early 20th century. Although one could view this as a kind of exclusionary strategy, the construction of the Woman's Campus allowed Harris to build the sort of separate sphere from which women students could derive strength and in which they could develop organizational and leadership skills.

The Woman's Campus included classrooms, dormitory space, and meeting rooms. Harris took special pride in the women's gymnasium, which opened in 1933, the very heart of the Great Depression. She soon discovered, however, that such modern facilities still had to be protected from the men students.

On learning that a group was petitioning for use of the swimming pool, Harris warned Ethel J. Saxman, professor of physical education, "that the granting of this request would be a serious blow to the progress of the education of women at the University of Alabama." Having struggled for nearly 6 years to build a comprehensive program for women, Harris was adamant that her efforts not be diminished, and she reminded her colleague that not only did the women students consider the gymnasium and its facilities among their "most precious possessions," but also that many parents in the region had sent their daughters to the University of Alabama precisely because it offered them access to college facilities comparable to those of men.[8]

CONTROL OF WOMEN'S SPORT ON
COEDUCATIONAL CAMPUSES

When Sarah Gibson Blanding became Dean of Women at the University of Kentucky in 1923, an active, professionally staffed physical education program for women had been in existence for over 2 decades. Early in her term, Blanding, unlike either Bowersox or Harris, confronted the more nuanced issues of configuration and control of women's sport on campus. What should an athletic program for women include? What should it prohibit? Who, within the university structure, would exercise ultimate control?

Close examination of this story includes both of the components of contemporary sport history that Patricia Vertinsky (1994) identified. It is the story of Sarah Blanding and of several other strong academic women who did not shrink, however complex and perhaps questionable their motives, from challenging the male-dominated institutional structure to secure control over women's sport. It is also the more complex story of gendered power relations among Blanding and her professional colleagues in physical education and three groups: the male athletic structure on campus, the university administration, and a vocal portion of women students.

In the fall of 1924, authorities at the University of Kentucky abolished intercollegiate basketball for women. For over 20 years, the sport created great excitement on the campus and in the city of Lexington, as players, students, and local fans thrilled to the exploits of the Kittennettes. During her undergraduate career, Blanding served as captain and as one of the more skilled players, under the tutelage of assistant basketball coach Albert B. "Happy" Chandler, who subsequently became governor of Kentucky and commissioner of baseball. By 1924, however, Blanding, having served as dean of women for barely a year, orchestrated the attack on women's intercollegiate basketball and rejoiced in the university's decision to abolish the program.

Contemporary historians of women of sport derive provocative conclusions from this administrative decision at a struggling public land grant institution in the economically depressed South of the 1920s. What began as an opportunity for innocent physical fitness and fun among college women became, instead, a battleground on which women's physical educators, male coaches, and administrators struggled to define the right relationship between women and athletics. What seemed on the surface to be a routine administrative decision was, in fact, a combination of cultural fiat and professional pragmatism. To appreciate these events and Blanding's role in them, it is essential to outline the course of women's basketball at the University of Kentucky, the philosophy of professional women physical educators toward college women and sport, and the conclusions historians draw from these actions.

The early 20th century appeared full of promise for proponents of a women's sport program at the University of Kentucky. Despite persistent traditional gender distinctions, it seemed that officials at the university wanted southern collegiate women in this new century to reflect not only academic success but also athletic ability. In 1901, the university established a physical education department and hired Florence O. Stout as director of physical education for women.

Hardly a decade had elapsed since the first women's collegiate basketball contest, in 1892, at Smith College when women at the University of Kentucky established their first basketball squad in 1902. In his study of the fortunes of women's basketball at the university, Gregory Stanley (1995) found that women students responded enthusiastically to this new campus activity. Stout, however, concluded that were the contests to continue because of their wide popularity, they would do so only under her strict control. By 1905, she banned men students from viewing the women's games, citing issues of propriety.

Frustrated by such stringent restraints on the quality of their collegiate experience, a contingent of women students petitioned the university administration, asking that the women's basketball team operate under the aegis of the male-dominated Athletic Association. Women students found powerful allies among the faculty, and, most important, in the new president, Henry Barker. Despite Stout's vehement protests, in 1910, the women's basketball team became the province of the Athletic Association, under the control of male physical educators and publicists.

For the subsequent 14 years, women's basketball flourished at the University of Kentucky. Collegiate opponents included Western Kentucky Normal, Kentucky Wesleyan, and Chattanooga. According to Peg Stanaland (1991), the Kittennettes also regularly played high school teams, with intermittent success. Under control of the Athletic Association, the women's team garnered enthusiastic support for its spirited athletic performance. Such enthusiasm was short-lived, however, for with the appointment of Frank L. McVey as president in 1917, Florence Stout gained an essential confederate in her battle to cancel the women's basketball program.

Gregory Stanley (1995) found that like Stout, McVey objected to women's intercollegiate basketball on both physiological and cultural grounds. First, he maintained that such an active sport excessively taxed women's physical strength. Furthermore, he questioned the propriety of a group of women athletes, with few chaperones, traveling across the state and region for games.

Three years after McVey's arrival, Stout persuaded him to establish the Women's Athletic Council, which the dean of women and the head of women's physical education controlled. With this administrative vehicle in place, she recommenced a more concerted, and ultimately successful, campaign to discontinue women's intercollegiate basketball. Crucial to her strategy was the support of Sarah Gibson Blanding, who became dean of women in 1923.

Thus, in her very first year as dean of women, Blanding found herself at the heart of a university-wide crisis concerning the quality of women's collegiate experience. To appreciate her support for canceling women's intercollegiate basketball, it is essential to reiterate Blanding's ties to her two professional mentors—Florence Stout and Frances Jewell McVey. Stout, like Blanding, was an alumna of the New Haven Normal School of Gymnastics. Thus, the two shared a powerful professional perspective on the nature of women's athletics. McVey not only played a pivotal role in Blanding's appointment to the deanship, but also took a deep personal interest in her professional welfare.

Such an alliance brought results, despite intense student protest. In November 1924, the University of Kentucky agreed, on recommendation of the Women's Athletic Council, to end women's intercollegiate basketball. Thus Blanding, after a relatively short time in office, played a crucial role in wresting control of women's sport at the university from the male power structure.

What did such a victory signify? What concerned these women about the increased interest in sport among college women? Whom did this circumstance most threaten? What mechanisms did women physical educators create to combat such a threat?

Gregory Stanley (1995) contends that the cooperation of two strong-minded women—physical educator Florence Stout and Dean of Women Sarah Gibson Blanding—played a decisive role in the demise of women's basketball at the University of Kentucky. Such a collaboration was no surprise. Stout and Blanding shared not only an alma mater but also an emerging women's profession. The two also shared an explicit philosophy concerning the proper relation between women and sport, a philosophy that underlay their determination to control and to configure women's athletics at the University of Kentucky.

Pioneer women physical educators moved expeditiously in the early 20th century to define the goals of the profession and the right relation between women and sport. Shrewdly they recognized that young women, in their desire to experience athletic opportunity, challenged a far more gendered reality than either the voting booth or the classroom or the professions—the almost primordial association between men and physical strength. Susan Cahn (1994) concludes that nothing less stood in the balance than the basis of traditional gender boundaries.

Central to the philosophy of women physical educators was an unequivocal opposition to intercollegiate sport programs for women. They concluded that these programs, almost invariably employing male coaches, benefitted only a small proportion of college women. Furthermore, this elite group of athletes, while enjoying the immediate accolades of sports fans, actually suffered both short- and long-term damage. Male coaches, often anxious to boost attendance and revenues, demanded that women wear inappropriately revealing costumes, which detracted from their dignity as college women. More serious long-term damage, however, included intemperate physical exercise and psychological pressure.

Determined to control and to configure women's sport on campus, women physical educators developed what Susan Cahn (1994) terms "a woman-centered philosophy of sport" (p. 9), predicated on moderation. These women, Joan Hult (1991) maintains, did not unequivocally oppose athletic competition for college women, only "the 'wrong kind' of competition" (p. 64)—that is, varsity, inter-collegiate contests. Women physical educators instead advocated a broad-based sport program that served the interests of the largest number of women. The Women's Division of the National Amateur Athletic Association (NAAF), founded in 1923, encapsulated this philosophy in the slogan "A Sport for Every Girl and Every Girl in a Sport."

Gregory Stanley (1995) found that in her attack on intercollegiate basketball for women at the University of Kentucky, Blanding invoked the democratic goals of the Women's Division. Such a stance followed directly from her initial professional training in physical education and her close association with Florence Stout. During the crisis over the fate of the Kittennettes, Blanding, who assumed a crucial role, did not hesitate to remind university officials of both the physical and the emotional pressures inherent in such contests.

Why did Blanding and numerous women's physical educators advocate discontinuing women's intercollegiate athletics, particularly basketball? Did they do so purely in response to cultural fiat? Was such a policy, at least in part, an act of professional pragmatism?

Close analysis of the local dispute in Lexington, Kentucky, is instructive on two levels. First, it reflects a far larger national phenomenon from which historians draw provocative conclusions. Second, it reminds historians that deans of women such as Blanding, however admirable their achievements on behalf of college women, seldom operated solely from altruistic motivation.

In her examination of the response of professional women physical educators to the growing popularity of women's intercollegiate sport, Susan Cahn (1994) identifies a fundamental conflict encompassing both gender and philosophy of sport. Throughout the 1920s, women physical educators and male coaches and promoters clashed repeatedly, especially over the propriety of intercollegiate basketball contests. Issues of configuration and control of women's athletic programs dominated the discussion.

Despite their thorough disagreement, women physical educators and their male antagonists shared certain common assumptions. Both agreed that college women should have access to sport. Both acknowledged the cultural fear that sport might masculinize women. Both sought to combat this fear, albeit through dramatically different representatives of athletic womanhood, under the control of diametrically opposed supervisors.

Woman physical educators, Cahn (1994) found, combined "female athleticism with a middle-class concept of womanhood" (p. 74). Eschewing provocative dress and professional sport marketing, the "'wholesome, modest athlete'" (p. 57) competed only in intramural contests under the supervision of women physical educators. Concerned primarily with good health and good fun, such student athletes welcomed a woman-centered, woman-directed sport program.

Male promoters and coaches, however, perennially alert to the economic main chance, created what Cahn (1994) considered the very antithesis of this unassuming combatant—"the 'athlete as beauty queen'" (p. 57). Drawing on the popular culture of the 1920s, this model of female athleticism celebrated her femininity through revealing uniforms and her physical strength through an aggressive style of play. Cognizant of the marketing value of this variant of womanhood, male coaches and promoters hesitated not in the least to emphasize these aspects of women's intercollegiate sport.

Cahn (1994) maintains that nothing less was at stake in the struggle between women physical educators and male coaches and promoters than the social control of gender identity. Such a conflict unfolded during the 1920s on collegiate basketball courts across the country, including the one at the University of Kentucky. Intercollegiate basketball proved for the women physical educators to be an especially provocative venue for combat. With its propensity for excessive physical exertion, psychological stress, titillating dress, and commercialism, basketball encompassed women physical educators' worst fears concerning the intersection of women's intercollegiate sport and male control.

Historians concur in their analysis of both the national response of women physical educators and the local response in Lexington, Kentucky, of Sarah Gibson Blanding to male-administered women's intercollegiate basketball. Similar factors motivated their determination to control and to configure women's sport on the college campus. Women physical educators' reasons, Cahn (1994) contends, reflect both a class-based conception of female propriety and a single-minded instinct for professional survival.

Two recent accounts of Blanding's role in the banning of women's intercollegiate basketball at the University of Kentucky support Cahn's (1994) interpretation. Terry Birdwhistell (1994), in his study of the impact of Frances Jewell McVey on the fortunes of women students at the university, explores the relationship between the president's wife and her protégé, Blanding. Both McVeys, of course, staunchly supported Blanding in her quest to dismantle the women's basketball program. While drawing no direct conclusions on the question of motive, Birdwhistell nevertheless contends that the ending of women's intercollegiate basketball dramatically detracted from the quality of women's collegiate experience at a time when the institution spent generously on all varieties of men's sport.

Far more explicit in his analysis of Blanding's role in the basketball controversy, Gregory Stanley (1995) found her antipathy to the program to be not only "more than a little ironic" (p. 442) but also a thoroughgoing repudiation of her own active life and natural athletic skill. She, like other women physical educators, unabashedly appropriated traditional arguments concerning the unsuitability of women and certain varieties of sport for individual self-interest. Blanding's "swift and remarkable conversion," Stanley concludes, merely confirms "the political realities of the athletic ban" (p. 444).

Consistent with Patricia Vertinsky's (1994) assessment of contemporary scholarship in the history of women and sport, these stories reflect two primary trends. First, they reveal the forthright efforts of three strong-minded individuals—Katherine S. Bowersox, Agnes Ellen Harris, and Sarah Gibson Blanding—to establish, maintain, configure, and control women's athletics on the coeducational campus. Second, they also reflect the larger cultural and professional context in which these deans of women formulated policy.

CONCLUSION

From their earliest appearance on previously all-male campuses, women students raised issues concerning not only the allocation of space and finances but also the establishment of academic honor societies and campus rituals. During the early decades of the 20th century, as the number of women on coeducational campuses increased, these concerns continued to dominate the actions of deans of women and other administrators. However, with the advent of the new century, women students, through their additional request for athletic programs with intercollegiate competition, tendered a provocative request. As a consequence, a spirited conflict occurred between deans of women and women physical educators, on the one hand, and male coaches on the other, concerning nothing less than the right to amend or control traditional conceptions of gender.

On their respective campuses, Bowersox, Harris, and Blanding confronted these identical problems. From both a personal and a professional perspective, they recognized the value of physical activity in the lives of young women. Throughout their own long lives, Bowersox and Blanding relished proximity to nature and participation in physical activity.

Determined that their women students enjoy full, autonomous lives, these deans also perceived the connection between academic achievement, physical health, and economic independence. Convinced that personal health was an essential component in the lives of educated women, Bowersox, Harris, and Blanding sought to establish, maintain, configure, and control athletic opportunity for women students on the coeducational campus.

This analysis of the efforts of these three women to foster such programs fills a significant gap in the literature of college women and sport. Historical analysis of women students' athletic experiences on campus focuses disproportionately on single-sex institutions. Perceptive accounts of the relationship between academic women and the outdoors, between students and athletic competitions in women's colleges, dominate the literature.

However, deans of women such as Bowersox, Harris, and Blanding, who sought to expand women students' athletic programs on coeducational campuses, came into direct conflict with the male campus power structure. In their debate over the configuration and control of women's sport programs, they confronted an issue central to the cultural perception of maleness. Accounts of their struggles, however complex the motivation, however varied the result, raise provocative questions and enrich historical perception of the power of the social construction of gender.

In 1932, Agnes Ellen Harris became the first woman from a college or university in the Deep South to serve as President of the National Association of Deans of Women. (William Stanley Hoole Special Collections Library, The University of Alabama)

CHAPTER 6

"We Who Live 'Off on the Edges'"

Academic Women and Professional Organizations

Agnes Ellen Harris's schedule in December 1933 was even more hectic than usual. In addition to her responsibilities as dean of women, since the summer of 1932, she also served as president of the National Association of Deans of Women (NADW). In both capacities, Harris continually faced the financial ramifications of the Great Depression for her women students and professional colleagues. As the fall term drew to a close, she contended not only with routine campus matters, but also with final arrangements for the NADW's annual meeting, to be held in Cleveland, in February 1934.

This conference marked a crucial juncture in the brief life of the profession. After decades of sustained growth, the NADW suffered a membership loss of 13% during Harris's first year in office. Following substantial reductions in salaries, hundreds of members were unable to pay the $9.00 dues promptly, if at all. As a result, the organization found itself operating on a month-to-month basis, trusting that the necessary funds would be forthcoming.[1] Anxious to resolve this crisis, Harris and her colleagues considered the Cleveland meeting an auspicious opportunity to rally the membership and preserve the association.

For NADW members, the association not only provided professional education and support but also fostered, through its annual meeting, essential social connections among women at a wide variety of institutions. Deans of women working at colleges and universities in the South, who faced persistent regional isolation, eagerly awaited the opportunities for professional and social contact. However, as the Great Depression intensified throughout the region, many deans of women, who often suffered substantial reductions in salary, faced the almost inevitable prospect of missing the annual meeting, if not leaving the NADW altogether. Cognizant of the value of the organization and of the financial realities deans of women in the South, including herself, faced, Harris explained to a colleague in the Northeast the especial importance of the NADW in their careers and in hers: "We who live 'off on the edges' probably gain much more from the Association than you in the educational centers do."[2]

Harris cut to the heart of the role that professional organizations assumed in the lives of deans of women on coeducational campuses in the South. Indeed, the story of Bowersox, Harris, Stamp, and Blanding and of their search for professional and social outlets for themselves and their colleagues reinforces, in both a literal and a metaphorical sense, the troubled relationship between women and physical space on coeducational campuses. Women students and a significant number of deans of women usually lived on the geographic edge of the campus, in rooming houses or recently constructed dormitories.

Local, regional, and cultural geography furthermore consigned these academic women to the edges of social life in the profession. Eminently cognizant of this circumstance, Bowersox, Harris, Stamp, and Blanding met the challenge of claiming social space for academic women. The four vigorously pursued access to professional and social outlets at the regional and national levels for themselves and for their colleagues.

At the regional level, they served as founders and perennially active forces within the growing contingent of state associations of deans of women. At the national level, they forged alliances that during the 1930s successfully challenged entrenched leadership within the NADW, opening the organization to women from a wider range of institutions.

STATE AND REGIONAL DEANS' ASSOCIATIONS

Among their many off-campus commitments, Bowersox, Harris, Stamp, and Blanding maintained a unique bond with their professional colleagues in the South. Deans of women throughout the region confronted a complex problem. Before they could function as effective advocates for either women students or faculty members, these women first had to establish themselves on campus, not as substitute mothers or gracious hostesses, but as professional administrative officers.

To meet such a challenge, Bowersox, Harris, Stamp, and Blanding found their connections with professional colleagues, at both regional and national levels, of inestimable value. Other deans working throughout the South shared these same concerns. However, many of these women, often working at small, poorly funded institutions, were unable to join the NADW, let alone attend its annual conventions. Consequently, many of them turned to state and regional deans' associations in search of professional stimulation, renewal, and support.

Bowersox, Harris, Stamp, and Blanding sensed these problems and with the energy typical of all their undertakings became active leaders among deans of women in their own states and across the South. Sensitive to financial realities, yet unwilling to acquiesce before them, these four women worked to draw deans of women within their states and throughout the South into a self-sustaining regional professional community. The founding of state associations of deans had actually preceded the establishment of the NADW. In 1915, deans of women in Wisconsin formed the first state organization (Sayre, 1950). By 1931, 39 grassroots associations served the profession, including 32 state, 5 city, and 2 regional organizations (Report of the Membership Committee, 1931).

Not surprisingly, the establishment of state associations reflected membership patterns within the NADW. Between 1916 and 1938, the Midwest and the Northeast dominated not only NADW leadership but also its membership. In fact, approximately 70% of the total number of members were from these areas. For the same period, White institutions in the southern states supplied the smallest regional contingent, contributing only about 14% of the organization's membership. Deans of women from Black institutions in the region joined in even more modest numbers, comprising only .4% of NADW membership. State associations reflected this trend as well.

Despite the South's small contribution to NADW membership, three southern states—Kentucky, Maryland, and Alabama—boasted some of the oldest state associations. The Kentucky Association of Deans of Women, founded in 1921, was the first southern state association established east of the Mississippi. Two years later, deans of women in Maryland founded an organization, which by 1927 evolved into the Regional Association, including Maryland, Delaware, the District of Columbia, and Virginia.[3] In 1926, the Alabama Association of Deans and Advisors of Girls appeared among the NADW listing of state organizations (*Proceedings of the Thirteenth Regular Meeting*, 1926).

It is no coincidence that these states were leaders in the establishment and expansion of the profession in the South. Bowersox, Harris, Stamp, and Blanding were highly involved with professional activities at the grassroots level—as founders, officers, committee members, and speakers in their respective states. Through their participation in deans' associations at the state and regional level, these four women continued to combine their sensitivity to marginal groups with their belief in the reforming potential of institutions to foster professional fellowship among deans of women across the South.

In 1926, the Alabama Association of Deans of Women and Advisors to Girls was one of only 6 southern state associations among the 33 regional, state, and city organizations listed in the NADW *Proceedings* (*Proceedings of the Thirteenth Regular Meeting*, 1926). Of the 3 states in question—Alabama, Kentucky, and Maryland—Alabama had the smallest number of members in the NADW. As a consequence, state association activities were of great importance to Alabama deans of women, many of whom were employed at small, poorly funded institutions.

Because of her previous work as a professional home economist and educator, Agnes Ellen Harris clearly recognized the value of professional societies for academic women, especially in the South. During the frustrating years as Dean of Women at Alabama Polytechnic Institution, she sensed her own need for professional support in her new career. Consequently, Harris joined the Alabama Association of Deans of Women and Advisors to Girls and subsequently served the profession at the state and regional levels in a variety of capacities. The membership, acknowledging her organizational skill and professional dedication, elected her vice-president in 1927 (*Proceedings of the Fourteenth Regular Meeting of the National Association of Deans of Women*, 1927, p. 12).

Despite her extensive commitments at the University of Alabama, Harris nevertheless participated in professional activities both in the Alabama association and throughout the region. In 1933, as chair of the NADW's University Section, she traveled across the South, supporting state associations during some of the profession's darkest days. While addressing deans' organizations in Georgia and Mississippi, Harris, ever the apostle of NADW membership, encouraged her colleagues to make every effort to join and to participate in the annual meeting.[4] One of the few southerners in the NADW leadership, she believed strongly in the value of affiliating with the national organization.

As NADW president, Harris persisted in her commitment to the development of strong state and regional associations. In 1932, in an effort to recognize grassroots leadership, the NADW instituted a luncheon honoring state and regional association presidents.[5] Cognizant of the value of cooperation between the NADW and local organizations and of the dedication of their presidents, Harris continued the practice and insisted that NADW Executive Committee members attend. Cordial relations between the NADW and regional networks, she maintained, were "essential to the welfare" of the profession.[6]

As the University of Maryland's first Dean of Women, Adele H. Stamp faced an especially formidable challenge. Thus, she recognized the importance of professional support. With customary dispatch, then, Stamp founded the State Association of Deans of Women and Advisors to Girls after only one year in College Park. Deans of women from the surrounding area, with no professional society of their own, soon appreciated the value of this organization, and, in 1927, Delaware, the District of Columbia, and Virginia joined with Maryland to form the Regional Association.[7]

During her long career, but especially in her early years as dean of women, Stamp constantly confronted the central issue in the profession—the perception of the dean of women. As a novice in the field, lacking any graduate training in personnel work, she initially drew on the organizational skills she had developed while involved with the YWCA. Even as an experienced administrator, known and respected throughout the profession, Stamp never forgot her uncertain initial years in office and gladly shared with younger deans of women the strategies she used to enhance the prestige and effectiveness of the office. Central to her success, she maintained, were the professional ties established through the Regional Association. Thirty-three years after its founding, Stamp cited the personal and professional significance of this organization in her career and consistently advised her colleagues to build such connections.[8]

The significance of professional societies at the state or regional level is especially evident in the case of the Kentucky Association of Deans of Women (KADW). Among the oldest, most active, and well-documented organizations of deans in the South, it built strong programs, engaged effective speakers, and served its members well, despite the grinding poverty of the state, especially during the Great Depression. Founded in 1921, initially for college and university deans of women, the organization soon included secondary school deans as well ("Honor for Berea," 1923).

Katherine S. Bowersox and Sarah Gibson Blanding made two valuable contributions to the KADW and to its members. As convention coordinators and speakers, they successfully fulfilled the organization's central mission, that is, the encouragement of a professional spirit among deans of women. In addition, through their personal example in the NADW, Blanding and Bowersox proved that deans of women from marginal institutions in the South could rise to positions of leadership within a national professional organization.

Although Kentucky deans of women were among the most active southern members of the NADW, a large number were unable to join or to attend the association's annual meeting. Consequently, for many of the women, the state convention offered their only opportunity for professional stimulation and fellowship. On numerous occasions, the society held its annual meeting either at Berea College or the University of Kentucky. In each instance, Bowersox and Blanding served as hostess ("Kentucky Deans of Women," 1925). Neither woman dismissed this task as purely ornamental or beneath her dignity as a leader. Instead, both realized that their efforts produced an environment in which deans of women could share experiences and reaffirm their professional status.

For its annual meeting in Lexington in 1935, the KADW invited Dorothy Stratton, Dean of Women and Director of Purdue University's graduate training program for deans, to address the problem of advising women students during times of economic uncertainty (Program of the Fourteenth Annual Meeting, 1935).

Stratton reminded her colleagues that many women students, not unlike some faculty personnel and members of the general public, still considered the dean of women solely a disciplinarian. She recalled the story of two young girls who saw a dean of women on a city street. "One little girl said to the other, 'Who is that woman?' and the other replied, 'I think they call her the demon of the college.'"

Particularly in times of financial stress, which threatened "youth's sense of security," Stratton insisted that the dean of women must reach out to the women students, convincing them of her understanding and discretion. She also stressed that college women in the 1930s, still anomalies among their sex, faced vexing questions concerning their vocational and marital prospects and asserted that frank discussion of these issues could both alleviate fear and establish bonds of trust and friendship between the dean of women and her students.[9]

Blanding suggested an additional way by which her regional colleagues could strengthen their sense of professionalism. She recognized that to fulfill her campus responsibilities successfully, the dean of women needed not only administrative support but also faculty approbation. Whether her training was in personnel work or some other discipline, she must command respect as an expert in her field. Particularly sensitive to this issue, Blanding took a year's leave from her duties for further graduate study at the London School of Economics in 1928 ("Vassar Picks a Woman," 1946). In a presentation before the KADW annual meeting in 1931, she reflected on that experience and emphasized its value for the dean of women in securing the esteem of her faculty colleagues. Nothing, she believed, could more decisively dispel the stereotype of the dean of women than proof of scholarly dedication.

THE NATIONAL ASSOCIATION OF DEANS OF WOMEN

The NADW survived the 1930s in large measure because of the leadership that Adele H. Stamp, Agnes Ellen Harris, and Sarah Gibson Blanding provided. Between 1929 and 1941, they consistently held major positions of responsibility within the organization. As Headquarters Committee Chair for 4 years (1929–1933), Stamp devoted countless hours to ensuring the survival and growth of this central agency of the profession. From 1930 to 1935, these three women dominated the leadership of the organization's influential University Section, which included deans of women from land grant institutions. Building on that constituency, Harris (1932–1935) and Blanding (1939–1941) became the first NADW presidents from public coeducational institutions in the South. These deans realized that their grassroots activism in state organizations provided not only enhanced visibility within the profession but also a solid voting block of devoted southern colleagues on which to build national support.

Stamp, Harris, and Blanding brought unique skills to their task. Their early occupations, dedicated to social reform, defined their approach to leadership within the NADW. Their sensitivity to marginal groups prepared them well to bring the organization through its most arduous decade. Consistent with their activism on behalf of students and academic women, these deans sought not only to preserve the association but also to integrate deans of women from southern institutions more fully into its professional and social activities.

Agnes Ellen Harris became president of the NADW through an unusual stroke of fate. In June 1932, Florence K. Root, Dean of Women at Cleveland College, resigned as the president of the NADW because of her impending marriage. Anxious to maintain the status quo, Harris prudently reminded her colleague that "marriage does not disqualify you to continue as president."[10] Not one to vacillate, however, she quickly accepted her new responsibility and questioned her predecessor concerning the organization's current financial status and forthcoming annual meeting.[11] Harris's presidency, from 1932 to 1935, marked a turning point in the organization's leadership. Of her seven predecessors, only one, Dorothy Stimson, Academic Dean at Goucher College in Maryland, had worked at an institution outside the Northeast or the Midwest (Catton, 1956).

As a consequence of her obvious leadership skills and forceful personality, Sarah Gibson Blanding also held positions of responsibility in the NADW. Between 1933 and 1935, she chaired the organization's prestigious University Section, and in 1939 she became the NADW president. She was only the second woman from a public institution in the South to serve as president of the NADW. Her Kentucky colleagues took great pride in her accomplishments, which strengthened their belief that neither geographical location nor institutional affiliation need restrict opportunity.

The Great Depression accentuated for deans of women the problem of perception. Throughout the decade, salary reductions and lost positions seriously threatened the future of the NADW. Central to its survival, however, were the leadership skills that Stamp, Harris, and Blanding brought to the task. Throughout their careers, these women drew on their experience off on the geographical and professional edges. They drew on such understanding of those circumstances, even as officers in the NADW during its most crucial decade, and dedicated themselves to claiming for those deans of women who, like themselves, worked in marginal institutions access to the leadership opportunities, services, and professional and social connections the organization offered.

Regional Politics in the NADW

Throughout the perilous 1930s, the old struggle between academics and practitioners, coupled with geography, determined political dimensions within the NADW. Since the establishment of the organization in 1916, Teachers College had played a growing role in the life of the profession. Its alumnae not only founded the NADW, but also profited from the institution's training program. Furthermore, two of its faculty, Ruth Strang and Sarah Sturtevant, were recognized authorities in the field of student personnel work, directing graduate research and publishing numerous studies of the profession. Although neither had practical experience as a dean of women, both became influential forces within the NADW.

Acutely attuned to these political differences, Stamp characterized the combatants in succinct terms: "the Sturtevant-Amos group"[12] versus "our gang."[13] Thyrsa W. Amos, Dean of Women at the University of Pittsburgh and former president of the NADW, led an unsuccessful campaign to close the Headquarters Office, so essential to deans of women on the geographical margins. Despite this setback, however, she and Sturtevant continued to be potent forces within the NADW. From New York and Pennsylvania, respectively, Sturtevant and Amos also exerted great influence in the two states that supplied the largest contingents of NADW members.

Unlike the Sturtevant-Amos faction, Stamp and the majority of her allies, or "my crowd,"[14] as she termed them, worked at land grant institutions, not as academics but as practitioners, confronting daily a host of problems with no textbook solutions. These deans, she believed, represented the heart of the profession. Among her partisans, the dean counted colleagues not only from isolated areas such as the South and the Far West but also from the traditional areas of NADW leadership, the Midwest and the Northeast. This faction, however, like the profession itself, also included deans from secondary schools, private institutions, and women's colleges. Rather than graduate school affiliation, however, the common denominator for this group was their status as practitioners who struggled on the front lines, often at isolated nonelite institutions, to claim for women students their right to a comprehensive collegiate experience.

Throughout the 1930s, these groups struggled over various issues crucial to the future of the NADW and the profession, the most significant being the quality of the organization's leadership and the maintenance of the Headquarters Office. For Stamp, Harris, and Blanding, however, the central question remained one of access. They believed that deans of women at marginal institutions needed a voice in the organization's leadership and in determining its agenda. They accomplished both. The election of Sarah Gibson Blanding to the NADW presidency in 1939 began an era in which deans of women from a broader range of institutions and regions led the organization and defined its goals.

Stamp and Harris wanted NADW leadership to reflect more accurately the organization's diverse membership. Although Harris served a second presidential term, both she and Stamp acknowledged the unique circumstances surrounding her assumption of office. Resolved that this shift in leadership would not be an anomaly, these deans, along with Blanding, led a campaign that opened the NADW leadership to women from a wide variety of institutions throughout the country.

Harris had been out of office hardly a year before the struggle began. Irma Voigt, Dean of Women at Ohio University, her staunch ally, supported Harris as president, but soon, for reasons that remain unclear, she severed her connections with the Stamp–Harris crowd.[15] Consequently, the elections of 1936 assumed great importance for continuing the achievement of Harris.

Traditionally, the Nominating Committee had presented one slate of officers for consideration. In 1936, it nominated Voigt for president, and Anna Dudley Blitz, Dean of Women at the University of Minnesota, as first vice-president. Neither the committee nor Stamp herself imagined that the young Blanding would object to this practice. Describing the scene to Evelyn Jones, Dean of Women at the University of Arizona, the dean recalled that "little Sue [Blanding] got up and said she thought it was un-democratic to have only one nominee, only one ticket."[16] For first vice-president, Blanding nominated Alice Lloyd, Dean of Women at the University of Michigan. "Result," Stamp rejoiced, "election of Alice Lloyd. Surprise to everyone, even our gang."[17]

Determined that the Sturtevant–Amos group not retain the NADW presidency, Stamp pursued a vigorous campaign to capture the office for "my crowd." The site of the annual meeting for 1937, New Orleans, served her purposes well, for both she and Harris tirelessly encouraged deans, particularly those from southern institutions, to attend. Speculating on their chances for success, Stamp admitted to Evelyn Jones that "the thing that counts, or rather I should use the plural, are the votes, and if we can't corral them in New Orleans we ought to lose."[18]

Although she maintained that "Sue [Blanding] would make a corking president,"[19] Stamp conceded that Lloyd, because of her more extensive experience, would be the stronger candidate. "Confidentially," she speculated to Evelyn Jones, "I think we stand a better chance of electing Alice this time and Sue [Blanding] the next."[20] If she were to succeed, Stamp knew that she must muster national support for the candidate. Enlisting Jones in the campaign, she asked her to encourage Edna McDaniel, Dean of Women at the University of Oklahoma, to attend the New Orleans conference.

Outlining her overall strategy for preparing for the election, Stamp warned Jones to "steer clear of the Columbia crowd," most of whom remained hostile toward both Lloyd and Blanding. "You see Alice never did take Sarah's famous deans' course," she reminded Jones, "and does not think that Columbia is 'hot,' so I would keep mum about Alice to Sarah's crew."[21]

As events unfolded, neither Lloyd nor Blanding was willing to consider accepting the nomination. When Jones suggested to Stamp that she stand for the presidency, the dean refused. "I could not be considered a dark horse in any sense of the word." Although content with the role of strategist, Stamp also recognized that despite her success, she had made powerful enemies. "I have been too actively associated with our group for the past six years," she reminded her friend, "to be considered at all."[22]

Stamp soon learned that members of the opposition considered Sarah Sturtevant a likely candidate. Dismayed by this prospect, the dean reminded Lillias MacDonald, Dean of Women at the University of Buffalo, that the professor "is not eligible since she is not a real dean of women—she just teaches how to be one and does not practice."[23] In the end, however, a Sturtevant ally, Eugenie Leonard, Vice President and Dean of Women at San Francisco Junior College, entered the race against Harriet Allyn, Academic Dean at Mt. Holyoke College.

Stamp maintained that Dean Allyn, although not her first choice, would make an effective president. Nevertheless, she also perceived the serious problems inherent in the race. Because of her publications and ties to the Sturtevant group, Dean Leonard was well known throughout the country.[24] Furthermore, Stamp realized that deans in both the Midwest and the Far West "have a prejudice against women's colleges and will think of Miss Allyn as an impossible New Englander."[25]

Throughout the campaign, Stamp adamantly opposed Leonard's election, which she believed would be a "grave mistake." In a trenchant letter to Jones, Stamp outlined her principal objections to Leonard. "She has not been a dean very long and after her brief term at Syracuse, which I understood was her first place, she went to this combination of junior college, finishing school and what not in California."[26] Determined to prevent her election, Stamp lobbied colleagues across the country, encouraging them to come to New Orleans. "The question of a President this time is going to be a serious one," she cautioned Maria Leonard, Dean of Women at the University of Illinois, "and we are going to need everyone's vote."[27]

The annual convention of the NADW in 1937 was unique for several reasons. Not since the Dallas Convention 10 years earlier had the organization met in the Deep South. Furthermore, as Stamp observed, deans of women, like other conventioneers, were not immune to the city's festive atmosphere. "New Orleans has certainly corrupted the deans," she apprised Jones, who had been unable to attend. "The cocktail bar was filled with them every night." Despite her own, more serious agenda, Stamp missed no opportunity to introduce her colleagues to the city. "Lillias [MacDonald] and myself betook ourselves to Antoines and there drank a Silver Fizz. It was Lillias' first one and she found it very potent, and very delicious." (A rather arcane and cloying potion, the Silver Fizz includes lemon juice, powdered sugar, dry gin, egg whites, carbonated water, and ice.)

Still the tension of the presidential campaign permeated the meeting. Stamp observed that "Leonard was there politicking for all she was worth." Meanwhile, Stamp, Harris, Blanding, and their allies did their work well. Harriet Allyn was elected to the NADW presidency, and the trio believed that the election "was a decided victory for our side." Impressed by Allyn's competence and demeanor, Stamp assured Jones that "she will hold the Sturtevant-Amos group in check and scare off some of the others."[28]

Following Harriet Allyn's election to the NADW presidency, Stamp, Harris, and Blanding continued to strengthen their coalition. In 1939, "after all these years of plotting and planning,"[29] Blanding became NADW president. Her election, unlike that of Harris, represented no vagary of fate, but rather a tribute both to her obvious administrative abilities and to the skill with which Stamp and Harris drew deans of women throughout the country into a vibrant, long-lived political coalition that would dominate the organization's leadership for the next decade. Blanding's successors, from Michigan, Illinois, Kentucky, and Texas, themselves representing a wide variety of institutions, ensured that deans of women from diverse backgrounds would enjoy access to the organization, its services, and its professional connections.

The NADW and the Issue of Race

Despite the festive atmosphere of New Orleans, yet another persistent, unresolved problem plagued the annual meeting. On their home campuses, Stamp, Blanding, and Harris confronted, with varying degrees of success, issues of space and gender. Like other enlightened White professional women, they faced the even more perplexing calculus of space, race, and gender at NADW conventions. Prior to the 1937 annual meeting, NADW Executive Secretary Kathryn G. Heath advised all Black members of the regulations on which the convention hotel insisted. Thirty-eight years later, at the 1975 annual meeting, she reiterated these indignities. When entering and exiting the hotel, Black members were to "use the back entrance . . . [and] . . . the freight elevators. Once inside they could join in a reception or a meal in a private room where no other hotel guest could see what was going on. Even then, the hotel indicated that the staff might not be receptive to serving any Black women" (Heath, 1975).

This problem neither originated in 1937 nor remained restricted to cities in the South. Although Black NADW members attended the 1928 and 1929 annual meetings, respectively, in Boston and Cleveland, without incident, they discovered in 1930 that the convention hotel in Atlantic City refused to welcome them. In response to Black members' consternation, NADW Executive Secretary Gwladys W. Jones insisted that the source of the problem was not "the liberality of the [White] deans" but the larger issue of "autonomy." The NADW held its annual meeting in conjunction with the National Education Association (NEA), which unfortunately "makes a choice of the annual meeting place."[30]

Not surprisingly, Black deans of women adamantly protested such a policy. Lucy D. Slowe, Dean of Women at Howard University and the first Black member of the NADW, challenged Jones's claim concerning the society's relationship to the NEA. "I do not think that our organization ought to admit that it has not any control of its meetings."[31] Marion V. Cuthbert, Dean of Women at

Talladega College, concurred. "It seems to me that any acceptance of such dicta-
tion is as much an affront to the autonomy of the Association as it is a humiliation to the women at whom it is aimed."[32] (See also Brett, Calhoun, Piggott,
Davis, & Bell-Scott, 1979.)

Such humiliation touched Black members in 1930 and remained a painful
memory. Despite her anger, Cuthbert reminded Jones that "we hope to meet the
present situation with tenacity, . . . and not docility, and we are keenly aware
that the very nature of the trouble forces the white members . . . in the front of
the attack. We should like nothing better than to bear the heaviest part of the
fight alone."[33] Hilda A. Davis, a protégé of Lucy Slowe, attended that NADW
meeting in Atlantic City. Nearly 50 years later, she reflected on her disappoint-
ment as a new member of the profession and of the association. "The few Ne-
groes in attendance stayed in small Negro hotels and boarding houses or with
Negro families several blocks away from the Boardwalk" (Brett et al., 1979,
p. 10).

The NADW faced this same problem in 1937, when it met in New Orleans.
This time, however, NADW leadership formally protested such policies. Executive Secretary Kathryn Heath deplored the fact that racial prejudice forced Black
deans to endure personal insult or "to forgo a membership privilege for which
they had paid their hard-earned depression dollars" (Heath, 1975). After com-
posing a letter outlining the problem, she invited Dean Slowe to the Headquarters Office in Washington. That action alone, Heath recalled, represented "one
little dent in the armor of white supremacy."

Black deans of women also protested this policy. Lucy Slowe approved
Heath's letter, which went to the NADW membership. Furthermore, Hilda
Davis, then president of the Association of Deans of Women and Advisors to
Girls in Negro Schools, exhorted her colleagues "as professional women not to
accept these conditions, therefore not to attend this convention." Recounting the
event over 40 years later, Davis proudly asserted that "only one Negro dean of
women did attend" (Brett et al., 1979, p. 10).

Financial Challenges

Harris desired that her colleagues in the South join the NADW and attend its
convention. Conscious of her unique status as president from a southern state,
she aggressively encouraged deans throughout the region to attend the meetings
in St. Paul, in 1933, and Cleveland, in 1934. Correspondence concerning these
conferences reflects dramatically the financial problem from which both members and leaders suffered.

An enthusiastic supporter of the Harris presidency, Inez Stacy, Dean of
Women at the University of North Carolina, nevertheless doubted that she could
attend the St. Paul meeting. "The University can give no financial assistance at

all," she stated, "and salaries are so reduced that a 'live at home' program is forced upon us."[34] In 1933, Irene Dillard Elliott, Dean of Women at the University of South Carolina, reported an equally grim situation in her state, where "our Legislature is cutting the appropriation exactly in half as compared with last year."[35] Nevertheless, she somehow found the money to attend the national meeting in 1934. On the eve of the conference in Cleveland, Elliott informed Harris, with ironic good humor, that "this time at last, my check is actually in the mails; if the banks hold I'll probably be an actual member of the National Association again!"[36]

NADW leaders were no less susceptible to the monetary crisis. In addition to association business, Harris and Stamp frequently discussed conditions in their respective states. "Alabama is having a mighty struggle," Harris lamented. "We have had a thirty percent [budget] cut . . . and haven't had a penny from the state in over a year."[37] Stamp indicated that circumstances were even worse in Maryland, which suffered a 40% budget reduction. "That means, of course," the dean recounted, "salary reductions, no travel allowance . . . and [even then] something will have to be cut out." With her typical verve, however, Stamp assured her friend that "I will be at the conference . . . if I have to hitch-hike."[38]

The president solicited southern involvement in the NADW for personal, as well as for professional, reasons. Conscious of the national perception of the region, which the Great Depression had intensified, Harris urged deans of women across the South to attend the annual conventions because "we do not want the rest of the U.S. to think we are absolutely buried under our difficulties."[39] Furthermore, as a consequence of the political divisions within the organization, both Harris and Stamp considered it vital that southern deans demonstrate their support for leaders from their region. Drawing on her extensive personal connections with deans across the South, Harris petitioned her closest friends, including Blanding, to "be a committee of one in your state to give encouragement to the others . . . to attending this meeting."[40] Leaving nothing to chance, however, Harris herself sent hundreds of letters apprising deans in the region of the national conferences.[41] Anticipating the headquarters fight at the convention in 1933, the president reminded her regional colleagues that "I am very anxious to have an unusually good representation of southern deans at the meeting in St. Paul."[42]

Beyond considerations of either ego or politics, however, Harris maintained that southern deans of women would genuinely benefit from NADW conferences. "I do not believe that the program is as important in these difficult times," she confessed to Irene Dillard Elliott, "as is the association of the deans of the nation."[43] Harris knew that meeting with women from across the country who shared the problems of adequate finances and facilities for the women students would decrease this sense of isolation. From a more politically practical perspective, however, Harris, eager to increase southern membership, also reminded

Blanding that at the St. Paul meeting "the Southern deans may be able to work out some plan of gaining strength in the South."[44]

Because of her gregarious nature, her long and varied career, and her professional activism in the South, Harris had formed an extensive network of friends who responded enthusiastically to her presidency. Her close friend Harriet Greve, Dean of Women at the University of Tennessee, assured her that as a consequence of her new status, "we southern deans [are] all swelled up with pride."[45] Despite often serious financial constraints, these women energetically supported their friend at the conferences over which she presided. Charlotte M. Beckham, Dean of Women at Harris's beloved Florida State College for Women, best expressed the regional enthusiasm: "Indeed you can count on me one hundred percent in every way. I am very proud that the National Association has recognized your ability as we have always done."[46]

Such comments reflect a sense of the pervasive economic and cultural struggle that deans of women in the South shared. They also testify to their corporate joy in the success of Agnes Ellen Harris and Sarah Gibson Blanding within the NADW. Using their administrative and political skills to best advantage, Stamp, Harris, and Blanding expanded the parameters of national leadership within their profession.

CONCLUSION

Because of their long experience on geographic, professional, and social margins, Bowersox, Harris, Stamp, and Blanding understood clearly questions of credibility and access. Through their involvement with regional deans associations and the NADW, the four worked energetically to claim access for themselves and their colleagues to social and professional outlets. To retain professional status in face of economic uncertainty, these three deans, as leaders of the NADW, addressed the crucial issues of leadership and community within the profession.

Conscious of the challenge of marginality, both on the coeducational campus and within the NADW itself, Harris and Blanding maintained that many of their colleagues at small, isolated institutions throughout the country required access to the professional and social opportunities the NADW provided. They knew that NADW leadership, in order to address the needs of all the members, must reflect the geographic, educational, economic, and racial diversity within the profession itself. Unwilling to remain "off on the edges" any longer, between 1929 and 1941, these deans built alliances that transformed the NADW into a somewhat more inclusive institution.

Katherine Bowersox (right) and faculty colleagues Mary Welsh (left) and Carol Hill (center) on the Berea campus in 1909. (Archives and Special Collections, Berea College)

CHAPTER 7

"Always a Dear Friend"

Academic Women, Family, and Friendship

In 1939, Agnes Ellen Harris served as toastmistress for the Founders' Day banquet, commemorating the 10th anniversary of Delta Kappa Gamma, an honor society for women educators founded by her professional associate and friend Annie Webb Blanton. In this convivial, yet emotional, setting, the two friends reestablished a connection forged two decades earlier, during Harris's tenure as State Superintendent of Home Economics in Texas, and for too long severed. "I have not had in a long while," Blanton wrote after the meeting, "a joy such as I felt when I saw you in Asheville." She assured Harris that across the years that separated them "you were just exactly the same Agnes Ellen that I loved so much when we were together in the State Department of Education." Despite the differences in age and in rank, Blanton maintained that "I never thought of myself as your boss. You were always . . . a dear friend."[1]

In her discussion of the art of feminist biography, Joyce Antler (1992) reminds historians that "material considered irrelevant by biographers of male subjects or other traditional historians may hold enormous value to those writing women's lives" (p. 113). Such is surely the case with the stories of Bowersox, Harris, Stamp, and Blanding. To appreciate their lives more fully, one must address one additional question. How, despite demanding administrative jobs in coeducational institutions, did these women fashion satisfying private lives?

What constitutes irrelevant material in a traditional biography but provides the stories of women with a richer cultural context? This is a provocative question, especially when considering the lives of professionals who in the 20th century redefined the American middle class. In the late 19th and early 20th centuries, leaders in higher education in the United States, the majority of whom were men, commanded significant respect. For them and for their biographers, gender was a fact rather than an issue. However, for the few women leaders, including Bowersox, Harris, Stamp, and Blanding, gender remained an inescapable impediment, touching every corner of their public and private lives.

Significant factors in private lives fall into two categories: elements of responsibility and opportunities for respite. The former encompasses matters of family and of health. The latter could include personal relationships of various kinds.

THE FAMILY CLAIM

Academic women and men, especially those employed in coeducational colleges and universities, experience private life in fundamentally different ways. The key to such dissonance lies in the institution of marriage, most particularly with the assistance that virtually all male leaders expected from that most invisible, but invaluable, of academic support personnel—the dutiful wife. Almost invariably she shielded her spouse from distracting matters of personal responsibility and enhanced his opportunities for personal respite.

Bowersox, Harris, Stamp, and Blanding, like most of their women colleagues, remained single. Furthermore, unlike the majority of academic women, these four worked on coeducational campuses, which provided fewer possible configurations for the conduct of private life than did women's colleges. Hence, for the biographer of Bowersox, Harris, Stamp, and Blanding, seemingly irrelevant material concerning personal responsibilities and respite is crucial to appreciating their stories and those of other academic women in coeducational institutions.

Carolyn Heilbrun (1988) concludes that there remains some confusion concerning "what a woman's biography should look like" (p. 27). She suggests that scholars not merely focus on their subject in her youth but also consider her in "middle age or active old age" (p. 28). The stories of Katherine S. Bowersox and Agnes Ellen Harris—midcareer, single women professionals with family obligations—offer an instructive place to begin.

Cultural expectations concerning gender and caregiving generally work to the disadvantage of women. This was a particularly poignant dilemma for single women professionals. "Nearly one third of my [women] colleagues . . . have one or more people dependent upon them in whole or in part" concluded an academic woman (Tanner, 1907, p. 23).

Bowersox and Harris numbered among those women. For the first 11 years of her employment at Berea College, as she had done since her own student days, Bowersox not only cared for her mother and brother but also provided them with a home—all the while holding a demanding job hundreds of miles from them. Such an additional burden resulted in some rather forthright salary negotiations with President W. G. Frost. "I feel that you will do what is right and just in the matter of salary," she commented. "I have undertaken a mortgage on our home which has given me some little concern." Cognizant that her circumstances represented no anomaly, she informed Frost that "it seems to be universally decreed that daughters should take care of their parents. I hire what help I can and try to take care of my mother in absentia nine months of the year."[2]

Following her mother's death in 1918, Bowersox continued to care for her younger brother, Rollin, a commitment that she honored until the end of her life over 40 years later ("Dean Bowersox," 1918). Available sources reveal only scant information about the dean's relationship with either of her two brothers. In 1927, Rollin G. Bowersox accepted employment at Berea College, responsible for the "care and improvement of the campus" ("New Teachers," 1927).[3] Archives suggest that he held the job for barely a year, but provide no clue to the circumstances of his dismissal. Additional knowledge of Bowersox's relationship with her brother comes not from her own correspondence, which reveals nothing, but from the private papers of her colleague and closest friend, Mary E. Welsh, who documents their retirement years.

Gender, rather than age, marital status, or profession, determined Bowersox's relationship with her mother and her brothers. Despite the fact that her other brother held a responsible administrative job and lived far closer to his family, it was the only sister who assumed the role of lifelong caregiver. Paradoxically, while Bowersox provided a home for her mother and brother, she lived in the dormitory for her entire working life, both at Carlisle and at Berea.

One wonders about Bowersox's almost total archival silence concerning either of her brothers. Were she and her older brother estranged? Was Rollin's disability a problem she hesitated to confide to anyone? Was his abortive employment at Berea a source of embarrassment? Was she too harried to commit her thoughts to paper? Did she, a dutiful daughter, merely shoulder the burden without complaint, secure in the support of her closest friend?

Between 1930 and 1940, Agnes Ellen Harris also experienced the dilemma of a woman professional caring for an aging parent while holding a demanding job and numerous other commitments. Like Bowersox, she had several siblings, two brothers and a sister. She too was an eldest daughter. Since childhood, Harris had been particularly devoted to her father and remained so throughout his long struggle with cancer. Nevertheless, correspondence reveals a persistent conflict in Harris's life, between the devoted daughter and the devoted professional. In the end, she honored both commitments, but at a price.

When Harris's father entered the hospital in Charlotte, North Carolina, in 1930, for the beginning of many visits, his eldest daughter realized that a fundamental shift in the roles of parent and child had occurred. "It hurts me to see him so weak," the dean confided to Florence Ward, a friend from the U.S. Department of Agriculture (USDA). "I feel for the first time in my life that he needs my help and strength. This situation has turned my thinking topsy turvy."[4]

So began for Harris a decade-long struggle between public and private obligations. One wonders why she felt this burden to be hers alone. James Harris's second wife was alive and well, as were his three other children. The dean's papers disclose little concerning her relationship either with her siblings or with her stepmother during this period.

Juggling the claims of family and profession proved to be no simple task, especially when several hundred miles divided the two. However, in the midst of her father's illness, Harris realized a long-cherished dream, a home of her own, after 10 years of living on campus. "My plans are moving forward for my house," she wrote her closest friend and colleague, Henrietta Thompson. "I am getting very enthusiastic about it."[5] At last, instead of making numerous trips to her parent's home, she could bring them to Tuscaloosa.

However convenient this might have appeared, Harris soon realized that even close proximity did not resolve the conflict between the professional and the personal. "I am so glad I have a home for them," she confided to Elizabeth Skinner Jackson, a friend of long standing. "Right now [however] I am being much more of a hostess . . . than I am being a Dean of Women. This is rather hard on the position."[6]

In the spring of 1938, Harris's father returned to the hospital, this time in Philadelphia. "Commencement and my father's illness make things very complicated," she explained to Elizabeth Baldwin Hill, a friend from Montgomery, Alabama, "but somehow we are always able to climb out of our difficulties."[7] Although her father rallied briefly, he returned to Philadelphia later that summer. Despite her anxiety, the dean remained on the job in Tuscaloosa. "I am trying not to go," Harris informed Hill, "but let other members of the family have the privilege of being with him. If I do go, it will be after commencement."[8]

In November, Harris returned to her father, who was visiting doctors in New York City, for what became an especially memorable visit for them both. Still, the decision to leave her work was no simple one. "We had a wonderful weekend," Harris assured Henrietta Thompson. "He adored it and I loved being there with him." Such contentment, however, did not prevent the dean from anxiety over her responsibilities to the university. She admitted to Thompson that "I am afraid I cannot do anything professional. It takes all my time doing the little things . . . for father."[9]

In the early months of 1940, James Harris's condition worsened dramatically. His eldest daughter's correspondence now reflected the years of strain and prospect of imminent loss. She conceded that "I am endeavoring not to do things that will take . . . enthusiasm because I just can't muster it. . . . For the first time in eleven years I am not going to the meeting of the National Association of Deans of Women."[10]

Her beloved father died in June 1940. After 10 years of balancing professional and family claims, Harris, despite her grief, knew that it was time to reorder her life and admitted this to her friend Winifred Collins. "I have been endeavoring to do more things than I could do well and last Spring . . . I tried to teach and . . . carry the responsibilities of this office while making several trips to New York," where her father was in the hospital.[11] The dean concluded that she must, however, relinquish her teaching responsibilities and devote her energies to administrative work.

During the decade of her father's illness, Harris reached her peak as a woman professional. On campus, she managed the Office of the Dean of Women and the School of Home Economics, either one a daunting job. Off campus, she continued her speaking schedule and became the first woman from an institution in the Deep South to serve as president of the National Association of Deans of Women (NADW). No less active in her private life, Harris finally made a home of her own, which she filled with family, friends, and laughter. Furthermore, she chose to honor her beloved father with quiet, consistent devotion. One must conclude that Agnes Ellen Harris did exactly what she wanted to do, however painful and challenging it might have been, and that she did it very well.

PERSONAL RELATIONSHIPS

To whom do single academic women working in coeducational institutions turn for support? Often removed from traditional family networks, these women, unlike many of their counterparts in women's colleges, worked in an environment in which married men with families predominated. Often they did not find the patterns of faculty social life welcoming. As a consequence, the few academic women on coeducational campuses often turned to each other to fashion rewarding personal lives.

Despite their hectic schedules, family responsibilities, and health problems, Bowersox, Harris, Stamp, and Blanding found time for travel, for parties, for picnics, and for correspondence with a wide variety of women friends. The verve and love of life that characterized their professional careers also colored their personal connections. Two sorts of relationships held a special place in their lives. Sarah Gibson Blanding and Agnes Ellen Harris formed especially close ties with older women who were their professional mentors. Katherine S. Bowersox, on the other hand, shared with a colleague a companionate relationship of nearly 50 years.

Discovering and evaluating such relationships among single academic women presents a distinct challenge and responsibility for historians of women. Oftentimes these women worked side by side for decades; hence, little correspondence exists—or, if it does, it is of an almost purely professional nature. Of course, some women protected their private lives by destroying papers. Such questions surely surround the life of Adele H. Stamp, who, unlike her three colleagues, left no private or professional correspondence suggesting any close women friends.

Then there is the puzzle of language. What did women write to each other, and what did it mean? Are terms of endearment and evocative language a regional peculiarity of the South, or is such language universal among persons of either gender who love each other? Do verbal expressions of affection require physical intimacy? Perhaps it is sufficient to conclude that life as an unmarried academic woman did not mean life without either joy or deep personal commitment and that the precise form of expression of these emotions often remains relatively difficult, if not impossible, to determine.

Among the many strong-minded women in Sarah Gibson Blanding's life, without a doubt the most influential was Frances Jewell McVey. In 1946, Blanding, the new president of Vassar College, delivered the principal address at the posthumous presentation of her mentor's portrait to the University of Kentucky. Blanding recalled their initial meeting at registration for the fall term of 1919. "Like many September registration days, it was hot and sultry. . . . The two lines in front of the English table were long, but finally . . . I was standing in front of Miss Jewell. . . . To a rather bewildered uncomfortable young woman who was both an instructor and a freshman, this first meeting marked the beginning of a new, thrilling adventure."

In Frances Jewell, Blanding found a woman who balanced faculty and administrative responsibilities with remarkable skill and tact. A student in one of Jewell's first-year English sections, Blanding observed that the young instructor "sometimes came into class a little breathless, but who, doing as much as she was, would not have been." Years later, after she became an administrator of national reputation, Blanding deferred to Jewell's talent. "I have known many deans of women, but Frances outstripped us all."[12]

Frances Jewell McVey possessed the acuity to recognize and to promote the career of her devoted student and protégée. Over the years, deep affection and respect developed between Blanding and both of the McVeys. A busy and sometimes brusque individual, Blanding nevertheless thrived on a friendship in which she could candidly express her anxieties and her emotions. "I wish we could be near each other," she wrote to her mentor, "[so] that I might enjoy the attention which would be good for my soul."[13] A private woman despite her occasionally obstreperous comments, Blanding was genuinely amazed that Frances McVey could "keep so many in your heart . . . [including] people like me who stretch out eager hands to receive."[14]

At several points during her long career, Agnes Ellen Harris accepted employment in agencies where women not only assumed significant leadership roles but also predominated as workers and as clients. As Dean of Home Economics at Florida State College for Women (FSCW), as a field agent for the U.S. Department of Agriculture (USDA), and as State Supervisor of Home Economics in Texas, Harris worked among independent women who advocated the advancement of women. Consequently, she formed an extensive network of friends, with whom she corresponded for decades.

Notable among those independent women was Annie Webb Blanton, who, between 1918 and 1932, served two terms as State Superintendent of Public Instruction in Texas and held a faculty position in the College of Education at the University of Texas. In her biography of Blanton, Debbie Mauldin Cottrell (1993) concludes that Blanton's major contribution was the founding in 1929 of Delta Kappa Gamma, an honor society for women educators. Cottrell found the organization to be "a unique combination of feminism, femininity, and meritocracy" (p. 107). Blanton was determined to create a society in which scholarly and practical experience and long service among women educators could be recognized and rewarded. Until her death in 1945, she worked relentlessly for Delta Kappa Gamma, as founder, first president, and tireless publicist. By 1945, the organization of 23,000 members had chapters in every state and constituted a network that connected a wide variety of women teachers. Such an achievement, Cottrell concludes, is entirely consistent with one who "made women the focus of both her personal and professional life" (p. 25).

Despite her not inconsiderable administrative experience when she left FSCW for Texas in 1919, Agnes Ellen Harris respected, loved, and learned much from this single-minded woman. Assessing Blanton's tenure as State Supervisor of Home Economics, Harris indicated that "the year I was in Texas [was] one of the greatest years I have ever had."[15] Nevertheless, time, space, and circumstances dictated that Harris and Blanton saw little of each other after she began her career as dean of women. Interestingly enough, however, the two women reaffirmed their friendship at a time of great stress for Harris, who confronted the impending death of her father. Appropriately, it was Delta Kappa Gamma, fulfilling one of its major functions for women professionals, that reunited them at the annual meeting of 1939, held in Asheville, North Carolina.

Their friendship renewed, Harris and Blanton corresponded regularly for the next few years. Early in 1940, facing her father's final illness and heavy responsibilities at the university, Harris considered curtailing additional professional commitments. When the president of Delta Kappa Gamma asked that she serve on the Nominating Committee, the dean's first inclination was to refuse. However, remembering her mentor and her unwavering devotion to the advancement of women, Harris confessed to Blanton, "I thought—well, Annie Webb Blanton would not have done this kind of thing."[16] She accepted the job.

Two years later, Delta Kappa Gamma held its annual convention in Birmingham, Alabama, and the two friends eagerly anticipated their reunion. "Now if you make an engagement to go off and speak somewhere else at that time," Blanton warned her peripatetic friend, "I'll never love you any more and you are my favorite of all."[17] Harris had no intention of missing the meeting. In fact, she hoped that Blanton could visit her beloved and hard-won home in Tusca-loosa. "How long can you stay with me?" the dean asked. Despite wartime restrictions, Harris assured Blanton that "I will save my gas and take you to Birmingham in my car. Nobody could visit me now that would give me more pleasure than [you]."[18]

The renewed friendship with Annie Webb Blanton came at an opportune time for Agnes Ellen Harris. Distressed by her father's death, she sincerely appreciated the older woman's concern and counsel. Doubtless, for them both, the letters and visits reinforced their memories of an especially challenging and productive period in their distinguished careers. The reunion, however, was all too short. In the fall of 1945, Blanton died after a brief illness. Even in the final months of her life, she remained active in her work for women teachers. Such professionalism in face of adversity stood as her final legacy to Agnes Ellen Harris, her cherished friend and colleague.

Katherine S. Bowersox, like so many single academic women of her gener-ation, survived frustration and savored success because of a supportive network of women friends. In the early 20th century, Berea College attracted an impres-sive cohort of strong women to its faculty. Often diverse in their economic background and formal education, they nevertheless shared a common dedica-tion to the institution's mission in the mountains. Bowersox made many friends among those women, but her deepest commitment was to her colleague Mary Elizabeth Welsh, with whom she shared nearly 50 of her 92 years.

Born in 1862 in Gloucester, Massachusetts, Mary Elizabeth Welsh was the eldest child of John H. Welsh, a sea captain engaged in the South American trade. An ardent traveler all her life, the child took her very first sea voyage at the age of 2, from Gloucester to Boothbay, Maine, to see her father's parents. Determined that his seven children know the world beyond the rural Maine to which the family relocated, he took them all on a voyage to South America. In her last year of high school, Mary Welsh described in her senior essay her adventures along the Amazon River.[19]

Captain Welsh not only wanted his children to be well traveled, he was determined that they be well educated. Unlike many men of his era, John Welsh sent all five of his daughters to college. Mary Welsh's choice, Wellesley Col-lege, from which she graduated in 1885, reveals much about her character. Pre-sided over by its energetic president Alice Freeman, inaugurated in 1881, Wellesley alone of the elite women's colleges in the Northeast boasted not only a woman president but also the only faculty composed entirely of women. In this atmosphere of intellectual rigor, dedication to the interests of women, and belief in the value of service, the young Mary Welsh grew to womanhood.

For the 17 years following her graduation, Welsh worked at a number of women's academies in the Northeast. Apparently these jobs failed to fulfill her deep sense of religious dedication, for around the turn of the century, she contemplated entering the mission field in India. Fortunately, Welsh answered the call of Berea College, another, equally fertile, mission field in the hills of Kentucky, and in 1902 joined the faculty.

President W. G. Frost hired Welsh to bring high culture to Berea College. In pursuance of this goal, she taught a variety of subjects and continued her formal education. Initially, she served as instructor of Latin and Greek. Soon, however, Frost provided support for additional training, in French, German, and art. Welsh studied at the most prestigious institutions in the United States and in Europe, including Harvard, the University of Marburg, and the Art Institute of Chicago.

Five years after Welsh's arrival at Berea, Katherine S. Bowersox joined the faculty. At first glance, the two seemed quite dissimilar. After losing her father when she was a child, the young Bowersox worked from adolescence to support herself and her family. Welsh, by contrast, lived in a large, devoted family, with no pressing economic problems. While Welsh was a world traveler before she was 18, Bowersox spent the first four decades of her life in central Pennsylvania. The two differed most dramatically in their academic credentials. Welsh attended one of the most exclusive women's colleges in the country. Bowersox, like so many young women of her generation, paid her own way to attend, but not graduate from, the nearest state teachers college.

Despite these obvious differences, four important factors bound Bowersox and Welsh together in the service of Berea College and in companionship with each other. Both women loved adventure. They traveled extensively, by ocean liner to Europe and by Welsh's series of Ford automobiles from Boothbay, Maine, to St. Petersburg, Florida. The two combined a zest for adventure with a great love of nature. Localities as diverse as the hills of Kentucky, the broad beaches of Florida, and the rugged coastline of Maine provided the backdrop for many hikes and picnics.

The two shared similarities of the heart and spirit as well. Religion played a major role in the daily lives of both women. Coupled with their faith was an abiding belief in the dignity of service to others. These factors, more than any other, drew Bowersox and Welsh to Berea College, where they found both meaningful work and enduring companionship.

Katherine S. Bowersox and Mary Elizabeth Welsh, like virtually all single faculty women at Berea College, worked at a variety of tasks. In addition to administrative and teaching responsibilities, both women lived in the dormitory for their entire careers, superintending student behavior. "As assistant to Miss Bowersox in Ladies Hall," Welsh performed an astonishing array of jobs, including supervising the cleaning of the lounges, the personal cleanliness of the students, and the enforcing of study hours. As if this were not sufficient service, Welsh assured President Frost in her annual report that "[I] hold myself ready to help Miss Bowersox in any emergency, or to relieve her when necessary."[20]

Keenly aware of her colleague's loyalty and effectiveness, Bowersox praised Welsh in no ambiguous terms. "A position which could easily be mere drudgery, through her unselfish interest has not only been endurable but pleasant."[21]

Despite such persistent obligations, the two somehow found time to join and to assume leadership roles in professional societies. "I attended the meeting of the Kentucky Deans of Women held at the State University," Welsh reported, "where Miss Bowersox and I were the guests of Mrs. McVey." She also reminded Frost of her friend's prominence in the organization. "We are honored having our . . . Dean as President of the State Association and look forward . . . to entertaining the women deans . . . at Berea at their next annual meeting."

Bowersox and Welsh also found time to enjoy life. They regularly partook of the natural beauty of Berea, going on countless hikes and picnics. Their opportunities for recreation and travel expanded dramatically, however, in 1920, when, as Welsh noted in her diary, two liberating events for these women occurred—"woman's suffrage—bought first Ford."[22] For the next 30 years, Bowersox and Welsh periodically took to the road, happily relinquishing their professional responsibilities and embracing the variety of natural beauty.

Bowersox did most of the driving. For its inaugural trip, Bowersox, Welsh, and her nephew drove the Model T Ford from Berea to Boothbay, Maine, a journey of approximately a week at that time. Thus did the two establish what would become their annual routine for the rest of their lives—summers in Boothbay, winters in Florida.

Mary Elizabeth Welsh owned a home on Sawyer's Island, just outside of Boothbay, Maine. "You asked me to tell of my island," Welsh wrote to her Wellesley classmates. "It is a small island close to the shoreline of Boothbay and is connected by two bridges. There are about twenty-two houses, all owned by people who seem to love the island as much as I do."[23] Welsh's home was a simple clapboard house, with a generous open porch overlooking the bay. She and Bowersox took hikes, went on picnics, visited friends, read the Bible, and rested. Never one to ignore any pleasure that nature might offer, the 65-year-old Bowersox informed President and Mrs. William J. Hutchins that "the water is cold—but I take a *dip* every day!"[24]

Like so many Americans in the 1920s, Bowersox and Welsh fell in love with the last frontier of the American South—Florida. Train trips to the Sunshine State suited neither woman. In the years between Welsh's retirement in 1932 and Bowersox's in 1939, the two regularly drove yet another Ford from Boothbay or Berea to Florida. "We left Boston on Friday, the thirteenth," Welsh reported to friends, "and, all superstitions to the contrary, we had a most delightful trip." On their arrival, the two rented "a good apartment in the very center of Miami. We have only to cross beautiful Biscayne Avenue to be on the bayfront." Here they read, swam, wrote letters, and observed the tourists. Unwilling to be sedentary for long, Welsh added that "we . . . also enjoy the many beautiful drives in the vicinity, thanks to Miss Bowersox, our skillful driver."

Between 1920 and 1950, Bowersox and Welsh took many trips together. Some of them had great sentimental value. In 1935, for instance, Bowersox drove her friend to Wellesley for the 50th reunion of the class of 1885. The trips they enjoyed most, however, were their annual retirement journeys to Maine and to Florida. When Bowersox bought a home in St. Petersburg, Florida, in 1938, the first she had ever owned, the two finally shared equally in fashioning a rewarding retirement.[25]

At first glance, Bowersox and Welsh seemed unlikely candidates for a friendship of nearly 50 years. From the outset, however, many factors bound them together. Both came to Berea College after years of independent living and working. While sharing the multifarious duties of faculty women at Berea, they became devoted friends. Soon they discovered their common love of adventure and of nature. Most important, however, they recognized their shared spiritual devotion—to their religion, to the dignity of service to others, and, finally, to the bond of friendship they formed.

CONCLUSION

Historians who write the lives of single academic women in coeducational institutions often encounter interpretive and archival challenges when examining the private lives, especially family responsibility and personal friendship. Only recently have scholars begun to examine the lives of single, economically independent women. With few examples to guide them, historians of single academic women must approach these lives with a spirit of adventure, recognizing that traditional categories for analysis of male life may be virtually useless.

Scholars, however attuned to innovative questions and categories, also face unique dilemmas in the discovery and interpretation of primary sources. If women worked in close proximity with other women, how does one discern the nature of their friendship? Across generations of cultural and linguistic evolution, how does one decode the language of friendship?

As single academic women in coeducational institutions in the South, Bowersox, Harris, Stamp, and Blanding lived professional and personal lives fundamentally different from those of their male colleagues. Gender, marital status, and to a lesser degree, region continually challenged their professional aspirations. No strangers to challenge, however, whether in obtaining education and employment or in claiming for women students access to the full range of campus life, the four successfully fulfilled family responsibilities while fashioning rewarding personal lives.

Sarah Blanding reached the pinnacle of her career in 1946, when she became the first woman president of Vassar College. (William F. Draper, *Portrait of Sarah Gibson Blanding*, 1955. The Frances Lehman Loeb Art Center, Vassar College, Poughkeepsie, New York)

"Lost Down in Kentucky"

Deans of Women and the Challenge of Historical Recovery

On Friday, October 11, 1946, Vassar College inaugurated Sarah Gibson Blanding as its first woman president. Numerous dignitaries attended the ceremony, including Virginia Gildersleeve, Dean of Barnard College, who conveyed congratulations from women's colleges across the country. Praising Blanding's contributions as Dean of the School of Home Economics at Cornell University, President Edmund E. Day reminded the audience that in 1941 "'we found this lady. She was lost down in Kentucky'" (*New York Times*, October 12, 1946, p. 12).

Among the early generations of academic women, those employed at coeducational institutions remain relatively obscure. Scholars have turned their attention to the significant number of women employed as faculty members at women's colleges. Furthermore, President Day's comments reflect an even more troubling perception concerning southern academic women. Often "lost" to the larger professional community in their own day, most of them remain lost to contemporary historians as well. To encourage historical recovery of academic women in the South, it is instructive to evaluate the remarkable careers of Bowersox, Harris, Stamp, and Blanding to assess the breadth and depth of pertinent contemporary historical scholarship and to suggest avenues for additional research.

Women faculty members, a minority on the coeducational campus, held mostly low-level positions in primarily feminized fields. As a consequence of their small numbers, Geraldine Clifford (1989) maintains, they remained both "invisible and extravisible" (p. 29). Faculty women at coeducational institutions rarely attained high academic rank, substantial salaries, or adequate funds for research. Yet in other ways their numbers ensured high visibility, for instance, as the only woman in a department or on a committee.

As the highest ranking, if not only, woman administrator on the coeducational campus, Bowersox, Harris, Stamp, and Blanding numbered among the most "extravisible" of academic women. These were very busy women, as their correspondence frequently reveals. Describing her responsibilities as dean of women, Sarah Gibson Blanding observed that the work constituted "a twenty-four hour job."[1] In her annual report of 1910, in which she enumerated her myriad teaching and administrative responsibilities, the forthright Katherine S. Bowersox penciled the comment "Too Much"[2] into the margin, one suspects not entirely as an afterthought.

Agnes Ellen Harris expressed more explicitly the dilemmas inherent in her hectic life. "I do not remember a day," she concluded after 6 years in Tuscaloosa, "when I have not had more work to do than the hours in which to do it. . . . I really do not take time to even darn my hose or black my shoes."[3] Most significantly, however, Harris articulated on several occasions the pivotal conflict in the lives of single women professionals. Proud of her home and eager to share it with friends, the gregarious dean remarked after two large dinner parties that "such activities make a rather heavy demand on the professional woman who is also a housekeeper."[4] Although Harris refused to relinquish or to curtail her social life, she nevertheless concluded that "the dual personality of homemaker and jobber is difficult to maintain."[5]

Despite overburdened schedules, the story of Bowersox, Harris, Stamp, and Blanding is not the story of victims. If they were in some sense "lost" geographically in academic circles in the United States, in no way were they lost either as professionals or as women. The four led full, rich, and committed lives.

To assess their careers perceptively, one must remember what Bowersox, Harris, Stamp, and Blanding brought to the job. They were experienced administrators. They were innovators. Recognizing the relative youth and fluidity of their profession, the four defined the job broadly to enhance their power. Advocacy for them encompassed far more than claiming space and extracurricular opportunities for women students. The four considered themselves advocates for academic women in an all-encompassing sense, including women faculty on their respective campuses and deans of women throughout the South. To achieve their goals, they used their considerable administrative skills to reform campus governance and to establish accessible, regional professional opportunities for deans of women.

Bowersox, Harris, Stamp, and Blanding recognized that the position offered them a unique opportunity to showcase both their skill as professionals and the concerns of a wide range of educated women. Consequently, they embraced extensive commitments both on and off campus. Their on-campus work included responsibilities of two varieties, imposed and embraced. Off campus, they participated in numerous organizations as speakers in the service of women's interests.

Like virtually all faculty members and administrators, Bowersox, Harris, Stamp, and Blanding fulfilled the most common of imposed campus responsibilities, service on college and university committees. For example, Adele H. Stamp participated on a wide-ranging array of committees concerned with administrative, curricular, financial, and social concerns.[6] This last, however, is of special importance because it clearly reflects ingrained cultural assumptions concerning gender roles. Throughout her career at College Park, in addition to her administrative responsibilities as dean of women and as university committee member, Stamp also served as a sort of hostess for university social occasions. She superintended many luncheons and receptions commemorating such institutional milestones as Charter Day, and marking the sesquicentennial of the university and the centennial of the Maryland Agricultural College.[7] Each year, Stamp also planned social activities such as the luncheon and dance for the university's homecoming celebration.

Male university officials were, of course, prompt and effusive in their gratitude. Following the homecoming festivities in 1947, David L. Brigham, University Alumni Secretary, assured the dean that "your statement 'Now David this is one thing you can drop from your mind for we'll take care of it' came at a time when it was sorely needed."[8] Of course university officers need not worry because for all such activities, Stamp always sought and obtained help from the unpaid labor force of American higher education—wives of faculty members and administrators. One wonders, of course, if she were the only administrator without a spouse. One does not wonder, however, why tasks such as this fell to the dean of women.

Institutions varied in their assignments for the dean of women. While the University of Maryland expected Stamp to radiate the social graces, Berea College expected Bowersox to reflect the pioneer spirit. For many years, as a part of Berea's mission to the mountains, the dean used a part of her summer to visit communities in Appalachia. Bowersox reported that in the summer of 1917, she and her assistant and closest friend, Mary Elizabeth Welsh, "spent two weeks in a backwoods county in the interior of West Virginia. . . . We walked about twenty miles and drove at least fifty, over very bad roads. We visited a number of families. . . . Also made some speeches in churches and schoolhouses."[9] Expeditions such as this testify to both the physical and spiritual strength of the 47-year-old Bowersox and the 55-year-old Welsh.

However persuasive they might be, Bowersox, Harris, Stamp, and Blanding discerned that one extravisible woman—the dean of women—could not alone secure permanent, tangible benefits for either women students or women faculty members. For this to occur, women in positions of governance in institutions of higher education in the United States must cease to be the exception, or the anomaly. Harris and Bowersox, the oldest and most seasoned of the four, were quite vocal in their support for women's inclusion at the highest level of institutional control, the board of trustees.

"Since there is a vacancy on the Board of Trustees of the University now,"

Agnes Ellen Harris wrote to a board member in 1936, "we . . . urge the Trustees . . . to consider the appointment of a woman member."[10] By virtue of their numbers on the campus and by virtue of women's status as voters and taxpayers in Alabama, the dean maintained that women merited a voice, a presence to begin with, in the major governing body of a public, tax-supported institution. "About 1,182 women are enrolled at the University this year. . . . The appointment of a woman . . . would be a great service to the work for women in the university."[11]

Katherine S. Bowersox was no less adamant in her support for the fair, and not token, representation of women on the Board of Trustees of Berea College. "We have traveled a great distance," she reminded President William J. Hutchins, "from the time when Mary Lyon sat outside the corridor while her board of trustees discussed the management of Mt. Holyoke, but we have a distance yet to go to catch up with the ideal that men and women should work together." Cognizant of Berea's commitment to coeducation from its founding, Bowersox urged Hutchins to fulfill that commitment at every level within the institution. Her comments reflected the hope and the frustration of academic women across the country. "A coeducational school should have women on the Board of Trustees and all executive boards. It is only by persistent . . . speaking that we have been able to get women's interests into the limelight so that a reasonable and just consideration can be had."[12]

Consistent with their lifelong commitment to the interests of women, Sarah Gibson Blanding and Agnes Ellen Harris maintained extremely active off-campus speaking schedules. This facet of their work as deans of women merits examination because it reveals the two women at very different stages in their careers. For the young Blanding, these opportunities offered a valuable training ground for one who would assume a major role in higher education in the United States in the post–World War II era. For Harris, they represented the culmination of decades of speeches to a number of audiences in an array of locations, including college women and home economists at Florida State College for Women (FSCW), farm wives and their husbands on the courthouse square in rural Kissimmee, Florida.

Blanding and Harris addressed similar agencies, including high schools, colleges, civic organizations, church groups, and professional societies. Several engagements deserve particular notice. In 1941, during her term as president of the National Association of Deans of Women (NADW), Blanding reached across racial barriers to speak to a group of Black deans of women in Louisville, Kentucky (*Lexington Herald Leader*, April 8, 1941). Harris became the first woman to deliver the commencement speech to the graduates of Georgia State College for Women, in Valdosta, Georgia, in 1931.[13] She also returned to her beloved FSCW several years later to address the founding members of the campus chapter of Alpha Lambda Delta, an undergraduate women's honor society.[14]

Although Blanding and Harris delivered speeches that were doubtless valuable in and of themselves, those speeches and the women who made them assume a larger cultural significance as well. In the early decades of the 20th century, southern women and men needed to see articulate women professionals claim their share of one of the most traditionally masculine of public spaces—the speaker's platform. In occupying it with such persistence and persuasiveness, Blanding and Harris not only enhanced their own reputations and those of their institutions but also sent a powerful message concerning the capabilities of college-educated women professionals in the South.

How successful were Bowersox, Harris, Stamp, and Blanding in their efforts to meet challenges to the advancement of women both on the coeducational campus and in their profession? If enrollment figures, building construction, and extracurricular opportunities indicate success, then these women effected major changes in the coeducational institutions they served. Furthermore, it is unlikely that such changes would have occurred without the presence of a strong dean of women, the one administrative officer dedicated solely to the interests of women.

Despite the dramatic increase in the number of women attending coeducational institutions after 1900, many skeptical presidents remained reluctant to hire deans of women. Alongside the obvious financial consideration was the question of necessity. Did women students actually require a special administrative office dedicated solely to their interests?

This study shows that indeed they did and, perhaps, still do. Although institutional authorities appreciated the monetary advantage of admitting women students to the classroom, most remained reluctant to appropriate any additional funds for dormitory, athletic, or social facilities. Advocates such as Katherine S. Bowersox, Agnes Ellen Harris, Adele H. Stamp, and Sarah Gibson Blanding, however, recognized that granting women access to the academic spaces of the campus fulfilled but one component of a much more complex collection of needs. Throughout their careers, these women insisted that without access to every aspect of college life, including its social, extracurricular, and athletic activities, women students would not enjoy a full collegiate experience.

They also understood that deans of women working in marginal institutions, in rural areas and small towns, could not enjoy rewarding professional lives without access to the connections that regional and national organizations provided. Within their home states, Bowersox, Harris, Stamp, and Blanding founded and served regional societies that fostered professional ties for deans of women who often could not afford to join or attend meetings of the NADW. Most dramatically, through shrewd political maneuvering and proven administrative skill, Harris, Stamp, and Blanding transformed the NADW, opening its leadership ranks to women from a wide variety of institutions and regions.

Margaret Ripley Wolfe (1995), in her comprehensive assessment of the history of southern women, concludes that the whole of "historical southern women" has, for too long, remained "in the proverbial wilderness . . . looking for the promised land" (p. 2). Such a diaspora, she contends, is fast coming to an end. Thoughtful historians, in the last 20 years, have produced "a veritable avalanche of scholarship" (p. 4) concerning the history of women in the South.

Instructively, however, Wolfe (1995) presents only limited consideration of both the role of higher education in the lives of southern women and the contributions of academic women to a meaningful college life. In her brief discussion of the higher education of women in the postbellum period, Wolfe focuses entirely on the Progressive era, outlining the role of public and private women's colleges and the struggle for coeducation in the region. While a significant component of her work is the recognition of activist women in a variety of fields, Wolfe identifies only two notable academic women. This definitive study reflects, yet again, a disturbing reality. Historians of southern women have barely embraced the essential and rewarding mission of the historical recovery of the lives of academic women in the region.

Why do competent, discerning historians continually ignore the history of academic women in the South? Elizabeth Fox-Genovese (1997) offers an instructive framework in which to consider this question. She contends that national reaction to education in the South has perennially ranged "from condescension to contempt" (p. 203). However valid Fox-Genovese's comment may be for the general population, historians seem stubbornly impervious to any such emotional excesses. While scholars of women's education in the Northeast have produced "a dense and satisfying [historical] account" (p. 203), the prospect of historical recovery of the lives of academic women in the South has failed, until recently, to generate spirited response from historians.

What portion of Wolfe's (1995) "veritable avalanche of scholarship" (p. 4) assesses the history of women and higher education in the South? While scholars in the last 20 years, replicating her conclusions concerning the field of southern women's history, have produced a growing number of dissertations and conference papers concerning the fortunes of academic women, unfortunately, all too few of these ultimately appear as journal articles or books. However, those that have been published reflect the full spectrum of academic women—students, faculty, and administrators.

Historians have produced and published a number of thoughtful accounts of the collegiate experiences of southern women. Christie Farnham's (1994) assessment of the role of higher education in the maintenance of the antebellum class system fundamentally revises historical understanding of women's higher education in this period. Amy Thompson McCandless (1987), Helen Delpar (1989), and Pamela Dean (1991) offer perceptive accounts of student life, in both single-sex and coeducational institutions in the postbellum era. Lynn Gordon (1990) interprets the significance of two of the region's premier women's colleges, Sophie Newcomb and Agnes Scott, within the national context of Progressivism.

Two historians offer thoughtful interpretations of the problematic experience of those women professionally trained to be faculty members in the South. Anne Firor Scott (1993) poignantly reflects the blatant discrimination and professional frustration the earliest professional trained women historians in the South faced. Nevertheless, she also celebrates their formidable personal resilience and professional skill in the face of almost insurmountable cultural circumstances. Debbie M. Cottrell's (1993) account of the career of Annie Webb Blanton, summarized in Chapter 7, integrates this strong-minded woman into the larger history of Progressivism and reflects the unique challenges and achievements of a member of a women's profession in the South in the early 20th century.

Published historical inquiry into the lives of women administrators in higher education in the South focuses almost exclusively on the dean of women. Karen Anderson (1989) and Linda Perkins (1996), in their studies of the career of Lucy Slowe, Dean of Women at Howard University, have produced pioneer work not only on the office of dean of women but also on the role of the Black deans of women, who faced challenges unknown to their White professional colleagues. I have expanded my own study of the dean of women in the South to the career of Bowersox's successor at Berea College, Julia F. Allen, who served that institution from 1935 to 1959. A lifelong activist, molded by her education at Mt. Holyoke and her tenure as a missionary in China, Allen enlarged her role as dean of women, introducing Berea students to farm labor organization in the 1930s and to involvement in the modern civil rights movement (Bashaw, 1996, 1999).

Despite this undoubtedly growing interest in the historical recovery of the lives of academic women in the South, what avenues for additional research should historians explore? Jacquelyn Dowd Hall (1994), speaking at a conference at the Schlesinger Library, suggests a productive context in which to cast future investigation. She contends that a perennial debate in most societies at some point, particularly in the United States at the turn of the 20th century, concerns "who should control modernization and for what purposes" (p. 43). Contrary to cultural stereotyping, Hall maintains that the South—its men and women—played significant roles in this process.

What questions then, should historians ask of academic women in the South in order to ascertain their role as agents of change in the development of higher education—surely one of the benchmarks of modernization? Should such questions encompass only their public activities? Should the whole of their lives be open to historical inquiry? To discern the contributions of these women to the achievement of meaningful collegiate experiences for women students and growing professional opportunities for academic women, one should address questions concerning institutions, impediments, initiatives, infrastructure, and intimacy.

Where did these women work? The South, in yet another facet of its unique configuration, contained more different kinds of institutions of higher education for women than did any other region of the country. What role did the dean of women and her faculty colleagues play in public land grant institutions? How significant was the office in public teachers colleges, where women often comprised the majority of the student population? Private coeducational institutions in the South also employed deans of women. Were their roles different in these colleges and universities? Did academic women in private institutions such as Duke and Tulane universities, which established separate, coordinate colleges for their women, experience professional life differently from their regional colleagues?

A particularly provocative field for historical inquiry remains the Black coeducational institution, which, like its White counterpart in the South, assumed multiple forms. A minority of elite institutions such as Howard University offered African Americans a liberal arts education, which prepared them for further professional training. Southern states also established public vocational colleges—the Agricultural and Technical schools. Did the dean of women's role differ in these institutions? Exploration of the calculus of gender, race, and professionalization both on campus and in the larger culture will decisively enhance historical understanding of the lives of Black academic women.

What challenges did deans of women face? Were presidents their staunch allies, as in the cases of Sarah Gibson Blanding and both the McVeys, Agnes Ellen Harris and George Denny? Were women students their devoted supporters? Exploration of the relationship between deans of women and their charges might well refute stereotypical assumptions concerning this office.

What did deans of women achieve? To what extent did they succeed in claiming campus space and financial consideration for women? Did institutional authorities support their efforts to establish academic societies and inclusive college ritual? Like Sarah Blanding, did many deans of women pursue a complex strategy in their desire to control women's sport on campus? Examination of personal correspondence between deans of women and alumnae may well deepen scholarly appreciation of their success in forging a meaningful college experience for women.

Did deans of women establish supportive professional regional and national networks? How active were deans of women, the majority of whom worked at underfunded institutions, in state and regional deans' associations? What ties existed between these women and southern leaders at the national level, including Stamp, Harris, and Blanding? Certainly Stamp's and Harris's correspondence reflects the pride women across the South took in the success of their colleagues.

Did deans of women fashion satisfying private lives as single women professionals? Increasingly, historians of women, including Estelle Freedman (1979), Helen Horowitz (1984, 1994), Patricia Palmieri (1995), and Blanche Wiesen Cook (1977), recognize the value of recovering and communicating the role that private lives assumed in the careers of active single professional women. Gender ensured that they experienced the professions differently. Their culturally mandated single status as women ensured that they experienced the professions differently. Within this context, and as deeply as primary sources allow, historians must consider the role that family, colleagues, and friends assumed in the lives of these professional women in the traditional South.

In her discussion of the writing of women's biography, Lois Rudnick (1992) maintains that "scholarship must include the full range of female personalities, just as it must include the full range of gender and class identities" (p. 131). Central to an even more comprehensive scholarship is the recognition of the significance of regional identity as well. Jacquelyn Dowd Hall (1992) provides yet another useful framework for understanding the significance of this omission—the dilemma of "triple invisibility" (p. 144).

Bowersox, Harris, Stamp, and Blanding suffer triple invisibility. They represent an unknown chapter in the history of higher education, a field in which historians have ignored or dismissed the South. They held leadership positions in a conservative society. They worked in a woman's profession in academia. Nevertheless, if the expansion of higher education and the growth of the modern professional ethic defined, in part, the coming age of the United States in the early 20th century, then women's experience as administrators in newly coeducational institutions remains a significant component in any comprehensive analysis of the period.

Notes

INTRODUCTION

1. Text of speech honoring Katherine Bowersox on the occasion of her retirement from Berea College, April 1939, Katherine S. Bowersox Collection, Hutchins Library, Berea, Kentucky. (Hereafter cited as Bowersox Collection.)

2. Mary E. Welsh Papers, in the possession of William B. Welsh, Boothbay, Maine. (Hereafter cited as Mary E. Welsh Papers.)

3. Francis Hutchins to Bowersox, April 18, 1950, Bowersox Collection.

4. Bowersox to Francis Hutchins, May 30, 1950, Bowersox Collection.

5. "Presentation of Miss Bowersox," June 1950, Bowersox Collection.

6. Bowersox to Charlotte Ludlum, 1950, Bowersox Collection.

7. Francis Hutchins to Mrs. Nicholas Cherkroff, 1951?, Bowersox Collection.

8. Mary E. Welsh Papers.

9. Bowersox to Charlotte Ludlum, 1955?, Bowersox Collection.

10. Lillian B. Storms to Harris, April 1, 1944, Agnes Ellen Harris Collection, Box 10, Folder 716, W. Stanley Hoole Special Collections Library, Tuscaloosa, Alabama. (Hereafter cited as Harris Collection.)

11. Dixie Bibb Graves to Mrs. Ira B. Moody, February 14, 1943, Harris Collection, Box 10, Folder 716.

12. Mary Robertson to Harris, March 1, 1944, Harris Collection, Box 3, Folder 156.

13. Transcript of George Denney's comments at the presentation of the portrait of Agnes Ellen Harris, 1944, Harris Collection, Box 10, Folder 716.

14. Harris to The Honorable A. H. Carmichael, January 28, 1946, Harris Collection, Box 7, Folder 465.

15. Harris to Eleanor Livingston, June 27, 1945, Harris Collection, Box 38, Folder 4496.

16. Eleanor Livingston to Harris, June 10, 1945, Harris Collection, Box 38, Folder 4496.

17. Harris to Henrietta M. Thompson, May 29, 1937, Henrietta M. Thompson Collection, Box 1439, Folder 326, W. Stanley Hoole Special Collections Library, Tuscaloosa, Alabama. (Hereafter cited as Thompson Collection.)

18. Notes on the last week of Agnes Ellen Harris's life, Harris Collection, Box 37, Folder 4462.

19. Stamp to Anne Irvine, July 12, 1956, Adele H. Stamp Papers, Series I, Box 5, McKeldin Library, College Park, Maryland. (Hereafter cited as Stamp Papers.)

20. Letter from Committee for Adele H. Stamp Memorial Fund, November 1974, Stamp Papers, Series IV, Box 14.

21. Sarah B. Holmes to Frank and Frances McVey, February 27, 1940, Frances J. McVey Papers, Box 4, Folder 26, Margaret I. King Library, Lexington, Kentucky. (Hereafter cited as Frances J. McVey Papers.)

22. Blanding to Thomas P. Cooper, March 18, 1941, Herman Lee Donovan Papers, Box 32, Special Collections and Archives, Margaret I. King Library, Lexington, Kentucky. (Hereafter cited as Donovan Papers.)

23. Blanding to Frank McVey, March 13, 1940, Frank LeRond McVey Papers, Margaret I. King Library, Lexington, Kentucky. (Hereafter cited as Frank McVey Papers.)

24. Francis Hutchins to Mary E. Welsh, March 14, 1951, Mary E. Welsh Papers, Faculty Record Group 9, Hutchins Library, Berea, Kentucky.

CHAPTER 1

1. Bowersox to W. J. Hutchins, June 5, 1922, Bowersox Collection.

2. "Berea College—Description of a Worker," Bowersox Collection.

3. Bowersox to W. G. Frost, June 17, 1907, Bowersox Collection, Folder 1.

4. Bowersox to Frost, June 17, 1907, Bowersox Collection, Folder 1. See also Bowersox to Frost, July 11, 1907, Bowersox Collection, and C. F. Rumold to Frost, June 23, 1907, Bowersox Collection, Folder 1. Rumold, one of Bowersox's colleagues at Carlisle, wrote a letter recommending her for the post at Berea.

5. Bowersox to Frost, July 11, 1907, Bowersox Collection.

6. Bowersox to Frost, June 17, 1907, Bowersox Collection.

7. Harris to Bess Furman, December 31, 1941, Harris Collection, Box 38, Folder 4496.

8. Harris to Edith L. Getchell, October 15, 1935, Harris Collection, Box 8, Folder 4509.

9. Harris to Furman, December 31, 1941, Harris Collection, Box 38, Folder 4496.

10. Harris to Getchell, October 15, 1935, Harris Collection, Box 8, Folder 4509.

11. Harris to Furman, December 31, 1941, Harris Collection, Box 38, Folder 4496.

12. Ibid.

13. "Academic and Professional Record—Agnes Ellen Harris" (n.d.), Harris Collection, Box 33, Folder 4301.

14. Harris to Rosa Longmire Williams, November 12, 1942, Harris Collection, Box 38, Folder 449.

15. Harris to Dean W. G. Dodd, February 19, 1938, Harris Collection, Box 8, Folder 564.

16. Harris to Elizabeth Forman, July 25, 1941, Harris Collection, Box 8, Folder 565.

17. "Academic/Professional Record—Agnes Ellen Harris" (n.d.), Harris Collection, Box 38, Folder 4497.

18. Harris to Bess Furman, December 31, 1941, Harris Collection, Box 38, Folder 4496.

19. Harris to Furman, December 31, 1941, Harris Collection, Box 38, Folder 4496.

20. "How the 'Little Reb' Met General Grant," 6–7, Sarah Gibson Blanding Collection, Manuscript Collection, Arthur and Elizabeth Schlesinger Library, Cambridge, MA. (Hereafter cited as Blanding Collection, Schlesinger Library.)

21. Transcript of interview with Sarah Blanding, 5, Blanding Collection, Schlesinger Library.

22. "'Little Reb,'" 6, Blanding Collection, Schlesinger Library.

23. Transcript of interview with Sarah Blanding, 2, 18–19, Blanding Collection, Schlesinger Library. Only in this interview does Blanding mention the woman physician. She does not, however, indicate her name.

24. Sarah Gibson Blanding interview with Bill Cooper, May 23, 1976, Lakeville, Connecticut; transcript, Alumni/Faculty Oral History Project, Margaret I. King Library, Lexington, Kentucky, 1–2. See also P. P. Boyd to Frank L. McVey, June 13, 1919, Frank L. McVey Papers, Box 30.

25. Blanding interview with Bill Cooper, Alumni/Faculty Oral History Project, 5. See also Minutes of the Executive Committee of the Board of Trustees, University of Kentucky, Vol. 7, November 21, 1923, 142; and "U of K Says 'Goodby' to Dean Sarah Blanding," *The Louisville Courier-Journal*, June 24, 1941.

26. Mrs. Henry G. Leach to Frank L. McVey, February 26, 1940, Frank L. McVey Papers, Box 30.

27. McVey to Mary C. Woodworth, March 22, 1940, Frank L. McVey Papers, Box 30.

28. Blanding to McVey, March 13, 1940, Frank L. McVey Papers, Box 30.

CHAPTER 2

1. "Dedication—Margaret Brent Hall," Text of speech by Mrs. Charles E. Elliott, December 1, 1931, Stamp Papers, Series I, Box 6.

2. Bowersox, "A Woman in the Making," n.d., Address to Berea Woman's Club, 1.

3. Annual Report of the Office of the Dean of Women—Bowersox, 1917, 2–3, Special Collections, Hutchins Library, Berea, Kentucky. (Hereafter cited as Annual Report of the Dean of Women—Bowersox.)

4. Stamp to Tom Orpwood, April 25, 1956, Stamp Papers, Box 14.

5. Jurgen Habermas (1964) defines the public sphere as "a realm of our social life in which something approaching public opinion can be formed" (p. 49). Restricted to no permanent setting, any location, he claims, becomes public space when people gather to discuss an issue. Although Habermas maintains that "access [to the public sphere] is guaranteed to all citizens" (p. 49) he adopts the term *citizen*, which, in the 19th-century context of his work, excludes women. Ryan (1990) instead defines public space as "an arena where women can strive, along with men, for empowerment and justice" (pp. 11–12). On the college and university campus, this means that students or faculty mem-

bers—regardless of gender or size of the contingent—could discuss their grievances and express them to the administration. See also Fraser, 1985.

6. Annual Report of the Office of the Dean of Women—Bowersox, 1925, 5, William J. Hutchins Papers, Series V. (Hereafter cited as Hutchins Papers.) See also Annual Report of the Office of the Dean of Women—Bowersox, 1910, 6; 1911, 2; 1915, 6. See also Bashaw, 1991.

7. Woods–Penniman Papers, Record Group 5, Folder 39, Special Collections, Hutchins Library, Berea, Kentucky. (Hereafter cited as Woods–Penniman Papers.)

8. Annual Report of the Office of the Dean of Women—Bowersox, 1926, 6, Hutchins Papers, Series V.

9. Bowersox to Hutchins, January 2, 1930, Folder 1, Bowersox Collection.

10. Adele H. Stamp, "Physical Education for Women—1932," Stamp Papers, Series IV, Box 14.

11. Stamp to R. A. Pearson, September 30, 1930, Stamp Papers, Series I, Box 5.

12. Stamp to Major E. Brooke Lee, November 29, 1930, Stamp Papers, Series IV, Box 14.

13. Stamp to S. M. Shoemaker, May 20, 1931, Stamp Papers, Series I, Box 4. See also Minutes, Board of Regents, University of Maryland, May 25, 1931, 4, Harry C. Byrd Collection, Series I, Subseries I, Box 1, Maryland Room, McKeldin Library, College Park, Maryland. (Hereafter cited as Byrd Collection.)

14. "Material Placed in Cornerstone for Women's Field House, June 8, 1931," Stamp Papers, Series I, Box 6.

15. Stamp, "Dean of Women—1932," Stamp Papers, Box 14.

16. Stamp, "Budget for 1932–33," September 27, 1933, Stamp Papers, Series IV, Box 14.

17. Annual Report, Office of the Dean of Women—Blanding, 1939–1940, 341. See also Bashaw (1991).

18. Annual Report, Office of the Dean of Women—Blanding, 1929–1930, 161.

19. Blanding to Frank L. McVey, September 4, 1924, Frank L. McVey Papers, Box 28, Folder 4. See also Blanding to Frank L. McVey, September 3, 1936, Frank L. McVey Papers, Box 28, Folder 4.

20. Annual Report, Office of the Dean of Women—Blanding, 1937–1938, 324. See also Blanding to Frank L. McVey, October 24, 1936, Frank L. McVey Papers, Box 28, Folder 4.

21. Annual Report, Office of the Dean of Women—Blanding, 1940–1941, 387–388.

22. Minutes of the Executive Committee, Board of Trustees, University of Kentucky, Vol. 10, June 1, 1933, 177.

23. Blanding to Frances J. McVey and Frank L. McVey, September 5, 1932, Frank L. McVey Papers, Box 28, Folder 4.

24. Frank L. McVey to Blanding, September 22, 1932, Frank L. McVey Papers, Box 28, Folder 4.

25. Blanding to Frances J. McVey and Frank L. McVey, September 5, 1932, Frank L. McVey Papers, Box 28, Folder 4.

26. Ibid. See also "UK Woman's Building to Be Opened April 19," *The Lexington Herald Leader*, April 9, 1933.

27. Annual Report, Office of the Dean of Women—Blanding, 1933–1934, 203.

28. Annual Report, Office of the Dean of Women—Blanding, 1936–1937, 285.

29. Annual Report of the Dean of Women—Bowersox, 1914, 5–6. See also Annual Report of the Dean of Women—Bowersox, 1908, 6; and Bowersox to Frost, July 4, 1914, Bowersox Collection. See also Bashaw, 1991.

30. Annual Report of the Dean of Women—Bowersox, 1914, 6. See also Bowersox to Frost, July 4, 1914, Bowersox Collection.

31. Bowersox to Frost, April 5, 1919, Bowersox Collection.

32. Annual Report of the Dean of Women—Bowersox, 1908, 6.

33. Annual Report of the Dean of Women—Bowersox, 1918, 1.

34. Annual Report of the Dean of Women—Bowersox, 1913, 5.

35. Annual Report of the Dean of Women—Bowersox, 1908, 8. See also Bowersox to W. J. Hutchins, August 10, 1920, Bowersox Collection; and Mary E. Welsh, Annual Report, 1917, 2, Mary E. Welsh Papers.

36. Berea College, Faculty Club Records, 1930–1962, Special Collections, Hutchins Library, Berea, Kentucky. (Hereafter cited as Faculty Club Records.) These records indicate that between 1925 and 1929, the Log House served as a center for faculty socialization. In essence, Bowersox's persistence paved the way for the founding of the Woods-Penniman Building in 1926 and the Faculty Club in 1930.

37. Bowersox to W. J. Hutchins, June 3, 1922, Bowersox Collection.

CHAPTER 3

1. Annual Report of the Dean of Women—Bowersox, 1917, 5.

2. Annual Report, Office of the Dean of Women—Blanding, 1933–34, 197.

3. Harris, "Memo to Women Faculty—University of Alabama," September 6, 1932, Harris Collection, Box 8, Folder 566.

4. Harris, "Memo to UA Alumnae," March 18, 1933, Harris Collection, Box 8, Folder 566.

5. Annual Report, Office of the Dean of Women—Blanding, 1933–34, 196.

6. Annual Report, Office of the Dean of Women—Blanding, 1936–37, 281.

7. Bowersox to William J. Hutchins, February 27, 1932, Bowersox Collection, Folder 2.

8. Annual Report, Office of the Dean of Women—Bowersox, 1915, 7. See also Annual Report of the Dean of Women—Bowersox, 1917, 7.

9. Annual Report, Office of the Dean of Women—Bowersox, 1915, 7. See also Annual Report, Office of the Dean of Women—Bowersox, 1917, 6.

10. Annual Report, Office of the Dean of Women—Bowersox, 1917, 5.

11. Bowersox to Mr. Huntington, May 29, 1935, Bowersox Collection, Folder 4. See also Bowersox to William J. Hutchins, August 15, 1933, Bowersox Collection, Folder 3.

12. Bowersox, "A Letter to Berea Girls," n.d., 3, Bowersox Collection.

13. Bowersox to W. J. Hutchins, September 25, 1931, Bowersox Collection, Folder 2. See also Report of Dress Committee to W. J. Hutchins, March 3, 1932, Bowersox Collection.

14. Bowersox, "A Letter to Berea Girls," 8.

15. In 1908, Bowersox and a colleague visited 13 schools in Carter County, in Northeastern Kentucky. See Annual Report of the Dean of Women—Bowersox, 1908, 1. The dean also visited homes in Owsley County, not far from Berea. See Bowersox, "A Home in Owsley County," n.d., Bowersox Collection, Folder 1.

16. Bowersox to W. J. Hutchins, September 25, 1931, Bowersox Collection, Folder 2.

17. Bowersox to W. J. Hutchins, December 1933, Bowersox Collection, Folder 3.

18. Bowersox to W. J. Hutchins, August 25, 1930, Bowersox Collection, Folder 2. See also Annual Report of the Dean of Women—Bowersox, 1922, 2.

19. Annual Report of the Dean of Women—Bowersox, 1925, 4.

20. Bowersox to Dress Committee, March 10, 1938, Bowersox Collection, Folder 5.

21. Bowersox, "Dress Code," March 13, 1939, Bowersox Collection, Folder 5.

22. Bowersox to W. J. Hutchins, September 25, 1931, Bowersox Collection, Folder 2. See also Bowersox to Dress Committee, March 10, 1939, Bowersox Collection, Folder 5.

23. Annual Report, Office of the Dean of Women—Blanding, 1937–1938, 331.

24. Annual Report, Office of the Dean of Women—Blanding, 1924–1925, 103–104. See also Annual Report, Office of the Dean of Women—Blanding, 1933–1934, 200; and "Miss Sturtevant Heard by Coeds," *The Lexington Leader*, November 5, 1937.

25. Annual Report, Office of the Dean of Women—Blanding, 1931–1932, 154. See also Annual Report, Office of the Dean of Women—Blanding, 1932–1933, 177–178.

26. Annual Report, Office of the Dean of Women—Blanding, 1923–1924, 84.

27. Annual Report, Office of the Dean of Women—Blanding, 1939–1940, 342.

28. "Vocational Information Conference," March 13–14, 1939, Office of the Dean of Women Papers, Special Collections and Archives, Margaret I. King Library, Lexington, Kentucky. (Hereafter cited as Office of the Dean of Women Papers.) See also Annual Report, Office of the Dean of Women—Blanding, 1938–1939, 328.

29. Harris to William E. Pickens, May 2, 1944, Harris Collection, Box 3, Folder 144.

30. Harris to Martha von Rensselaer, October 6, 1931, Harris Collection, Box 13, Folder 923.

31. Harris to Bernie Feld, February 11, 1937, Harris Collection, Box 10, Folder 745.

32. Harris to Ruth Bryan Owen, October 27, 1935, Harris Collection, Box 11, Folder 768. See also Harris to George Denny, March 8, 1941, Harris Collection, Box 8, Folder 520.

33. Blanding to Frank L. McVey, February 8, 1936, Frank L. McVey Papers, Box 30. See also Blanding to F. L. McVey, January 28, 1937, McVey Papers, Box 30.

34. Harris to Ralph Adams, July 2, 1938, Harris Collection, Box 5, Folder 312.

35. Blanding to Frank L. McVey, February 8, 1936, Frank McVey Papers, Box 30. See also Blanding to Frank L. McVey, January 14, 1937, and Frank L. McVey to Blanding, January 22, 1937, Frank L. McVey Papers, Box 30.

36. Adelyn Van Court Andrews to Harris, March 19, 1928, Harris Collection, Box 5, Folder 338.

37. Wilma G. Isbell to Harris, March 23, 1933, Harris Collection, Box 6, Folder 347.

38. Henry J. Early to Harris, July 7, 1928, Harris Collection, Box 5, Folder 342.

39. Marmie House to Harris, May 1, 1934, Harris Collection, Box 6, Folder 346.

40. Emma Aldredge to Harris, October 4, 1930, Harris Collection, Box 5, Folder 338. See also Ella Alexander to Harris, January 24, 1930, Harris Collection, Box 5, Folder 338.

41. Harry Riddle to George Denny, April 11, 1932, Harris Collection, Box 5, Folder 338. See also Bessie M. Henderson to Harris, April 30, 1928, Harris Collection, Box 6, Folder 346.

42. Mrs. M. B. Gilbert to Harris, February 16, 1928, Harris Collection, Box 6, Folder 345.

43. Mrs. Frank Andress to Harris, April 1, 1932, Harris Collection, Box 5, Folder 338.

44. Harriet B. Adams to Harris, May 28, 1932, Harris Collection, Box 5, Folder 338.

45. Mrs. M. B. Fly to Harris, April 26, 1929, Harris Collection, Box 6, Folder 344.

46. Harris to Mrs. John W. Brooks, January 28, 1935, Harris Collection, Box 5, Folder 339.

47. Harris to J. K. Dixon, March 17, 1933, Harris Collection, Box 6, Folder 350.

48. Harris to Mrs. S. C. Gentry, August 25, 1931, Harris Collection, Box 6, Folder 345.

49. Harris to Mrs. LaGrange Denny, January 16, 1932, Harris Collection, Box 5, Folder 342.

50. Harris to Mrs. Emmett W. Ledbetter, March 31, 1931, Harris Collection, Box 6, Folder 350.

CHAPTER 4

1. A 1928 committee on training of deans of women also outlined the duties of the dean of women on the same models as Mathews, Miller, and Bragdon. See Margaret Morris to Gwaldys Jones, December 17, 1928, NAWDAC Collection, Center for Archival Collections, Jerome Library, Bowling Green, Ohio, Box 3 (unprocessed). (Hereafter cited as NAWDAC Collection.)

2. "Senior Women's Honor Society Memory Book, 1929–1934," Stamp Papers, Series III, Box 13. See also Stamp to Kathleen Kuhlman, March 7, 1933, Stamp Papers, Series IV, Box 14.

3. Stamp to Kuhlman, March 7, 1933, Stamp Papers, Series IV, Box 14.

4. "Memory Book, 1929–1934."

5. Ruth Williams to Stamp, February 6, 1928, Stamp Papers, Series I, Box 3.

6. Dorothy O. Young to Albert F. Woods, March 9, 1926, Stamp Papers, Series I, Box 3. See also Woods to Young, March 15, 1926, Stamp Papers, Series I, Box 3.

7. Stamp to Gertrude Wilharm, January 12, 1925, Stamp Papers, Series I, Box 3.

8. Wilharm to Stamp, March 13, 1926, Stamp Papers, Series I, Box 3.

9. Wilharm to Stamp, January 23, 1926, Stamp Papers, Series I, Box 3. See also Stamp to Wilharm, February 2, 1926, Stamp Papers, Series I, Box 3.

10. Stamp to Katherine E. Kuhlman, March 7, 1933, Stamp Papers, Series IV, Box 14. See also Kuhlman to Stamp, September 15, 1933, Stamp Papers, Series I, Box 3.

11. Senior Women's Honor Society to Kuhlman, October 23, 1934, Stamp Papers, Series I, Box 3.

12. Stamp to Kuhlman, October 26, 1934, Stamp Papers, Series IV, Box 14.

13. See Stamp Papers, Series I, Box 6.

14. Stamp to Louise Reinohl, November 7, 1934, Stamp Papers, Series I, Box 3. See also Frances Gruver to Stamp, November 23, 1934, Stamp Papers, Series I, Box 3.

15. Harris, untitled, undated manuscript concerning the Women's Convocation, Harris Collection, Box 7, Folder 420. See also Harris, Memo to Women Faculty, December 8, 1933, Harris Collection, Box 9, Folder 643.

16. Harris, Memo to Women Faculty, October 8, 1944, Harris Collection, Box 9, Folder 646.

17. See "16th Homecoming Convocation of Alumnae and Women Students, 1943," Harris Collection, Box 9, Folder 645; and "17th Homecoming Convocation of Alumnae and Women Students, 1944," Harris Collection, Box 9, Folder 646.

18. Harris to Women Faculty, December 8, 1944, Harris Collection, Box 9, Folder 646.

19. *University of Alabama Bulletin*, 1944–1945, 10–25, J. Stanley Hoole Special Collections Library, Tuscaloosa, Alabama.

20. Mary Boniske to Harris, October 7, 1938, Harris Collection, Box 16, Folder 1331.

21. Boniske to Harris, October 7, 1938, Harris Collection, Box 16, Folder 1331. See also Harris to Boniske, November 28, 1938, Harris Collection, Box 16, Folder 1331.

22. Harris to Boniske, November 28, 1938, Harris Collection, Box 16, Folder 1331.

23. May Day Programs, 1937–1944, Stamp Papers, Series I, Box 2.

24. "May Day Presentation to Adele Stamp, 1937," Stamp Papers, Series I, Box 2. See also "May Day Program, 1937," Stamp Papers, Series I, Box 2.

25. Stamp to Governor Theodore R. McKeldin, May 10, 1956, Stamp Papers, Series I, Box 2.

26. "May Day, Stamp Are Symbols," *The Diamondback*, May 8, 1956, Stamp Papers, Series I, Box 2.

27. M. Eunice Hilton to Stamp, June 7, 1956, Stamp Papers, Series I, Box 2.

CHAPTER 5

1. Annual Report of the Dean of Women—Bowersox, 1926, 4. See also Annual Report, Office of the Dean of Women—Blanding, 1937–1938, 331.

2. "Mountain Day," Record Group 11, Mountain Day File, Special Collections, Hutchins Library, Berea, Kentucky.

3. Ibid.

4. Annual Report of the Dean of Women—Bowersox, 1909, 3.

5. Annual Report of the Dean of Women—Bowersox, 1926, 4.

6. Annual Report of the Dean of Women—Bowersox, 1908, 7.

7. Annual Report of the Dean of Women—Bowersox, 1926, 4.

8. Harris to Ethel J. Saxman, October 11, 1933, Harris Collection, Box 12, Folder 848.

CHAPTER 6

1. Harris to the NADW Executive Committee, August 10, 1933, NAWDAC Collection, Box 26 (processed).

2. Harris to Katherine S. Doty, December 11, 1933, Harris Collection, Box 38, Folder 4500.

3. Adele Stamp to Tom Orpwood, April 25, 1956, Stamp Papers, Box 14.

4. Annie P. Hopper to Harris, December 6, 1932, Harris Collection, Box 38, Folder 4500. See also Harris to E. Purnell Wilson, December 20, 1932, Harris Collection, Box 38, Folder 4500.

5. Harris to Grace L. Pinel, December 30, 1933, NAWDAC Collection, Box 15 (processed), Folder 15.

6. "Executive Committee Meeting," February 21, 1933, NAWDAC Collection, Box 1 (processed), Folder 1.

7. Stamp to Orpwood, April 25, 1956, Stamp Papers, Box 14.

8. Ibid.

9. Dorothy C. Stratton, "The Dean Looks at the Problems of Youth," 1, text of a speech delivered at the 1935 annual meeting of the KADW, Lexington, Kentucky, Office of the Dean of Women Papers.

10. Florence K. Root to Harris, June 3, 1932, NAWDAC Collection, Box 15 (processed).

11. Harris to Root, June 7, 1932, Harris Collection, Box 38, Folder 4498.

12. Stamp to Evelyn Jones, March 13, 1937, Stamp Papers, Box 8.

13. Stamp to Evelyn Jones, March 7, 1936, Stamp Papers, Box 8.

14. Stamp to Harris, April 25, 1933, Harris Collection, Box 38, Folder 4305.

15. The reasons behind this obvious breach are difficult to isolate. For some sense of the friction, see Stamp to Evelyn Jones, January 11, 1936, Stamp Collection, Box 8; and Stamp to Jones, March 13, 1937, Stamp Papers, Box 8.

16. Stamp to Evelyn Jones, October 28, 1936, Stamp Papers, Box 8.

17. Stamp to Evelyn Jones, March 7, 1936, Stamp Papers, Box 8.

18. Stamp to Evelyn Jones, November 11, 1936, Stamp Papers, Box 8.

19. Stamp to Evelyn Jones, October 6, 1936, Stamp Papers, Box 8.

20. Stamp to Evelyn Jones, October 28, 1936, Stamp Papers, Box 8.

21. Stamp to Evelyn Jones, November 11, 1936, Stamp Papers, Box 8.

22. Stamp to Evelyn Jones, November 23, 1936, Stamp Papers, Box 8.

23. Stamp to Lillias MacDonald, November 30, 1936, Stamp Papers, Box 8. See also Stamp to Evelyn Jones, November 23, 1936, Stamp Papers, Box 8.

24. Stamp to MacDonald, January 1, 1937, Stamp Papers, Box 8.

25. Stamp to Evelyn Jones, January 5, 1937, Stamp Papers, Box 8.

26. Stamp to Evelyn Jones, October 28, 1936, Stamp Papers, Box 8.

27. Stamp to Maria Leonard, December 7, 1936, Stamp Papers, Box 8.

28. Stamp to Evelyn Jones, March 13, 1937, Stamp Papers, Box 8.

29. Stamp to Blanding, June 2, 1939, Stamp Papers, Box 8.

30. Gwladys W. Jones to Marion V. Cuthbert, December 9, 1929, NADWAC Collection, Folder 6, Box 10 (unprocessed).

31. Lucy D. Slowe to Gwladys W. Jones, December 12, 1929, NAWDAC Collection, Folder 6, Box 10 (processed). See also Ruth Brett, Edna M. Calhoun, Lucille J. Piggott, Hilda A. Davis, and Patricia Bell Scott. "A Symposium: Our Living History: Reminiscences of Black Participation in NAWDAC," *Journal of NAWDAC* 42 (Winter 1979): 9.

32. Cuthbert to Gwladys W. Jones, November 25, 1929, NADWAC Collection, Folder 6, Box 10 (processed).

33. Cuthbert to Gwladys W. Jones, December 13, 1929, NADWAC Collection, Folder 6, Box 10 (processed).

34. Inez Stacy to Harris, January 17, 1933, Harris Collection, Box 38, Folder 4501.

35. Irene Dillard Elliott to Harris, February 16, 1933, Harris Collection, Box 38, Folder 4500.

36. Irene Dillard Elliott to Harris, January 6, 1934, Harris Collection, Box 38, Folder 4504.

37. Harris to Adele H. Stamp, May 3, 1933, Harris Collection, Box 38, Folder 4305.

38. Stamp to Harris, April 25, 1933, Harris Collection, Box 38, Folder 4305.

39. Harris to Nellie S. Keirn, January 14, 1933, Harris Collection, Box 38, Folder 4501.

40. Harris to Blanding, January 4, 1933, Harris Collection, Box 38, Folder 4501.

41. For samples of this extensive correspondence, see Harris Collection, Box 38, Folder 4501.

42. Harris to Nellie S. Keirn, January 4, 1933, Harris Collection, Box 38, Folder 4501.

43. Harris to Irene Dillard Elliott, January 14, 1933, Harris Collection, Box 38, Folder 4501.

44. Harris to Blanding, January 14, 1933, Harris Collection, Box 38, Folder 4501.

45. Harriet Greve to Harris, January 12, 1934, Harris Collection, Box 38, Folder 4504.

46. Charlotte M. Beckham to Harris, January 7, 1933, Harris Collection, Box 38, Folder 4501.

CHAPTER 7

1. Annie Webb Blanton to Harris, September 26, 1939, Harris Collection, Box 7, Folder 499.

2. Bowersox to W. G. Frost, June 18, 1908, Bowersox Collection.

3. The Berea archive contains three letters from President William J. Hutchins to Rollin Bowersox, all written between 1927 and 1928. There is one letter from Katherine Bowersox to Hutchins concerning Rollin's dismissal; however, the language is so euphemistic that it is virtually impossible to discover the actual facts of the case. However, it does appear that her other brother assisted with the problem. The dean informed Hutchins that Rollin would return to Pennsylvania to stay with his brother.

4. Harris to Florence E. Ward, January 21, 1930, Harris Collection, Box 15, Folder 928.

5. Harris to Henrietta Thompson, September 3, 1949, Thompson Collection, Box 1349, Folder 326.

6. Harris to Elizabeth Skinner Jackson, July 7, 1937, Harris Collection, Box 9, Folder 658.

7. Harris to Elizabeth Baldwin Hill, May 21, 1938, Harris Collection, Box 9, Folder 636.

8. Harris to Hill, August 9, 1938.

9. Harris to Henrietta M. Thompson, November 28, 1938, Thompson Collection, Box 1439, Folder 326.

10. Harris to Josephine Eddy, February 20, 1940, Harris Collection, Box 8, Folder 544.

11. Harris to Winifred Collins, February 10, 1941, Harris Collection, Box 7, Folder 484.

12. Remarks delivered by Sarah Blanding at the presentation of a portrait of Frances Jewell McVey to the University of Kentucky, May 14, 1946, 1–3, Frances J. McVey Papers.

13. Blanding to Frances J. McVey, October 2, 1936, Frances J. McVey Papers.

14. Blanding to McVey, January 6, 1937.

15. Harris to K. C. Gray, January 4, 1940, Harris Collection, Box 7, Folder 499.

16. Harris to Annie Webb Blanton, January 4, 1940, Harris Collection, Box 7, Folder 499.

17. Harris to Blanton, September 21, 1943.

18. Harris to Annie Webb Blanton, September 27, 1943, Harris Collection, Box 7, Folder 499.

19. Tape of interview with William B. Welsh, May 24, 1993, Boothbay, Maine, in possession of author.

20. Mary E. Welsh, Annual Report, 1911, 2, Mary E. Welsh Papers.

21. Annual Report of the Dean of Women—Bowersox, 1908, 6.

22. Mary E. Welsh Papers.

23. Mary E. Welsh, Alumnae File, Class of 1885, November 1954, Wellesley College Archives, Margaret Clapp Library, Wellesley, Massachusetts. (Hereafter known as Welsh-Alumnae File.)

24. Bowersox to President and Mrs. W. J. Hutchins, June 22, 1934, Bowersox Collection.

25. Mary E. Welsh Papers.

EPILOGUE

1. Sarah Blanding, Transcript of interview, 41, Blanding Collection.

2. Annual Report of the Dean of Women—Bowersox, 1910, 4.

3. Untitled, undated one-page typescript [1933?], Harris Collection, Box 38, Folder 4497.

4. Harris to W. G. Dodd, February 19, 1938, Harris Collection, Box 8, Folder 564.

5. Harris to Pearl B. Smith, April 15, 1938, Harris Collection, Box 12, Folder 864.

6. See General Administrative Board, Committee Reports 1937–1939, Stamp Papers, Series I, Box 1.

7. Charter Day marked the sesquicentennial of the University of Maryland. See Charter Day Banquet Committee, January 19, 1957, Stamp Papers, Series I, Box 1; and "Centennial Program," March 6, 1956, Stamp Papers, Series I, Box 1.

8. David L. Brigham to Stamp, November 4, 1947, Stamp Papers, Series I, Box 2.

9. Annual Report of the Dean of Women—Bowersox, 1917, 1.

10. Harris to Henry B. Foster, October 9, 1936, Harris Collection, Box 8, Folder 570.

11. Ibid. In 1967, 31 years after Agnes Ellen Harris made her case for the appointment of a woman to the Board of Trustees, Lurleen Wallace became the first woman to serve on that body by virtue of her position as Governor of Alabama. In 1979, Margaret Sims, of Huntsville, Alabama, was the first woman to hold an appointment to the Board of Trustees.

12. Annual Report of the Dean of Women—Bowersox, 1925, 6–7.

13. Winifred Collins to Harris, May 31, 1931, Harris Collection, Box 7, Folder 484. See also Harris to R. H. Powell, April 11, 1931, Harris Collection, Box 9, Folder 655.

14. Harris to Maria A. Leonard, April 12, 1941, Harris Collection, Box 9, Folder 673. Interestingly, the national president of Alpha Lambda Delta, Maria A. Leonard, Dean of Women at the University of Illinois, was a friend and colleague of Harris, demonstrating yet again the interconnectedness of the academic women of this generation.

Primary Sources

MANUSCRIPT COLLECTIONS

Bloomsburg University Archive, Bloomsburg, Pennsylvania
    Alumni List of Bloomsburg Literary Institute and State Normal School Sixth District, Pa. 1870–1902.
    The Philologian Advance. Vol. I, June 1893.
Center for Archival Collections, Jerome Library, Bowling Green, Ohio
    Membership Lists 1918–1953
    Minutes of the Executive Board 1922–1952
    National Association of Deans of Women (NAWDAC) Collection
    National Convention Proceedings 1903–1951
    Presidential Correspondence 1926–1953
    State and Regional Association Proceedings
Historical Manuscripts and Archives Department, McKeldin Library, College Park, Maryland
    Harry C. Byrd Collection, Series I, Subseries I
    Adele Hagner Stamp Papers 1922–1960
    The Diamondback 1922–1960
    University of Maryland Catalogue 1922–1960
Manuscript Collections, The Arthur and Elizabeth Schlesinger Library, Cambridge, Massachusetts
    Sarah Gibson Blanding Collection
Special Collections, Hutchins Library, Berea, Kentucky
    Annual Reports, Office of the Dean of Women 1907–1937
    The Berea Alumnus
    The Berea *Citizen*
    Berea College Catalogue 1907–1937
    Berea College Faculty Club Records 1930–1962
    Katherine S. Bowersox Papers
    Alice Kate Douglas Papers, Faculty and Staff Biographical File
    E. Henry Fairchild Papers
    W. G. Frost Papers, Series VI
    William J. Hutchins Papers, Series V
    Mary E. Welsh Papers, Faculty Record Group 9
    Woods Penniman Papers, Record Groups 5, Folder 39
    The *Pinnacle* 1907–1937

Special Collections, Milbank Memorial Library, Teachers College, New York
  "Sarah Martha Sturtevant." Personnel File, Public Relations Office, Record Group
      17
  Teachers College Catalogue 1915–1941
Special Collection, Robert Manning Strozier Library, Tallahassee, Florida
  Bulletin of the Florida State College for Women 1910–1919
  Dodd, William G. "Florida State College for Women: Notes on the Formative
      Years." Manuscript 1958–1959
  Flastocowo 1910–1915
  The Florida Flambeau 1915–1919
Special Collections and Archives, Margaret I. King Library, Lexington, Kentucky
  Annual Reports, Office of the Dean of Women 1923–1941
  Herman Lee Donovan Papers 1940–1941
  The Kentuckian 1919–1941
  The Kentucky Colonel 1919–1941
  Frances Jewell McVey Papers
  Frank LeRond McVey Papers 1923–1941
  Minutes of the Executive Board, Board of Trustees, University of Kentucky 1909–
      1941
  Office of the Dean of Women Papers
  University of Kentucky Catalogue 1920–1941
Tulane University Archives, Howard-Tilton Memorial Library, New Orleans, Louisiana
  The Jambalaya 1918–1921
U.S. Army Military History Institute, Historical Reference Branch, Carlisle Barracks,
Pennsylvania
  The Arrow 1904–1905
  The Indian Helper 1893–1894
  The Red Man and Helper 1900–1904
W. Stanley Hoole Special Collections Library, Tuscaloosa, Alabama
  The Corolla 1927–1947
  Agnes Ellen Harris Collection
  Henrietta M. Thompson Collection
  University of Alabama Bulletin 1927–1947
Wellesley College Archives, Margaret Clapp Library, Wellesley, Massachusetts
  Annals of the Class of 1885 1885–1898, 1906–1907, 1909–1910, 1915–1918, 1920,
      1935–1939, 1945
  Wellesley Alumnae Magazine 1940–1950, 1954
  Mary E. Welsh, Alumnae File

PRIVATE COLLECTIONS

Mary E. Welsh, Papers. In the possession of William B. Welsh, Boothbay, Maine

INTERVIEWS

Blanding, Sarah Gibson. Interview by Bill Cooper, May 23, 1976, Lakeville, Connecticut. Transcript, Special Collections and Archives, Margaret I. King Library, Lexington, Kentucky

Blanding, Sarah Gibson. Interview by Delores Greenberg, June 11, 1964, Poughkeepsie, New York. Transcript, Sarah Gibson Blanding Collection, Arthur and Elizabeth Schlesinger Library, Cambridge, Massachusetts

Welsh, William B. Interview by Carolyn Terry Bashaw, May 24, 1993, Boothbay, Maine. Tape in possession of author

References

Adele H. Stamp. (1976). *Who Was Who in America* (Vol. 1, 1974–1976). Chicago: Marquis Who's Who.

Alumni list of Bloomsburg Literary Institute and State Normal School, sixth district, Bloomsburg, PA 1870–1920. (n.d.). Bloomsburg, PA.

Annals of the class of 1885. (1945). Wellesley College Archive, Wellesley, MA.

Anderson, K. (1989). Brickbats and roses: Lucy Diggs Slowe, 1883–1937. In G. J. Clifford (Ed.), *Lone voyagers: Academic women in coeducational institutions, 1870–1937* (pp. 283–307). New York: Feminist Press.

Antler, J. (1987). *Lucy Sprague Mitchell: The making of a modern woman.* New Haven: Yale University Press.

Antler, J. (1992). Having it all, almost: Confronting the legacy of Lucy Sprague Mitchell. In S. Alpern, J. Antler, E. I. Perry, & I. W. Scobie (Eds.), *The challenge of feminist biography: Writing the lives of modern American women* (pp. 97–115). Urbana: University of Illinois Press.

Bashaw, C. T. (1991). To serve the people of the state of Kentucky: Sarah Gibson Blanding and the development of administrative skill, 1923–1941. *The Filson History Club Quarterly, 65,* 281–301.

Bashaw, C. T. (1996). One kind of pioneer project: Julia F. Allen and the southern tenant farmers union college student project, 1938. *Arkansas Historical Quarterly, 55,* 1–25.

Bashaw, C. T. (1999). The witness we tried to make: Julia F. Allen and racial justice at Berea College, 1935–1974. In W. J. Urban (Ed.), *Southern education in the twentieth century: Exceptionalism and its limits* (pp. 129–162). New York: Garland Press.

Bell-Scott, P. (1979). Schoolin' respectable ladies of color: Issues in the history of black women's higher education. *Journal of NAWDAC, 42,* 22–33.

Birdwhistell, T. L. (1994). *An educated difference: Women at the University of Kentucky through the second world war.* Unpublished doctoral dissertation, University of Kentucky, Lexington, KY.

Blakey, G. T. (1986). *Hard times and the new deal in Kentucky, 1929–1939.* Lexington: University of Kentucky Press.

Bordin, R. (1993). *Alice Freeman Palmer: The evolution of a new woman.* Ann Arbor: University of Michigan Press.

Breckinridge, S. P. (1921). *Madeline McDowell Breckinridge: A leader in the new South.* Chicago: University of Chicago Press.

Breed, M. B. (1908). The control of student life. *Journal of the ACA, Series III, 18,* 60–73.

Brett, R., Calhoun, E. M., Piggott, L. J., Davis, H. A., & Bell-Scott, P. (1979). A symposium: Our living history: Reminiscences of black participation in NAWDAC. *Journal of NAWDAC*, *42*, 3–13.

Brisbay, E. (1990). College women in the 1930s: The possibilities and the realities. *The Filson History Club Quarterly*, *64*, 32–59.

Brumberg, J., & Tomes, N. (1982). Women in the professions: A research agenda for American historians. *Reviews in American History*, *10*, 275–296.

Bulletin of the State College for Women, 1912–1913. (n.d.). Tallahassee: Florida State College for Women.

Cahn, S. K. (1994). *Coming on strong: Gender and sexuality in twentieth-century women's sports*. New York: Free Press.

Capstone to mark 50 years of co-education. (1943, May 16). *The Birmingham News-Age Herald*.

Catton, B. (1956). Our association in review. *Journal of NAWDAC*, *20*, 3–9.

City playgrounds to be formally opened tomorrow. (1921, 2 June). *The Lexington Herald*.

Clarke, E. H. (1873). *Sex in education: Or a fair chance for girls*. Boston: James R. Osgood.

Clifford, G. J. (1989). *Lone voyagers: Academic women in coeducational universities, 1869–1937*. New York: Feminist Press.

Cook, B. W. (n.d.). Female support networks and political activism: Lillian Wald, Crystal Eastman, and Emma Goldman. *Chrysalis*, *3*, 43–61.

Coon, H. (1947). *Columbia: Colossus on the Hudson*. New York: E. P. Dutton.

Cott, N. (1987). *The grounding of modern feminism*. New Haven: Yale University Press.

Cottrell, D. M. (1993). *Pioneer woman educator: The progressive spirit of Annie Webb Blanton*. College Station: Texas A&M University Press.

Dabney, V. (1981). *Mr. Jefferson's university: A history*. Charlottesville: University of Virginia Press.

Dean, P. (1991). Learning to be new women: Campus culture at the North Carolina Normal and Industrial College. *The North Carolina Historical Review*, *68*, 286–306.

Dean Blanding to leave U.K. (1941, April 29). *Lexington Herald Leader*.

Dean Bowersox called to her home. (1918, January 28). *The Berea Citizen*.

Delpar, H. (1989). Coeds and the lords of creation: Women students at the University of Alabama, 1893–1930. *Alabama Review*, *42*, 292–312.

Douglass, D. A. (1992). *Edward Clarke's "sex in education": A study in rhetorical form*. Unpublished doctoral dissertation, Pennsylvania State University, University Park, PA.

Edwards, E. B. (1982). *Profile of the past, a living legacy: Bloomsburg State College, 1839–1979*. Bloomsburg, PA: Bloomsburg State College Alumni Society.

Farnham, C. A. (1994). *The education of the southern belle: Higher education and student socialization in the antebellum South*. New York: New York University Press.

Fitzpatrick, E. (1990). *Endless crusade: Women social scientists and progressive reform*. New York: Oxford University Press.

Former university dean to retire from Vassar. (1964, April 29). *The Lexington Herald Leader*.

Fox-Genovese, E. (1997). Education of women in the United States South. *Journal of Women's History, 9,* 203–211.

Fraser, N. (1985). What's critical about critical thinking? The case of Habermas and gender. *New German Critique, 35,* 97–131.

Fraser, N. (1989). *Unruly practices: Power, discourse, and gender in contemporary social theory.* Minneapolis: University of Minnesota Press.

Frederickson, M. (1984). Recognizing regional differences: The southern summer school for women workers. In J. L. Kornbluh & M. Frederickson (Eds.), *Sisterhood and solidarity: Workers' education for women, 1914–1984* (pp. 149–186). Philadelphia: Temple University Press.

Freedman, E. (1979). Separatism as strategy: Female institution building and American feminism, 1870–1930. *Feminist Studies, 5,* 512–529.

Girls her hobby for 38 years. (1960, December 4). *Baltimore Sun.*

Glazer, P. M., & Slater, M. (1987). *Unequal colleges: The entrance of women into the professions, 1890–1940.* New Brunswick: Rutgers University Press.

Gordon, L. D. (1990). *Gender and higher education in the progressive era.* New Haven: Yale University Press.

Grabiner, D. (1983, September 12). Honoring a woman of vision. *Precis.* The University of Maryland, College Park, MD.

Graham, P. A. (1981). So much to do: Guides for historical research on women in higher education. *Teachers College Record, 76,* 421–429.

Habermas, J. (1964). The public sphere: An encyclopedic article. *New German Critique, 3,* 49–55.

Hall, G. S. (1904). *Adolescence* (Vol. 2). New York: D. Appleton.

Hall, J. D. (1992). Second thoughts on Jessie Daniel Ames. In S. Alpern, J. Antler, E. I. Perry, & I. W. Scobie (Eds.), *The challenge of feminist biography: Writing the lives of modern American women* (pp. 139–158). Urbana: University of Illinois Press.

Hall, J. D. (1994). Location, location, location. In S. Ware (Ed.), *New viewpoints in women's history: Working papers from the Schlesinger library 50th anniversary conference* (pp. 40–52). Cambridge, MA: Arthur & Elizabeth Schlesinger Library.

Hall, J. D., & Scott, A. F. (1987). Women in the South. In J. B. Boles & E. T. Nolen (Eds.), *Interpreting southern history: Historiographical essays in honor of Sanford W. Higginbotham* (pp. 454–509). Baton Rouge: Louisiana State University Press.

Harris, S. (1935). *James Coffee Harris and his family.* Birmingham, AL.

Hartman, M. S. (1990, July 5). Mills students provide eloquent testimony to the value of women's colleges. *The Chronicle of Higher Education,* p. A40.

Hay, M. P. (1980). *Madeline McDowell Breckinridge: Kentucky suffragist and progressive reformer.* Unpublished doctoral dissertation, University of Kentucky, Lexington, KY.

Hay, M. P. (1988). The Lexington civic league: Agent of reform, 1900–1910. *The Filson Club Quarterly, 62,* 336–355.

Heath, K. G. (1975). Our heritage speaks (Audiotape of speech delivered at the annual meeting of NAWDAC, 1975). Bowling Green, OH: Bowling Green State University.

Heck, E. D. (1960). *Kentucky division of the American Association of University Women 1930–1960.* Danville, KY: Advocate Messenger.

Heilbrun, C. G. (1988). *Writing a woman's life*. New York: Norton.

Henderson, J. B. (1932, March 21). Dishgirl's soliloquy. *The Pinnacle*.

Herrick, U. B. (1927). The dean's opportunity to encourage graduate study. In *Proceedings of the fourteenth regular meeting of the National Association of Deans of Women* (pp. 171–176). Dallas, TX.

Honor for Berea. (1923, November 11). *The Berea Citizen*.

Horowitz, H. L. (1984). *Alma mater: Design and experience in women's colleges from their nineteenth century beginnings to the 1930s*. New York: Knopf.

Horowitz, H. L. (1987). *Campus life: Undergraduate cultures from the end of the eighteenth century to the present*. New York: Knopf.

Horowitz, H. L. (1994). *The power and passion of M. Carey Thomas*. New York: Knopf.

How the "little reb" met General Grant. Blanding Collection. Schlesinger Library, Cambridge, MA.

Howe, F. (1984). Myths of coeducation. In F. Howe (Ed.), *Myths in coeducation: Selected essays, 1964–1983* (pp. 204–214). Bloomington: Indiana University Press.

Howes, A. (1885). *Health statistics of women college graduates: Report of a special committee of the Association of Collegiate Alumnae*. Boston.

Hult, J. S. (1991). The governance of athletics for girls and women: Leadership by women physical educators, 1899–1949. In J. S. Hult & M. Trekell (Eds.), *A century of women's basketball: From frailty to final four* (pp. 53–82). Reston, VA: American Alliance for Health, Physical Education, Recreation and Dance.

Ihle, E. L. (1976). *The development of coeducation in major southern state universities*. Unpublished doctoral dissertation, University of Tennessee, Knoxville, TN.

Industrial Committee of the War Work Council. (1918). *War work of the industrial committee*. New York: National Board of the YWCA.

Ingels, K. (1918). Report to the playground committee of the civic league, 1918 (Civic League Reports 1918–1931). Lexington, KY: City Records and Archives, Lexington-Fayette Urban County Government.

Interview with Sarah Blanding. Conducted by Bill Cooper, May 23, 1976. Transcript, Special Collections and Archives, Margaret I. King Library, Lexington, KY.

Interview with Sarah Blanding. Conducted by Delores Greenberg, June 11, 1964. Transcript, Arthur and Elizabeth Schlesinger Library, Cambridge, MA.

Jacobi, M. P. (1876). *The question of rest during menstruation*. New York: Putnam.

Jacobs, K. A. (1977). Adele Hagner Stamp. In W. G. Helmes (Ed.), *Notable Maryland Women* (pp. 354–356). Cambridge, MD: Tidewater Publishers.

Jambalaya, The. (1921). New Orleans, LA: The Sophie Newcomb College of Tulane University.

Jones, J. L. (1928). *A personnel study of women deans in colleges and universities*. New York: Teachers College Bureau of Publications.

Kentuckian. (1923). Lexington, KY: The University of Kentucky.

Kentucky deans of women express thanks to Berea. (1925, November 25). *The Pinnacle*.

Kerber, L. K. (1988). Separate spheres, female worlds, woman's place: The rhetoric of women's history. *The Journal of American History, 75*, 9–39.

Kett, J. F. (1985). Women and the progressive impulse in southern education. In W. J. Fraser, Jr., R. F. Sanders, Jr., & J. L. Wakelyn (Eds.), *Web of southern social relations: Women, family, and education* (pp. 166–180). Athens: University of Georgia Press.

Kunkel, F. M. (1926). To what extent should the dean of women function in dormitory management. In *Proceedings of the thirteenth regular meeting of the National Association of Deans of Women* (pp. 152–153). Washington, DC.

Lee, M. B. (1927). The dean as chief personnel officer. In *Proceedings of the fourteenth regulation meeting of the National Association of Deans of Women* (pp. 100–107). Dallas, TX.

Letson, D. (1994). *Industrial education for white women: The establishment of Texas Women's University.* Paper presented at the Third Southern Conference on Women's History, Houston, TX.

Lindley, B., & Lindley, E. K. (1938). *A new deal for youth: The story of the national youth administration.* New York: Viking Press.

Link, W. A. (1991). The social context of southern progressivism, 1880–1930. In J. M. Cooper & C. Neu (Eds.), *The Wilson era: Essays in honor of Arthur S. Link* (pp. 55–82). Arlington Heights, IL: Harlan Davidson.

Link, W. A. (1992). *The paradox of southern progressivism, 1880–1930.* Chapel Hill: University of North Carolina Press.

Martin, G. S. (1911). The position of dean of women. *Journal of the Association of Collegiate Alumnae Series IV*, 69.

Maryland's woman dean has world war experience. (1939, October 15). *The Baltimore Sun.*

Mathews, L. K. (1915). *The dean of women.* New York: Houghton Mifflin.

Maudsley, H. (1874). Sex in mind and education. *The Fortnightly Review, 88*, 473–477.

McCandless, A. T. (1984). From pedestal to mortar board: Higher education for women in South Carolina, 1920–1940. *Southern Studies, 23*, 348–362.

McCandless, A. T. (1987). Preserving the pedestal: Restrictions on social life at southern colleges for women, 1920–1940. *History of Higher Education Annual, 7*, 44–67.

McCandless, A. T. (1993). Progressivism and the higher education of southern women. *The North Carolina Historical Review, 70*, 302–325.

Memories of Blanding. (1985, March 27). *The Lexington Herald Leader.*

Merrill, R. A., & Bragdon, H. D. (1926). *The vocation of dean.* Washington, DC: Press and Publications Committee of the NADW.

Miner, F. H. (1921). Civic league report (Civic League Monthly Reports 1920–1930). Lexington, KY: City Records and Archives, Lexington-Fayette Urban County Government.

Moore, V. P. (1929). The history of home demonstration work in the state of Florida. In *Proceedings of the Silver Anniversary Cooperative Demonstration Work, 1908–1928* (pp. 131–137). Houston, TX.

Morton, L. (1962). How the Indians came to Carlisle. *Pennsylvania History, 29*, 53–73.

New Teachers in Berea. (1927, September 22). *The Berea Citizen.*

Newcomer, M. (1959). *A century of higher education for women.* New York: Harper & Brothers.

Nidiffer, J. (1994). *More than a wise and pious matron: Origins of the position of deans of women, 1895–1916.* Unpublished doctoral dissertation, Harvard University, Cambridge, MA.

Olin, H. R. (1909). The women of a state university. New York: G. P. Putnam's Sons.

Orr, M. L. (1930). *The state-supported colleges for women.* Nashville, TN: George Peabody College for Teachers.

Palmieri, P. (1981). *An Adamless Eden: A social portrait of the academic community at Wellesley College, 1875–1920.* Unpublished doctoral dissertation, Harvard University, Cambridge, MA.

Palmieri, P. A. (1995). *In Adamless Eden: The community of faculty women at Wellesley.* New Haven: Yale University Press.

Peck, E. (1982). *Berea's first 125 years.* Lexington: The University Press of Kentucky.

Perkins, L. (1996). Lucy Diggs Slowe: Champion of self-determination of African American women in higher education. *Journal of Negro History, 81,* 89–104.

Pherigo, A. S. (n.d.). *Playgrounds in Review—1900–1950* (Civic League Records). Lexington, KY: City Records and Archives, Lexington-Fayette Urban County Government.

Phillips, K. S. (1920). *The work of a dean.* Unpublished masters thesis, Columbia University, New York.

Phillips, K. S. (1953). Beginnings. *Journal of the National Association of Deans of Women, 16,* 143–145.

Phillips, K. S. (1964). *My room in the world: A memoir.* New York: Abingdon Press.

Phillips, Mrs. E. L., Kerr, M., & Wells, A. (1927). History of the National Association of Deans of Women. In *Proceedings of the Fourteenth Regular Meeting of the National Association of Deans of Women* (pp. 228–235). Dallas, TX.

Potter, M. R. (1927). History of the conferences of deans of women to the organization of the national association in 1917. In *Proceedings of the fourteenth regular meeting of the National Association of Deans of Women* (pp. 212–227). Dallas, TX.

President gives recognition in last chapel talk to retiring faculty members. (1939, June 1). *The Berea Citizen,* p. 2.

Priddy, B. L. (1922). Relation of the dean of women to the professional life of the student. In *Addresses and proceedings of the sixtieth annual meeting of the National Education Association* (pp. 788–793). Boston, MA.

Proceedings of the thirteenth regular meeting of the National Association of Deans of Women. (1926). Washington, DC.

Proceedings of the fourteenth regular meeting of the National Association of Deans of Women. (1927). Dallas, TX.

Program of the fourteenth annual meeting—Kentucky Association of Deans of Women. (1935). Lexington, KY: University of Kentucky.

Prominent guests honor Dean Stamp at dinner. (1956, May 10). *Diamondback.*

Prucha, F. P. (1984). *The great father: The United States government and the American Indian* (2 vols.). Lincoln: University of Nebraska Press.

Report of the membership committee. (1931). *Proceedings of the fifteenth annual meeting of the National Association of Deans of Women.* Detroit, MI.

Richards, F. L. (1918). What a dean may rightly expect from a president. In *Address and proceedings of the fifty-sixth annual meeting of the national education association* (pp. 399–402). Pittsburgh, PA.

Robinson, M. O. (1960). *Eight women of the YWCA.* New York: National Board of the YWCA of the USA.

Rosenberg, R. (1982). *Beyond separate spheres: Intellectual roots of modern feminism.* New Haven: Yale University Press.

Rossiter, M. (1982). *Women scientists in America: Struggles and strategies to 1940.* Baltimore: The Johns Hopkins University Press.

Rudnick, L. (1992). The male-identified woman and other anxieties: The life of Mabel Dodge Luhan. In S. Alpern, J. Antler, E. I. Perry, & I. W. Scobie (Eds.), *The challenge of feminist biography: Writing the lives of modern American women* (pp. 116–138). Urbana: University of Illinois Press.

Ryan, M. P. (1990). *Women in public: Between banners and ballots, 1825–1880.* Baltimore: The Johns Hopkins University Press.

Sarah Gibson Blanding. (1963, May 12). *The Courier Journal Magazine.*

Sayre, M. B. (1950). *Half a century: A historical analysis of the NADW, 1900–1950.* Unpublished doctoral dissertation, Teachers College, Columbia University, New York.

Schwager, S. (1987). Educating women in America. *Signs: Journal of Women in Culture and Society, 12,* 333–372.

Schwartz, R. A. (1990). *The feminization of a profession: Student affairs work in higher education, 1890–1945.* Unpublished doctoral dissertation, Indiana University, Bloomington, IN.

Scott, A. F. (1984). Education of women: The ambiguous reform. In A. F. Scott (Ed.), *Making the invisible woman visible* (pp. 398–412). Chicago: University of Illinois Press.

Scott, A. F. (Ed.). (1993). *Unheard voices: The first historians of southern women.* Charlottesville: University of Virginia Press.

Scott, R. V. (1970). *The reluctant farmer: The rise of agricultural extension to 1914.* Urbana: University of Illinois Press.

Simrall, J. P. (1925). The dean of women on the campus of 1925. In *Proceedings of the twelfth regular meeting of the national association of deans of women* (pp. 54–59). Cincinnati, OH.

Simms, M. S. (1950). *The YWCA: An unfolding purpose.* New York: Woman's Press.

Smith, M. M. (1939). Katherine S. Bowersox: She made a tradition. *Berea Alumnus, April,* 203.

Solomon, B. M. (1985). *In the company of educated women: A history of women and higher education in America.* New Haven: Yale University Press.

Some of the people you will meet at the mountain summer school. (1919, May 8). *The Berea Citizen.*

Stanaland, P. (1991). The early years of basketball in Kentucky. In J. S. Hult & M. Trekell (Eds.), *A century of women's basketball: From frailty to final four* (pp. 167–179). Reston, VA: American Alliance for Health, Physical Education, Recreation and Dance.

Stanley, G. K. (1995). And not to make athletes of them: Banning women's sports at the University of Kentucky, 1902–1924. *Register of the Kentucky Historical Society, 93,* 422–445.

Sturtevant, S. M., & Strang, R. (1928). *A personnel study of deans of women in teachers colleges and normal schools.* New York: Teachers College Bureau of Publications.

Sturtevant, S. M., Strang, R., & McKim, M. (1940). *Trends in student personnel work.* New York: Teachers College Bureau of Publications.

Talbot, M., & Rosenberry, L. K. M. (1931). *The history of the American Association of University Women, 1881–1931*. New York: Houghton Mifflin Company.

Tanner, A. (1907). The salaries of women teachers in institutions of collegiate rank. *Journal of the ACA, 15,* 10–24.

Todhunter, N. (1953, May 2). *Agnes Ellen Harris, a tribute.*

Treichler, P. A. (1985). Alma mater's sorority: Women and the university of Illinois, 1890–1925. In P. A. Treichler, C. Kramarae, & B. Stafford (Eds.), *For alma mater: Theory and practice in feminist scholarship* (pp. 3–61). Urbana: University of Illinois Press.

Tribute to a great woman educator. (1952, May). *The University of Alabama Bulletin.*

Tuttle, K. N. (1996). *What became of the dean of women? Changing roles for women administrators in American higher education, 1940–1980.* Unpublished doctoral dissertation, University of Kansas, Lawrence, KS.

University of Maryland honors Miss Stamp. (1960, December 5). *Baltimore Sun.*

University of Kentucky press release. (1946, October 8). Lexington, KY: University of Kentucky.

University of Kentucky press release. (1968, June 20). Lexington, KY: University of Kentucky.

Vassar picks a woman and breaks tradition. (1946, March 31). *The New York Times Magazine.*

Vertinsky, P. A. (1994). Gender relations, women's history, and sport history: A decade of changing inquiry. *Journal of Sport History, 21,* 1–24.

Wallace, M. (1929). Home demonstration work in Virginia. In *Proceedings of the silver anniversary cooperative demonstration work, 1903–1928* (pp. 123–125). Houston, TX.

Ware, S. (1981). *Beyond suffrage: Women in the new deal.* Cambridge: Harvard University Press.

Ware, S. (1992). Unlocking the Porter-Dewson partnership: A challenge for the feminist biographer. In S. Alpern, J. Antler, E. I. Perry, & I. W. Scobie (Eds.), *The challenge of feminist biography: Writing the lives of modern American women* (pp. 51–64). Urbana: University of Illinois Press.

Wolfe, M. R. (1995). *Daughters of Canaan: A saga of southern women.* Lexington: University Press of Kentucky.

Woody, T. (1929). *A history of women's education in the United States* (2 vols.). New York: The Science Press.

Wright, M. B. (Ed.). (1905). *History of the Oreal Collegiate Institute.* New Haven, CT: Tuttle, Morehouse & Taylor Company.

Index

Academic societies for women, 72–74
Active old age, concept of, 6
Adams, Ralph E., 61
Agnes Scott, 128–129
Alabama Association of Deans and Advisors of Girls, 97–98
Alabama Polytechnic Institute, 31, 97–98
Allen, Florence, 60
Allen, Julia F., 8, 129
Allyn, Harriet, 104–105
American Association of University Women (AAUW), 4, 60–61, 73
American Home Economics Association (AHEA), 61
American Red Cross, 34, 35
Amos, Thyrsa W., 102–103
Anderson, Karen, 14, 15, 129
Antioch College, 71
Antler, Joyce, 14, 111
Association of Collegiate Alumnae (ACA), 3, 4
Association of Deans of Women and Advisors to Girls in Negro Schools, 106
Athletic programs, 79–92
    control of women's sport on campus, 85–91
    establishment of women's sport on campus, 83–85
    love of nature and, 81–83
    women's intercollegiate basketball, 85–91

Bakeless, O. H., 24
Barker, Henry, 87
Barnard College, 4, 5, 123
Bashaw, C. T., 129, 137 n. 29

Beckham, Charlotte M., 108
Bell-Scott, Patricia, 14, 106
Berea College. *See also* Bowersox, Katherine S.
    athletic programs for women, 79–80, 84
    Bowersox retirement from, 1–2, 7–8
    dress code for women, 57–58
    honorary degrees for Bowersox, 8, 17, 22
    housing for women faculty, 48–50
    and Kentucky Association of Deans of Women, 99
    love of nature and, 81–82
    Mountain Day, 82
    student-labor program, 56–57
    Woman's Building, 44
Birdwhistell, Terry L., 90
Blakey, G. T., 56
Blanding, A. L., 36
Blanding, Sally Anderson, 13, 35–36
Blanding, Sarah Gibson, ix, 11–13, 35–39, 124. *See also* University of Kentucky
    athletic programs for women, 83, 85–91
    as Cornell University Dean of College of Home Economics, 12
    death of, 12
    and dormitories for women students, 46–47
    early work experiences, 36–37, 83
    education of, 20–21, 36, 83, 87–88, 100
    family connections, 35–36
    and financial support for women, 55, 56

Blanding, Sarah Gibson (*continued*)
    and Kentucky Association of Deans of
      Women, 99–100
    love of nature, 81, 82–83
    as NADW president, 11–12, 100, 101,
      102, 105, 108
    needs of women students and, 42–44
    personal relationships, 115, 116
    as president of Vassar College, 12,
      116, 123
    professional development and, 60–61
    resignation from University of Ken-
      tucky, 11–12
    retirement from Vassar College, 12
    speaking engagements, 126–127
    University of Kentucky dormitory com-
      plex named for, 12
    vocational counseling and, 58–59
    and Woman's Building at University of
      Kentucky, 47
Blanding, William de Saussure, 35
Blanton, Annie Webb, 30, 111, 117–118
Blitz, Anna Dudley, 103
Bloomsburg Literary Institute and State
    Normal School, 22, 24, 81
Boniske, Mary, 76
Bordin, Ruth, 3, 14
Bowersox, F. C., 24
Bowersox, Katherine S., ix, 7–9, 22–25,
    124. *See also* Berea College
    athletic programs for women, 79–80,
      84
    birth of, 22
    death of, 8
    dress code for women, 57–58
    early work experiences, 22–25, 81
    education of, 20–21, 22, 81
    family connections, 7, 22, 24, 112–113
    and financial support for women, 53,
      56–58
    honorary degrees from Berea College,
      8, 17, 22
    and housing for women faculty, 48–50
    and Kentucky Association of Deans of
      Women, 99, 120
    love of nature, 81–82

needs of women faculty members and,
    126
needs of women students and, 42–44
personal relationships, 115, 118–121
as Principal of Academy Department,
    24–25
professional activities of, 97
retirement from Berea College, 1–2, 7–8
social activities of, 23
and Woman's Building at Berea Col-
    lege, 44
Bowersox, Rollin G., 7, 24, 113
Bragdon, Helen, 68
Breckinridge, Madeline McDowell, 35–
    36, 37
Breckinridge, S. P., 37
Breed, Mary Bidwell, 68
Brett, R., 106
Brigham, David L., 125
Brisbay, Erin, 55–56
Brittain, Vera, 59
Brumberg, Joan Jacobs, 67
Bryn Mawr College, 11, 38
Byrd, T. B., 27

Cahn, Susan K., 88–90
Calhoun, E. M., 106
Carlisle Indian Industrial School (Pa.),
    22–24, 81
Case Western Reserve University, 11
Catton, B., 101
Chandler, Albert B. "Happy," 86
Clarke, Edward Hammond, 70
Cleveland College, 100–101
Clifford, Geraldine, 14, 15, 123
Coeducational institutions, 69–72
    academic societies for women and,
      72–74
    athletic programs for women and,
      83–92
    Black, 105, 129, 130
    campus ritual and, 74–77
    coordinate colleges versus, 71
    deans of women and. *See* Deans of
      women
    debate over, 69–70

early experiments, 71
number of women students attending,
    2, 70
private women's colleges versus, 71
women faculty members and, 123–127
Collins, Winifred, 114–115
Columbia University, 31
Conference of Deans and Advisors in
    State Universities, 4
Cook, Blanche Wiesen, 131
Coon, H., 26
Cooper, Thomas P., 12
Coordinate colleges, 71
Cornell University, 3, 5, 12, 59, 123
Cott, Nancy, 2, 67
Cottrell, Debbie Mauldin, 117, 129
Cronkhite, Bernice Brown, 59
Crow, Martha Foote, 4
Cuthbert, Marion V., 105–106

Dabney, V., 27
Dascombe, Marianne, 3
Davis, Hilda A., 106
Day, Edmund E., 123
Dean, Pamela, 71, 128
Dean of Women, The (Mathews), 67–68
Deans of women. *See also names of spe-
    cific deans*
    athletic programs for women and,
        79–92
    expectations for women, 14
    extent of employment, 2
    financial concerns of, 53–64
    innovations by, 3–5
    obstacles faced by, 2–3, 123–131
    public perception problem, 67–68
    revised interpretation of work of,
        14–15
    role of, 14, 42–51, 53
    well-known examples, 20
Delpar, Helen, 128
Delta Kappa Gamma, 117
Denny, George H., 9, 31, 85
Department of Agriculture, U.S. (USDA),
    27–31, 59–60, 116–117
Douglass, D. A., 70

Edwards. E. B., 22
Eisenmann, Linda, ix–x
Elliott, Irene Dillard, 107
Elliott, Mrs. Charles E., 41
Ernberg, Anna, 82

Farnham, Christie, 128
Federal Emergency Relief Agency
    (FEMA), 56
Financial support for women, 54–58
Fitzpatrick, Ellen, 3, 14
Florida State College for Women
    (FSCW), 27–29, 30–31, 108, 116–
    117, 126
Fox-Genovese, Elizabeth, 128
Fraser, N., 69, 135–136 n. 5
Frederickson, M., 32, 33
Freedman, Estelle, 131
Freeman, Alice, 48, 118
Frost, William G., 24–25, 44, 49, 56–57,
    112, 119–120

Georgia Normal and Industrial College
    for Women, 26
Gildersleeve, Virginia, 5, 123
Gill, Laura Drake, 4
Glazer, Penina M., 2–3, 15
Gordon, Lynn D., 34, 128–129
Goucher College, 101
Grabiner, D., 11
Graham, Patricia A., 15
Graves, Dixie Bibb, 9
Greve, Harriet, 108

Habermas, Jurgen, 135–136 n. 5
Hall, G. Stanley, 70
Hall, Jacquelyn Dowd, 15, 129, 131
Harper, William Raney, 3
Harris, Agnes Ellen, ix, 25–31. *See also*
    University of Alabama
    athletic programs for women, 85
    birth of, 25
    death of, 10
    early work experiences, 27–31,
        116–117
    education of, 20–21, 25–27, 31

Harris, Agnes Ellen (*continued*)
  family connections, 25–26, 113–115,
    118
  and financial support for women, 55
  housemothers program, 61–64
  as NADW president, 95–96, 98, 100–
    101, 102–103, 107–108, 115
  needs of women faculty members and,
    125–126
  needs of women students and, 42–44
  personal relationships, 111, 115,
    116–118
  professional development and, 60–61
  retirement from University of Alabama,
    8–10
  social activities of, 26, 124
  U.S. Department of Agriculture and,
    27–31, 59–60, 116–117
  vocational counseling and, 59–60
  Woman's Convocation, 75–76
  Women's Student Government Associa-
    tion, 75–76
Harris, Ellen Simmons, 25
Harris, James Coffee, 25–26, 113–114
Harris, Margaret, 25
Harris, Seale, 25, 59–60
Harris, William Julius, 59–60
Hartman, Mary S., 13
Hay, Melba Porter, 36–37
Heath, Kathryn G., 105, 106
Heilbrun, Carolyn, 6, 19, 112
Herrick, U. B., 68
Hill, Elizabeth Baldwin, 114
Hilton, M. Eunice, 77
Holmes, Sarah B., 11–12, 56, 60–61
Home demonstration movement, 27–31
Hopkins, Harry, 35
Horowitz, Helen L., 44, 48, 68, 72, 74,
  131
Housemothers program, 61–64
Howard University, 105, 129, 130
Howes, A., 70
Hult, Joan, 88–89
Hutchins, Francis, 1, 7–8, 17
Hutchins, William J., 22, 44, 50, 56, 120,
  126

Ihle, E. L., 5
Ingels, K., 37

Jackson, Elizabeth Skinner, 114
Jacobi, M. P., 70
Jacobs, K. A., 45
Jewell, Frances, 37
Jones, Evelyn, 103
Jones, Gwladys W., 105–106
Jones, J. L., 68

Kentucky Association of Deans of
  Women (KADW), 97, 99–100,
  120
Kerber, Linda K., 43–44
Kerr, M., 4
Kett, J. F., 29
Kittennettes (University of Alabama),
  86–91
Knapp, Seaman A., 27
Kunkel, F. M., 67

Lee, E. Brooke, 45
Lee, M. B., 67
Leonard, Eugenie, 104
Leonard, Maria, 104
Letson, D., 71
Lexington Civic League, 37
Lindley, B., 56
Lindley, E. K., 56
Link, William A., 58
Livingston, Eleanor, 9
Lloyd, Alice, 103
London School of Economics, 100
Ludlum, Charlotte, 8
Lyon, Mary, 126

MacDonald, Lillias, 104
Martin, Gertrude S., 3, 5
Mathews, Lois Kimball, 67–68
Maudsley, H., 70
McCandless, Amy Thompson, 71, 128
McDaniel, Edna, 103
McKeldin, Theodore R., 77
McKim, M., 68
McLean, Kathryn Sisson, 4–5

McVey, Frances Jewell, 11–13, 37–38, 46–47, 87–88, 90, 116, 120
McVey, Frank L., 11–13, 37–39, 56, 87
Mead, Margaret, 59
Merrill, Ruth, 68
Miner, F. H., 37
Mitchell, Lucy Sprague, 14, 20
Moore, V. P., 27–28
Mortar Board, 73–74
Morton, L., 22–23
Mt. Holyoke College, 48, 104, 126, 129

National Amateur Athletic Association (NAAF), 89
National Association of Deans of Women (NADW), 100–108
    Blanding as president of, 11–12, 100, 101, 102, 105, 108
    financial issues of, 106–108
    formation of, x, 5, 55
    Harris as president of, 95–96, 98, 100–101, 102–103, 107–108, 115
    professional development and, 60–61
    public perception problem, 67–68
    race as issue in, 105–106
    regional politics in, 101–105, 127
    Stamp as leader in, 98–99, 100, 102, 103–105, 107
    state and regional deans' associations and, 96–100
    University Section, 4, 98, 100
National Education Association (NEA), 4–5, 105
National Youth Administration (NYA), 56
Newcomb, Josephine LeMonnier, 34
Newcomer, Mabel, 54, 70
Nidiffer, Jana, 14
Northwestern University, 4

Oberlin College, 3, 11, 71
Ohio University, 102–103
Olin, H. R., 70
Oread Institute of Domestic Science, 26
Orr, M. L., 71
Owen, Ruth Bryan, 60

Palmer, Alice Freeman, 3, 14
Palmieri, Patricia A., ix–x, 15–16, 131
Patterson, James K., 47
Patterson, Walter K., 47
Paty, Raymond, 9
Pearson, R. A., 45
Peck, E., 24, 50
Perkins, Linda, 129
Pherigo, A. S., 37
Phillips, Kathryn Sisson, 5, 14
Phillips, Mrs. E. L., 4
Piggott, L. J., 106
Potter, M. R., 4
Pratt, Richard Henry, 22–23
Priddy, B. L., 68
Professional development, 60–61
Professional organizations. *See also* National Association of Deans of Women (NADW)
    regional, 96–100
    state, 96–100
Prucha, F. P., 22–23
PTA (Parent-Teachers Association), 73
Purdue University, 99

Race
    and black coeducational institutions, 105, 129, 130
    and NADW, 105–106
Regional Association, 97, 98–99
Regional deans' associations, 96–100, 127
Richards, Florence L., 60
Ritual, campus, 74–77
Robertson, Mary, 9
Robinson, M. O., 32
Root, Florence K., 101
Rosenberg, R., 3, 70
Rosenberry, L. K. M., 4
Rossiter, Margaret W., 2, 14
Rudnick, Lois, 131
Rutgers University, 13
Ryan, Mary P., 42, 135–136 n. 5

Salmon, Lucy, 48
San Francisco Junior College, 104

Saxman, Ethel J., 85
Sayre, Mildred Bunce, 14, 97
Schurz, Carl, 23
Schwager, Sally, 15
Schwartz, Robert, 14
Scott, Anne Firor, 13, 15, 129
Scott, R. V., 27
"Sex attraction" theory (Hall), 70
Sex in Education (Clarke), 70
Simms, Florence S., 32
Simrall, J. P., 67
Sims, Margaret, 144 n. 11
Slater, Miriam, 2 3, 15
Slowe, Lucy D., 14, 105, 106, 129
Smith, May M., 1
Smith, Septima C., 76
Smith, Sybil, 76
Smith College, 86–87
Solomon, Barbara M., 42, 70, 71, 79
Sophie Newcomb Memorial College, 31–
    32, 33–34, 71, 73, 128–129
Southern Association of College Wom-
    en, 4
Stacy, Inez, 106–107
Stamp, Adele H., ix, 31–36. *See also* Uni-
    versity of Maryland
  birth of, 31
  committee participation, 125
  death of, 11
  and dormitory for women students, 41,
    45–46
  early work experiences, 32–35
  education of, 20–21, 31–32, 33–34
  emeritus status at University of Mary-
    land, 11
  May Day festival, 75, 76–77
  Mortar Board and, 73–74
  as NADW leader, 98–99, 100, 102,
    103–105, 107
  needs of women students and, 42–44
  personal relationships, 115–116
  retirement from University of Mary-
    land, 10–11
  speaking engagements, 126–127
  Women's Field House, 46
  and the YWCA, 32–34, 98

Stanaland, Peg, 87
Stanley, Gregory K., 87–91
State Association of Deans of Women
    and Advisors to Girls, 98
State deans' associations, 96–100
State Teachers College (Nebraska), 4
Stimson, Dorothy, 101
Storms, Lillian, 9
Stout, Florence O., 86–88
Strang, Ruth, 4, 68, 101
Stratton, Dorothy, 99–100
Sturtevant, Sara M., 4, 68, 101–104
Syracuse University, 77

Talbot, Marion, 3–4, 5, 14, 20
Talladega College, 105–106
Tanner, A., 112
Teachers College, Columbia University,
    4–5, 26–27, 101
Thompson, Henrietta M., 9–10, 31, 61,
    114
Todhunter, Neige, 10
Tomes, Nancy, 67
Treichler, Paula, 14
Tulane University, 71
Tuttle, Kathryn, 14
Tutwiler, Julia, 9, 10, 31
Tydings, Joseph, 11

U.S. Department of Agriculture, 27–31,
    59–60, 116–117
University of Alabama. *See also* Harris,
    Agnes Ellen
  athletic programs for women, 85
  Harris' retirement from, 8–10
  housemothers program, 61–64
  vocational counseling and, 59–61
  Woman's Convocation, 75–76
  Women's Student Government Associa-
    tion, 75–76
University of Arizona, 103
University of Buffalo, 104
University of California at Berkeley,
    20
University of Chicago, 3–4, 5, 20
University of Illinois, 104

University of Kentucky. *See also* Bland-
  ing, Sarah Gibson
  athletic programs for women, 83, 85–91
  and dormitories for women students,
    46–47
  and Kentucky Association of Deans of
    Women, 99
  vocational counseling and, 58–59
  Woman's Building, 47
University of Maryland. *See also* Stamp,
  Adele H.
  dormitory for women students, 41,
    45–46
  and emeritus status for Stamp, 11
  May Day festival, 75, 76–77
  Mortar Board and, 73–74
  Stamp's retirement from, 10–11
  Women's Senior Honor Society and,
    73–74
University of Michigan, 103
University of Minnesota, 103
University of Missouri, 68
University of North Carolina, 106–107
University of Oklahoma, 103
University of Pittsburgh, 102
University of South Carolina, 107
University of Tennessee, 108
University of Virginia, 5

Van Rensselaer, Martha, 59
Vassar College, 37, 48
  Blanding as president of, 12, 116,
    123
  Blanding's retirement from, 12
Vernon, J. J., 27
Vertinsky, Patricia A., 80–81, 86, 91
Vocational counseling, 58–60
Voigt, Irma, 102–103

Wallace, Maude, 29–30
Ward, Florence, 113
Ware, Susan, 19, 60
Wellesley College, ix–x, 48
  Bowersox and, 3, 7
Wells, A., 4
Welsh, John H., 118
Welsh, Mary Elizabeth, 7, 8, 17, 82, 113,
  118–121, 125
Whitehurst, Mrs. John, 10
Winthrop College, 29
Wolfe, Margaret Ripley, 53–54, 127–
  128
Woods, Alfred F., 34, 73
Woody, T., 69, 70
Wright, M. B., 26

YWCA, Stamp and, 32–34, 98

About the Author

Carolyn Terry Bashaw is Professor of History at Le Moyne College, Syracuse, New York. She received her B.A. from Vanderbilt University and earned an Ed.D. and a Ph.D. from the University of Georgia. Dr. Bashaw has published articles concerning deans of women in the South and has won awards for her writing from the Alabama Historical Association and from the Filson Club Historical Society, in Louisville, Kentucky.